# America's Royalty

Theodore Roosevelt's daughter Alice Lee at age eighteen (1902). Photo courtesy of the Library of Congress.

# AMERICA'S ROYALTY

## All the Presidents' Children
### Revised and Expanded Edition

Sandra L. Quinn-Musgrove
*and* Sanford Kanter

**GREENWOOD PRESS**
Westport, Connecticut • London

**Library of Congress Cataloging-in-Publication Data**

Quinn-Musgrove, Sandra L.
America's royalty : all the presidents' children / Sandra L. Quinn-
Musgrove and Sanford Kanter.—Rev. and expanded ed.
p.   cm.
Includes bibliographical references and index.
ISBN 0–313–29535–2 (alk. paper)
1. Children of presidents—United States—Biography.   I. Kanter,
Sanford.   II. Title.
E176.45Q56   1995
973'.099—dc20
[B]        95–7545

British Library Cataloguing in Publication Data is available.

Library of Congress Catalog Card Number: 95–7545
ISBN: 0–313–29535–2

First published in 1995

Greenwood Press, 88 Post Road West, Westport, CT 06881
An imprint of Greenwood Publishing Group, Inc.

Printed in the United States of America

The paper used in this book complies with the
Permanent Paper Standard issued by the National
Information Standards Organization (Z39.48–1984).

10 9 8 7 6 5 4 3 2 1

**Copyright Acknowledgments**

Every reasonable effort has been made to trace the owners of copyright materials in this
book, but in some instances this has proven impossible. The author and publisher will be
glad to receive information leading to more complete acknowledgments in subsequent
printings of the book and in the meantime extend their apologies for any omissions.

*To an endlessly resourceful friend
and husband, Freddy Gene Musgrove*

*To my loving wife, Charlene Kanter*

# CONTENTS

# LIST OF PHOTOS

# PREFACE

America's presidents have fathered 157 children, two of whom were adopted, and eight of whom are generally accepted as the illegitimate offspring of three men who later became presidents. Six presidents had no children, five were married, and one never married. The lives of all of these men's children are chronicled in this book.

This second edition brings American presidents' families up to date. Since the first edition of this book there have been two more presidents who have added seven children to America's history: Bush with six children and Clinton with one. Many changes were prompted by the addition of information associated with aging, death, birth, marriage, remarriage, and the host of other life experiences common to all of us. Although some presidents' children died while very young, others grew up to add their adult contributions to society. Both the newest additions to the roles of America's "Royalty" and the added materials on the major changes that took place in the lives of each president's child are developed chapter by chapter in the chronological order of each man's presidency.

In the first edition, some of the presentations focused on the child's contributions as if derived only as a result of their presidential parent, unintentionally attributing the contributions as direct by-products of the parent while neglecting the perhaps solitary role of the child's skills, abilities, drive, ambition, and other characteristics each of us develop individually—regardless of parental contributions. On the other hand, each of us has friends and relatives who are responsible for directing, guiding, denying, or even boosting us into our life's role, and the children of presidents are no different. A review of the lives of presidents' children reveals that their parents have also helped and hindered their progeny.

Finally, throughout all of the accounts, some changes have been made, perhaps reflecting the maturing technical or mechanical skills of this edition's author. Thus, the book is replete with such changes, reflecting the belief that at no point of any writer's practice will writing reach perfection—despite the constancy of the quest.

Other than the changes identified in the foregoing, the book retains its basic structure of focusing on the lives of all of the American presidents' children. Stories of the six presidents without progeny are addressed in the first chapter of the book.

The use of this book's material can be varied. For teachers, however, the most dominant use remains as a means of stimulating or even motivating students in our college history and political science classes. Coming to understand that history and political science, or any other human endeavor, are products of humans is an excellent means of titillating further studies of human endeavors, regardless of the topic studied. Over, maybe even above, this valued use of the subject matter of this book is the satisfaction each of us finds in answering our own curiosity.

The first edition of this book developed after a curious question motivated the authors to find the answer: "Do you know the story of Lincoln's son, Bob?" asked a colleague. We didn't. We became curious. Our quest for the answer concluded only when we could answer to our own academic and human curiosity's satisfaction, "Yes, we know the story of Lincoln's son, Bob." Further, as the first research satisfied curiosity, academic uses for this and other information about all of the presidents' children prompted further reading and research.

On the way to the compilation of this book's materials, including reading and reviewing a seemingly endless list of biographies and autobiographies, as well as nonfiction books, documents, and newspapers—many of which are referenced in appropriate portions of this book—a variety of resources developed. Many individuals contributed both effort and inspiration to the accumulation of the materials in this updated version of stories about the presidents' children. Materials used include information from *Presidents' Sons,* authored by Joseph Perling, whose widow, Esther Ruth Perling, graciously granted permission for its use. Reference librarians in private and public San Antonio, Texas, libraries aided in our quest to update information. A variety of unseen faces, but known telephone voices, responded to both letter and phone requests from presidential library staffs aiding in this most recent quest for updates. Judy Larson, reference librarian at Our Lady of the Lake University in San Antonio, exhibited a constant willingness to aid in finding seemingly impossibly buried information. And, finally, not last but most, without the contributions of programming, researching, and editing and the general all around efforts of Freddy Gene

Musgrove, husband of Quinn-Musgrove, this edition could not have been completed.

It is sincerely hoped that you will enjoy the reading as much as the telling of the stories was enjoyed.

# INTRODUCTION

Who were the presidents' children? What are their vital statistics? What were their relationships with their families? Was it, or is it, an advantage to be born to a man who becomes the president of the United States? Do presidents' children share common characteristics with each other? Are they more political than average citizens? Do they form an elite group, in any sense, other than in being born of a man who becomes president of the United States? If so, in what way? Whom do the children of presidents marry? Is social equality an issue for American presidents' children in choices of their spouses? Do men who serve as American presidents transmit such special abilities to their offspring? What kinds of fathers do presidents make? Are strong presidents necessarily strong parents? Are the lives of the children of presidents markedly different from the lives of their contemporaries before and after their fathers' election to the presidency? Do presidents' children favor one occupation? Is a presidential father's career a "boost" for a son or daughter, assuring of the offspring's success? In fact, do presidential fathers regularly impact on the lives of their children more so than do other fathers seeking to aid their children in their life choices?

There is an assumption that being the child of a president assures a place in life somewhat larger than the ordinary. This commonly held view is apparent in a story attributed to John Adams. John Quincy Adams was elected president during his father's lifetime. During his first appearance before a joint session of Congress, his father, John Adams, second president of the United States, sat and listened with some of his closest friends. After the speech a friend leaned over and said, "You know, Mr. Adams, your son made a finer speech than you did at your inauguration." The old gentleman responded, "Yes, he did. And, he'll probably be a greater president than I was. And all of his speeches will be better. But, remember, he started where

I could not . . . from my shoulders." Even if true—and there are those who argue that John Quincy would have made it to the top regardless of his father's position—do the facts really support the senior Adams's inference that having a politically prestigious family heritage is an advantage in a democracy? Other presidents have also been very conscious of the role they would play in history, and they have admonished their children to be conscious of the historical impact their deeds may have. Often such admonishments were associated with public demonstrations by one or more of their children ill-suited to kindness by historians. Not only did Adams make periodic remonstrations to several of his sons, Andrew Jackson, Millard Fillmore, U. S. Grant, Chester Arthur, and Calvin Coolidge all made it clear that theirs is a special role in American history. As such, they observe, their childrens' position will also support or detract from the future's images of each man's presidency. Just how much do the lives of children impact on the evaluations of each man's presidency?

Answers to these and other questions may become apparent to the reader who absorbs all of the lives of the presidents' children presented in this book. However, the reader may also reach the conclusion that children of presidents have advantages little different from those afforded to the children of many of America's leading families.

Nonetheless, the position of American presidents' children is unique. Since there have been only forty-two presidents, six of whom did not sire children, the lives of these children hold a special intrigue perhaps merely by virtue of their infrequency. The authors have concluded that such attention reflects a constant curiosity, indeed even fascination, about children of powerful and successful leaders.

This second edition of *America's Royalty: All the Presidents' Children* is replete with much interesting history. Such history addresses conditions surrounding the period of each child's and their parents' lifetimes. Simply, as students of history, readers well know the value of a good story. How better to garner knowledge of the American experience than to study the lives of Abraham Lincoln's children? Learning about the death of Franklin Pierce's son, Benny, may help the reader appreciate the development of America's railway system after the mid-nineteenth century. How often have readers bitten into the chocolately, nutty candy bar "Baby Ruth," knowing that the confection's name is derived from a president's daughter; and even that the name was challenged by another hero of the early twentieth century—Babe Ruth? So often stories about real people add to the value of the study of history.

In the early 1980s, when the authors undertook to develop information about presidential children as yet another tool in the ongoing process of tempting our history and political science students to appreciate the subjects we teach daily, we were indeed naive about the task we had set for ourselves. We assumed that such information would exist in some, rather orderly, fashion. It did not. Instead, we found contradictions, and much information was available for some children and almost no recorded information was available for others.

After months of daily research, we collected a complete set of names with a lot of stories generally unknown to the public, much less to our students. The stories have proven to be enjoyable, average, coincidental, informational, sometimes boring, and sometimes tragic anecdotes about the families of America's highest office holders.

Certainly, this book may be read as a whole from beginning to end. It may be read as support material for various presidents and their times. The lives of each child may be read only for their human interest—and indeed to serve as a wonderful form of entertainment. Regardless of the way and purpose of the read, it is the sincere hope that each reader will have a "good read!"

# America's Royalty

# 1  CHILDLESS PRESIDENTS

Of the forty-two presidents of the United States through William Clinton, six had no children. Of the six, only one, James Buchanan, was a lifelong bachelor. The other five, Washington, Madison, Jackson, Polk, and Harding, were married only one time and each of these men's marriages lasted for many years. One of the five, Washington, acquired a family when he married a widow. Jackson adopted a child, and Harding allegedly parented at least one child in a relationship outside of his long-term marriage. Though these presidents sired no legitimate children, an explanation of each man's relationship to his wife and to the children he inherited, adopted, or fathered outside of marriage is interesting to the reader.

## GEORGE WASHINGTON

George Washington, first president of the United States, married the widow Martha Dandridge Custis, a mother of four children. Two of her children had died while very young, well before she married Washington. At the time of the marriage Washington was close to twenty-seven years of age and Martha was almost twenty-eight. She had become a widow when her husband, twenty years her senior, died from tuberculosis. Martha brought to her marriage both a large inheritance from her deceased husband and a ready-made family of a young daughter and son. The daughter, Martha, died unexpectedly when she was only thirteen years old; however, her son, John Parke Custis, knew Washington as the male parent in the Washington family household.

Young Custis served as Washington's aide-de-camp during the Revolutionary War. He was with Washington in all of the war's battles through the final British surrender at Yorktown. Shortly after the war young Custis died from a fever, leaving behind his wife and four small children to be provided for and raised. The two youngest, a three-year-old girl who died while still a small child, and little George Washington Parke Custis, only months old, were taken into the care of George and Martha Washington. Years later, some biographers refer to this child as Washington's adopted son; however, Washington did not adopt the boy. In correspondence, Washington referred to Martha's grandson as his ward.

Nonetheless, Washington did raise the boy, sending him to both St. Johns College and Princeton, though there is no record of any particularly special abilities demonstrated while he was in school. Leaving school when he was just seventeen years old, George went into the military, receiving a commission as an officer of dragoons. Washington wanted to see that the boy was secure and requested he receive a higher rank so that he might be a leader in battle should the need arise. Custis never did lead troops.

America's first president died in 1799, leaving his "inherited" namesake land, including property on the Potomac River. When George Washington Parke Custis was twenty-three years old, he married. He built a home on his inherited land on the west side of the Potomac River. He named his home Arlington in honor of his grandmother's husband's family home in England. Custis who then lived the life of a country gentleman, was periodically visited by the Washington, D.C., elite, including President Andrew Jackson. The couple's daughter married Robert E. Lee. In her later writings, she referred to her father as "the adopted son of George Washington," giving credence to the adopted-son hypothesis put forth by early Washington biographers.[1]

Maintaining pride in his heritage by association, Custis's final request was that, as the last descendant of George Washington, his only child, a daughter, would rename her son with the Washington name, to continue the name, if not the line. There is no record as to whether she complied with her father's dying wish.

## JAMES MADISON

The fourth president of the United States, James Madison, had no children. He married Dorothea "Dolley" Dandridge Payne Todd when he was forty-three and she was twenty-six. The marriage lasted for almost forty-two years. Dolley was the mother of two children, one of whom had died the year prior to her marriage to Madison. The other, John Payne Todd, was brought into their marriage. The boy evoked no interest in contemporary biographers or later chroniclers and thus disappeared from the pages of history.

## ANDREW JACKSON

Andrew Jackson married Rachel Donelson Robards, supposing her to be divorced from Lewis Robards. He later found his marriage to be invalid, necessitating a remarriage of the Jacksons.

At the time of their first, invalid, marriage, both were twenty-four years old. Their marriage lasted thirty-seven years, until her death. When no children were born to the couple after several years of marriage, they adopted a son. The boy, one of a pair of twins born to Rachel's brother's wife, was named Andrew Jackson, Jr. Although Jackson's career kept him from the young man during his early years, his wife wrote progress reports on their son and Jackson responded, frequently giving advice on how to raise Andrew, Jr.

Just as Andrew Jackson was elected to the presidency in 1828, his beloved Rachel died. Andy, Jr., divided his time among the family home, The Hermitage, supervising the plantation's overseers; Washington, D.C., with his father; and Philadelphia with his twin brother, who had been raised by his natural mother and who had accepted a government appointment. The young man was engaged twice before he settled upon Sarah Yorke for his wife. They were married in 1831. The president approved of his son's wife. Evidence of this fondness is apparent with his giving his beloved Rachel's jewelry to the girl, with the stipulation that it would be his granddaughter's—should the couple produce a daughter—and that they should name their daughter Rachel.

Jackson set his son to the task of learning to manage his extensive land holdings. In time, Jackson bought a plantation for Andy and Sarah very near The Hermitage. But his son was incapable of management and soon acquired major debts, which Jackson paid off repeatedly. During one period, when Jackson thought his life to be near an end, he wrote to his son:

My dear Andrew, I have been quite unwell. . . . My son, as my life is uncertain, and we know not at what moment we may be called hence, I now address you with the fondness of a father's heart. I wish to bring to your view the situation you now, and will hereafter, occupy, that it may be a stimulant to your proper conduct in all time hereafter. It is well known that I have adopted you as my own son and you are to represent me when I am called hence. Your conduct standing as my representative, the son of a President, draws upon you the eyes of the world, and the least deviation from the rules of strict decorum and propriety are observed and commented on by all our enemies.[2]

However, Jackson did not die at this time, but neither did his son observe any "propriety." Instead he continued to accumulate large debts, which his father continued to make good. Before Jackson died in 1845, he was advised to make his will in the name of Andy's wife, Sarah, but the senior Jackson felt that such an act would not show good faith. He left to Andy's guardianship massive holdings. The young man repeatedly risked the family's finances. Each time his ventures failed, exhausting funds further. Finally Andy sold the family home, The Hermitage, and its surrounding lands to the state of Tennessee, although Andy maintained the right to live in The Hermitage during his lifetime.

This adopted son survived his father by twenty years, dying in 1865 at the close of the Civil War. Although Andy maintained his neutrality during the Civil War two of his sons fought for the South.

While climbing a fence during a hunting expedition, Andy's gun accidentally discharged. He received minor injuries to his hand, but within a week he had died from lockjaw.

## JAMES KNOX POLK

The marriage of James Polk, the eleventh president, and Sarah Childress took place when he was twenty-eight and she was twenty years old. No children resulted from the twenty-five-year marriage. Sarah Polk, noted for her piousness, devoted her entire time and energy to her husband before and during his presidency.

## WARREN GAMALIEL HARDING

The fifth and final married president to have no children was the twentieth-century president Warren G. Harding and his wife, Florence Kling DeWolfe. Although this was the first marriage for Harding, Florence had been married and was divorced nine years prior to their 1891 marriage. Florence Harding, five years older than her husband, had a son, Marshall DeWolfe, who died of tuberculosis. The Harding marriage lasted for more than thirty-two years, and though there was a greal deal of gossip as to the quality of the marriage, officially Harding sired no children of record.

In 1963 love letters between Harding and Carrie Phillips gave credence to the story of a fifteen-year affair with the wife of one of his closest friends. However, this liaison is not credited with producing any children.

Instead, while Harding maintained his affair with Carrie Phillips, he entered into a relationship with a woman thirty years his junior. The woman, Nan Britton, and Harding continued their relationship even after he assumed the presidency. In 1919, just before Harding moved to the White House, Britton gave birth to a daughter whom she named Elizabeth Ann Christian. Harding supported the child with payments made through his White House Office. When Harding died, Britton sought support through a trust fund, but her quest was rejected. In 1927 she authored a book, *The President's Daughter*, and dedicated it to unwed mothers. The book became a best-seller of the era. Harding's mistress later moved to the Midwest, and allegedly the daughter of the union is alive today, living in the Far West.[3]

## JAMES BUCHANAN

The fifteenth president of the United States, James Buchanan, is the only president who never married. Buchanan remained a bachelor for all of his seventy-seven years, although he had been engaged to marry at the age of twenty-eight. His fiancée died from an overdose of a sedative in 1819. Never again was there any discussion of an engagement or a Buchanan marriage.

Such are the stories of the presidents to whom no children were born or sanctioned within their marriages. All other presidents produced heirs, some of whom survived long years, living full and influential lives. Some children developed as eccentrics; others lived lives not unlike those of children born to any citizen or resident of the United States.

It is the stories of these children that form the content of the rest of this book.

# 2  JOHN ADAMS'S CHILDREN

## ABIGAIL AMELIA ADAMS SMITH

First child of John Adams and Abigail Smith
*Born:* July 14, 1765     *Birthplace:* Braintree County, Massachusetts
*Died:* August 15, 1813     *Age at Death:* 48 years, 1 month
*Cause of Death:* Breast cancer     *Education:* Tutored at home
*Profession:* Housewife, mother     *Spouse:* William Stephens Smith
*Number of Children:* 4

Abigail Amelia Adams, known familiarly as Amelia, Nabby, or Emmy, was quiet and rather withdrawn. She had blue eyes, reddish hair, a round face, and a fair complexion. Educated at home, common to the era's upper-income family's women, Amelia was strongly influenced by her dominating parents and particularly her father. Whether by nature or nurture, Amelia was not the dominant voice in her adult relationships.

When Amelia was seventeen years old, she fell in love with a young lawyer, Royall Tyler, who had practiced law in Boston before his move to Amelia's home county, Braintree, Massachusetts. Royall, who defined his avocation as poetry, is described as classically tall, dark, and handsome. He was, therefore, very attractive to Braintree County's unmarried women, many of whom sought his attention. Eventually he courted Amelia, but the courtship did not go smoothly. The Adams family found Tyler lacking in qualities necessary for connection with their prominent family. Nevertheless, Amelia and Tyler became engaged.

Engagement or not, father John Adams was angered by his daughter's choice of a husband who did not fulfill the Adams's family standards. Hoping to break the engagement, Adams sent his Amelia to Boston. The maneuver did not work, and she returned to Braintree County, resuming her engagement. Next, Amelia's father ordered her, and her mother Abigail, to join him in Paris, where he was representing the United States. Amelia agreed to go to Paris on the condition that after one year, if she and Tyler maintained their affection for each other, Royall would travel to the Continent to marry her. After an initial flurry of frequent correspondence between the couple, the frequency of letters dwindled to a one-sided romance—from Amelia to Royall. As weeks passed, Amelia became dejected and even more withdrawn and silent than was normal for her.

In May 1785 John Adams was appointed America's first minister to England. Abigail, Amelia, and John Adams moved to London. From London, Amelia continued her regular correspondence with her brother, John Quincy, and maintained her unanswered correspondence with Royall. During a presentation at the Court of St. James, Amelia was introduced to her father's aide, the secretary of the American legation, William Stephens Smith, a New Yorker and former aide to General Washington. Smith, a veteran of the Revolutionary War, was the kind of man acceptable to the Adamses as a son-in-law. The introduction signaled the beginning of a relationship with Smith and the family's much sought end of Amelia's engagement to Royall. Amelia ended her correspondence with Royal, breaking their engagement with her letter stating, "Sir, Herewith you receive your letters and miniature with my desire that you return mine to Uncle Cranch, and my hope you will be well satisfied with the affair as is."[4] The response from Royall was unexpected. Royall wrote claiming he had corresponded with her regularly as he traveled seeking to expand his business interests. He pleaded that he had not received her letters except for the last. But he was too late. Amelia and Smith were in London. Royall was in the United States.

Amelia and Smith became constant companions. Smith gave letters and testimonials to his character to Mrs. Adams with his stated intent "to gain confidence of her daughter to lay a proper foundation for a future connection."[5]

Amelia's regular letters to her brother, John Quincy, now often spoke of "le colonel." On John Adams's recommendation, Smith was appointed consul general to Great Britain. Amelia became Smith's bride on June 26, 1786, and the couple made their home near her parents' London home. As the bridegroom continued to serve under John Adams, Amelia's life changed only with the addition of a husband, without lessening her position as the daughter of John Adams.

Back in the United States, Royall was crushed by news of Amelia's marriage. He left his law practice and returned to Boston. In time, Royall's poetic qualities brought him success when two plays he wrote became hits.

Upon the 1788 return of the Adams and Smith families to the States, the true character of Smith began to emerge. He disappeared for months on end. When he was home with Amelia, she complained he paid little attention to her.

During some of Smith's absences he was involved in an insurrection in Venezuela and in land speculations in the West. None of his ventures proved successful. Amelia developed breast cancer, and at the age of forty-eight she died in her home in the "wild west" of New York. Her brother later observed that Amelia was "an innocent victim of fortune's treacherous game."[6]

Ironically, the man the Adams family had successfully opposed as unsuitable for Amelia, Royall Tyler, achieved success in the law and became a chief justice of Vermont's Supreme Court. Upon his death he was honored as "universally loved and respected."[7]

## JOHN QUINCY ADAMS

Second child, first son of John Adams and Abigail Smith
*Born:* July 11, 1767      *Birthplace:* Braintree County, Massachusetts
*Died:* February 23, 1848      *Age at Death:* 80 years, 7 months
*Cause of Death:* Cerebral hemorrhage
*Education:* Tutors, Continental schools, Harvard University
*Profession:* Presidential aide, professor, diplomat, secretary of state, president of the United States
*Spouse:* Louisa Catherine Johnson
*Number of Children:* 4

John Quincy Adams, the eldest of John Adams's sons, graduated from Harvard in 1788. Before he had even reached the age of twenty-two, he had already crossed the Atlantic four times, including three trips during the Revolutionary War. While still in his teens John Quincy served as secretary and interpreter on the U.S. mission to the Russian court of Empress

Catherine. His linguistic skills were acquired when he studied in both Paris and Leyden during his father's diplomatic service. At Harvard, John Quincy specialized in literary and classical studies although he later turned to law.

Excelling in all he tried, this Adams son was described by one of his Harvard professors as the most brilliant student ever to study at Harvard. His drive to achieve would remain strong throughout his life, perhaps reflecting the strict, even rigid, standards established for all of the Adams children under the strict guidance of their father. The senior Adams constantly harangued his son, John Quincy, to surpass all others in scholarship. Social and emotional awareness were not typically characteristic of either John Adams or his son, John Quincy. Following his father's path into politics, he adopted his father's maxims as the rules upon which to run his life. It was the puritanical code of the seventeenth century that the elder Adams successfully imposed upon this brilliant son. John Adams admonished him, "Morals, my boy, morals should be, as they are eternal in their nature, the everlasting object of your pursuits."[8] It was this kind of advice that shaped the brilliant man with his haughty, stern character which closely resembled that of his father, John Adams.

Completing studies at Harvard, John was a lawyer in Boston for a brief period. But in 1794, he was appointed by President George Washington as minister to the Netherlands. From the Netherlands, he was sent to Sweden in 1798 to negotiate commercial treaties on behalf of the United States.

During a brief interlude in London, John Quincy met and married Louisa Catherine Johnson, the daughter of the American minister to England. A fiery character in her own right, though chronically suffering from numerous unspecified illnesses, in the twenty-five years of their marriage Louisa never claimed to really understand her husband.

By 1802 John Quincy, his wife, and child returned to the United States. Immediately he entered the political scene, and he was successively elected to the Massachusetts Senate and then to the U.S. Senate. While senator from Massachusetts, John Quincy also fulfilled the duties of professor of rhetoric and oratory at Harvard College. The assignment was given because of his personal experience in foreign affairs through the years America sought to establish its role among nations. (As had his father's experiences, John Quincy's contributions to the nation's interests had begun even before the nation was solidified under the Constitution of 1789.)

He was appointed as minister to Russia, leaving that nation only when he was appointed to the commission that negotiated the Treaty of Ghent, which ended the War of 1812 with England. Returning to the United States, John Quincy became secretary of state under President James Monroe. Many historians claim that he, alone, should be credited with the design and implementation of the 1823 Monroe Doctrine. The doctrine announced to the world that the United States was prepared to compete with the world's powerful nations, with its stated purpose of opposing growth of European colonies or the conquest of former colonies in the Western Hemisphere.

In 1825 John Quincy Adams became the only son of a president to follow his father into the presidency. Like his father, John Quincy was unpopular with the public. After a heated presidential campaign resulting in a 99 to 84 electoral college vote for the popular General Andrew Jackson, John Quincy became president only because the House of Representatives had the last word on the election's result; and they supported the experience of the former president's son.

In 1828 his single term in office ended with the popular election of his 1824 competitor, Jackson. Adams's attempt at reelection was the first real "gut-level," name-calling election in American presidential politics. Jackson called John Quincy extravagant, corrupt, and an aristocrat. Adams responded with a moral tone observing that Jackson was an ignoramus, a vulgarian, and a murderer, as well as an adulterer. The public overwhelmingly denied John Quincy's second presidential term, and he returned to his Massachusetts home for a short period. John Quincy Adams later returned to Washington as a member of the House of Representatives where he remained until 1848.

During his years in the House, his reputation was that of a moral fanatic. Said one observer about a discussion over slavery, an institution Adams violently opposed,

I remember the appearance of Mr. Adams as he sat day after day watching his opportunity to present his mammoth petition on the subject of slavery. Mr. Adams was excessively bald and as he sat in the middle of the House, with his immense petition rolled around a kind of windlass to sustain it, his excitement was manifest in the flaming redness of his bald head, which acted as a chronometer to his audience.[9]

It may well have been a petition such as the one he presented from several Massachusetts citizens, defiantly requesting the dissolution of the United States over the issue of slavery.

A solitary person before, during, and after his marriage, much of Adams is yet a mystery. To the public he had the appearance of a dour, bitter, and cranky old man. But to statesmen of his era, John Quincy Adams was known for his brilliance, tempered by a difficult and obstinate nature.

## SUSANNA ADAMS

Third child, second daughter of John Adams and Abigail Smith
*Born:* December 28, 1768     *Birthplace:* Boston, Massachusetts
*Died:* February 4, 1770     *Age at Death:* 1 year, 1 month
*Cause of Death:* Unknown

---

Susanna Adams was the only Adams child not to survive infancy. Life was very harsh for newborns even of wealthy families in the colonies. Susanna lived with the family in their Boston Brattle Square home just past her first birthday. (The Adams's Boston home was called "The White House" long before the title was given to the home of the chief executive in Washington, D.C.)

Susanna was the first child of a future chief executive to die, as Washington never fathered children. Abigail Adams is recorded as having long mourned the early death of her second daughter.

## CHARLES ADAMS

Fourth child, second son of John Adams and Abigail Smith
*Born:* May 29,1770     *Birthplace:* Boston, Massachusetts
*Died:* November 30, 1800     *Age at Death:* 30 years, 6 months
*Cause of Death:* Cirrhosis of the liver
*Education:* Tutors, private schools, Harvard University
*Profession:* Lawyer     *Spouse:* Sarah Smith
*Number of Children:* 2

---

In September 1779, Charles accompanied his older brother, John Quincy, to London, where their father was negotiating on behalf of the United States. In less than two years, he became so homesick that his father decided he should return home to preserve his health. Leaving London in August 1781, eleven-year-old Charles was stranded in Spain when the ship was sent into drydock for repairs. The family lost contact with him and believed he had been lost at sea. Four months later, Charles arrived home but was ever after to appear as a "lost" soul.

Charles attended Harvard with his younger brother, Thomas, where they studied law and later passed the bar. Charles was, however, actively involved in campus disputes during his days at the school. Despite completion of his law studies, Charles never went on to practice law. After college, he moved back to Boston and stayed with his mother's family. He fell in love with his cousin, Sarah, and despite family objections that he was too young, they married in August 1795.

How Charles came to be impoverished is unknown, but by 1797 he was already unable to support his wife and two children as he floundered in depression and alcoholism. In October 1800 his mother, Abigail, arrived at Charles and Sarah's home in New York City for a visit. Instead of finding a happy home she found Charles "upon a bed of sickness, destitute of a home. The kindness of a friend afforded him an asylum," and his wife no longer lived with him.[10]

On November 30, 1800, Charles died of cirrhosis of the liver. Charles was mourned by his mother and father, who commented on "the melancholy death of a once loved son."[11]

## THOMAS BOYLSTON ADAMS

Fifth child, third son of John Adams and Abigail Smith
*Born:* September 15, 1772    *Birthplace:* Quincy, Massachusetts
*Died:* March 12, 1832    *Age at Death:* 59 years, 6 months
*Cause of Death:* Unknown
*Education:* Tutors, Harvard University
*Profession:* Lawyer, politician, writer
*Spouse:* Ann Harod    *Number of Children:* Unknown

---

Thomas, the third son and last child of John Adams, was born shortly before his father assisted in creating the new American nation. Graduating from Harvard in 1790, Thomas studied law. During his law studies he also served as treasurer of Quincy, Massachusetts. Admitted to the bar in 1795, he joined his brother, John Quincy, as secretary in diplomatic posts on the Continent. Acting as chargé d'affaires of the American legation in the Netherlands and later as a secretary in Berlin—where his brother also served—Charles appeared to be following the paths of both his father and brother into diplomatic and political careers. So thinking, his father wrote, "I thank the supreme that I have yet two sons, who will give me some consolation by a perseverance in those habits of virtue and industry which they have hitherto preserved."[12] When Thomas returned to the United States, his father was president. Thomas lived with his father in Philadelphia, where the nation's new capitol had been transferred from New York City, though shortly the constitutionally created federal district, in Washington, the District of Columbia, would become the family's presidential home. Thomas decided to settle permanently in Philadelphia to practice law. But during his European residency he had developed a taste for luxury, though his earnings from the law did not pay for his newly acquired tastes. Nevertheless, Thomas did not allow his lack of funds to interfere with satisfying himself. He just spent far above his income, and although he eventually repaid his debts, his "high living" lifestyle caused great concern for both his ultra-proper father and his straightlaced brother, John Quincy.

Thomas married Ann Harod, returned to Quincy, and began again to practice law. In Quincy his law practice flourished and his reputation grew. Periodically, Thomas served on investigating commissions, and ultimately he became a Massachusetts state court judge. During this period of public service, Thomas also added to the Adams family reputation through scholarship in literature and philosophy. A reviewer of his writing said, "He [Thomas] honorably maintained the reputation of the family from which he is descended; which family is rendered noble, not by office and power in the State, but by a taste and capacity for acquiring ancient and modern literature."[13]

Thomas died at fifty-nine years of age, survived by his brother, John Quincy. His death caused little comment in newspapers of the day. Though successful in his own right, he failed by comparison to both his father and brother.

## FOR FURTHER READING

Burnham, Sophy. *The Landed Gentry: Passions and Personalities inside America's Propertied Class*. New York: G. P. Putnam's Sons, 1978.

East, Robert Abraham. *John Adams*. Boston: Twayne Publications, 1979.

Hess, Stephen. *America's Political Dynasties*. New York: Doubleday, 1966.

Levin, Phyllis Lee. *Abigail Adams: A Biography*. New York: St. Martin's Press, 1987.

Perling, Joseph J. *Presidents Sons: The Prestige of Name in a Democracy*. New York: Odyssey Press, 1947; Freeport, New York: Books for Libraries Press, 1971.

Vidal, Gore, et al. *Great American Families*. New York: W. W. Norton, 1977.

Whitney, David C. *The American Presidents*. 4th ed. Garden City, New York: Doubleday, 1978.

# 3  THOMAS JEFFERSON'S CHILDREN

## MARTHA (PATSY) WASHINGTON JEFFERSON RANDOLPH

First child of Thomas Jefferson and Martha Wayles Skelton
*Born:* September 27, 1772
*Birthplace:* Monticello, Albemarle, Virginia
*Died:* October 10, 1836     *Age at Death:* 64 years, 1 month
*Cause of Death:* Apoplexy
*Education:* Tutors, private schools in France
*Profession:* Housewife, mother, White House hostess
*Spouse:* Thomas Mann Randolph, Jr.     *Number of Children:* 12

Martha Washington Jefferson was only ten when her mother died. "Patsy," as she was called by her father, became the feminine head of her father's household, a position she never relinquished.

Described as bright and studious, bearing a strong resemblance to her tall, red-haired father, Patsy attended small private schools, studied the classics, and mastered the French language. An avowed advocate of education, Jefferson required his children be exposed to all possible formal educational opportunities. A cheerful, though obedient, Patsy, found it easy to follow the daily study practices her father prescribed for his daughters. His regimen was strict, and appeared as:

Practice music: 8–10 A.M.
Dance one day and draw another: 10 A.M.–1 P.M.
Draw on the day you dance; write a letter the next day: 1–2 P.M.

Read French: 3–4 P.M.
Exercise yourself in music: 4–5 P.M.
Read English and write: 5 until bedtime.[14]

The combination of Patsy's willingness and ability to study and her conformity to her father's requirements resulted in Patsy's acquiring a formal education far beyond that of most women of her era.

The bond between father and daughter was close, and it became even closer as the motherless young girl matured into a woman. Martha accompanied her father to Philadelphia when he attended the Continental Congress where he served as an elected representative for the new state of Virginia. In 1784 she traveled with her father to France, where they lived for several years.

In 1790, at the age of eighteen, Martha married a man she had known all of her life, Thomas Mann Randolph, Jr. The newlyweds moved to their plantation, Edgehill, nearby the Jefferson family home at Monticello. (The Jefferson family home had come to Thomas Jefferson through his wife, when laws of primogeniture required that the inheritance of a married woman become her husband's property with marriage.)

Between 1791 and 1818, Martha and Thomas had twelve children. Given the proximity of the Randolph home to Jefferson's home, the attachment between father and daughter remained intense, and she continued as hostess at Monticello, while she maintained her marital home at Edgehill. Monticello was a second home to Martha and her growing family.

Randolph was elected to Congress, though he served with a remarkable lack of distinction until he was elected as governor of Virginia, 1819–1822. (Martha was the first of two presidents' daughters to serve as Virginia's first ladies; with the election of Charles Robb as Virginia's governor in 1982, Lyndon Baines Johnson's daughter, Lynda Bird, became the second presidents' daughter to be the wife of a Virginia governor.)

But all was not smooth in the marriage. Randolph suffered a series of mental breakdowns and bankruptcies. In time, Randolph developed an anomosity toward his father-in-law. The Randolph family finances went from bad to worse. However, throughout the emotional and financial trials of her marriage, the single stable element in Martha's life remained: the love she had for her children and her father. When her sister, Polly—the only other surviving Jefferson child—died, father and daughter became even closer.

When Jefferson died in 1826, Martha's emotional and financial strength was gone. She inherited her father's considerable debts and considered selling Monticello or turning it into a school. Her husband, Thomas Randolph, had become remote from the family, and Martha bore the burden of both her own family and the problems associated with the Jefferson estate. However, both the family and the estate were saved when state legislatures of both South Carolina and Louisiana heard of her plight. Each state appropriated $10,000 for her maintenance.

Martha died of apoplexy in 1836, surviving her father by only a decade. She was buried not at the Edgehill home she shared with her husband, but rather at her heartfelt, lifelong home, Monticello.

## JANE RANDOLPH JEFFERSON

Second child, second daughter of Thomas Jefferson and Martha Wayles Skelton
*Born:* April 3, 1774     *Birthplace:* Monticello, Albemarle, Virginia
*Died:* September 1775     *Age at Death:* 1 year, 6 months
*Cause of Death:* Unknown

---

Jane Randolph, the second of the Jeffersons' six children, was born when the nation was heading for its dramatic separation from England. Not much is known about this child who lived only eighteen months, but it is clear that her birth was not difficult, unlike all of the following pregnancies of Martha Jefferson. Her father, Thomas, was home when she died. This little girl had lived long enough to be "greatly loved, and her death must have compounded Jefferson's reluctance to leave his wife."[15] Thus, as Jefferson was involved in the serious business of giving birth to a new nation, he was torn between his two loves, his family and his country. Martha, never a healthy woman, became progressively ill followng Jane's birth and childhood death.

## "SON" JEFFERSON

Third child, only son of Thomas Jefferson and Martha Wayles Skelton
*Born:* May 28, 1777     *Birthplace:* Monticello, Albemarle, Virginia
*Died:* June 14, 1777     *Age at Death:* 17 days
*Cause of Death:* Unknown

---

He was the only son of Thomas Jefferson and Martha Skelton, but he seems not to have been named. The short span of his life and the lack of a name suggest that his survival was questionable at birth. By the laws of primogeniture, property was inherited through the son in this period of American history. Thus, naming of an only son would have been of paramount importance to his parents, as this son would have become the heir to Jefferson's estate.

There is a certain irony that exists when we consider the birth and early death of Jefferson's only son. It was Jefferson who later successfully introduced laws into Virginia's legislature that eliminated the practice of primogeniture in the state. In a short time, the dissolution of such laws spread throughout the other states. Their elimination in the early stages of the nation's development may, indeed, be partly attributed to the early death of Jefferson's only son.

## MARY JEFFERSON EPPES

Fourth child, third daughter of Thomas Jefferson and Martha Wayles Skelton
*Born:* August 1, 1778      *Birthplace:* Monticello, Albemarle, Virginia
*Died:* April 17, 1804      *Age at Death:* 25 years, 8 months
*Cause of Death:* Childbirth complications
*Education:* Tutors, private school in France
*Profession:* Housewife, mother
*Spouse:* John Wayles Eppes      *Number of Children:* Unknown

Mary Jefferson, though called Polly or Marie by her family, lived her life in the shadow of her older sister, Martha. In an attempt to reassure Polly that her constant competitiveness with Martha was unnecessary, her stern, but fair, father wrote to her from the White House, shortly before the end of her life and during a time when she was suffering characteristics of depression. Jefferson wrote, "No, never imagine that there could possibly be a difference to me between yourself and sister. You have both such dispositions to engross my whole love and each so entirely that there can be no greater degree of it that each possess."[16]

Polly was educated in France under her father's advisement, and she attended a Catholic convent near Paris. Following the death of her sister,

Lucy II, from whooping cough, which she herself barely survived, nine-year-old Polly made the trip to Paris accompanied by a Jefferson family household slave, fourteen-year-old Sally Hemings. Separated from her father and sister for almost six years following her mother's death, it was two years after the death of her sister Lucy II before Polly got to Europe. (Jefferson had finally decided she was no safer from illnesses in the States.) When Polly arrived in Paris she just barely remembered her father and had no memory of her older sister, Martha.

Unlike Martha, Polly bore a strong resemblance to her mother and was considered very lovely. She married her cousin, John Wayles Eppes, whom she had known and loved all her life. The marriage further strengthed ties of the Jefferson family with the Wayles family—her mother's. Polly's husband became a member of the House of Representatives, and the economic and social strength of these united families represented a substantial power in Virginia and in all of the United States.

During the years of her marriage, Polly gave birth to several children, but the final birth ended Polly's life at age twenty-five. At the time of Polly's death, her father was in his second term as president of the United States. Distraught over the death of this daughter who had lived to adulthood, Jefferson formed an even closer relationship with his only surviving child, Martha.

## LUCY ELIZABETH JEFFERSON I

Fifth child, fourth daughter of Thomas Jefferson and Martha Wayles Skelton
*Born:* November 3, 1780      *Birthplace:* Richmond, Virginia
*Died:* April 15,1781      *Age at Death:* 5 months
*Cause of Death:* Unknown

Lucy Elizabeth, the first of two Jefferson daughters to be so named, was named after Jefferson's two sisters, eleven-year-old Lucy and twenty-one-year-old, mentally retarded Elizabeth. As a large, ten-and-one-half pound, baby, anticipation for her survival was high.

Jefferson was in the Virginia capitol of Richmond when Lucy Elizabeth died. He did not learn of her death until he returned to Monticello. The profound grief he felt at the death of this child was further deepened by the effects of this child's death on his wife, Martha. She fell into a deep state of melancholy, having had three of the five children she had given birth to die during infancy. She continued in this emotional state for the next seventeen months, when yet another birth caused her death.

## LUCY ELIZABETH JEFFERSON II

Sixth child, fifth daughter of Thomas Jefferson and Martha Wayles Skelton
*Born:* May 8, 1782    *Birthplace:* Monticello, Albemarle, Virginia
*Died:* November 17, 1785    *Age at Death:* 3 years, 6 months
*Cause of Death:* Whooping cough

---

Lucy Elizabeth Jefferson, the second Jefferson daughter named after his two sisters, was born a bit more than a year after the death of her sister, Lucy I. Lucy II was the last of Jefferson's legally accepted children. Her birth resulted in Martha's death.

Martha's successive pregnancies, often regularly resulting in miscarriages, was a factor in her death shortly after the difficult birth of the second Lucy.

Jefferson, who loved his wife passionately, was distraught. Monticello came to represent memories he was unable to bear. To escape the scene of his wife's death, Jefferson took the position of U.S. minister to France. He took with him only his daughter Martha and left his younger daughters, Polly and Lucy II, with his sister-in-law, Mrs. Eppes. Jefferson believed that by leaving the small children in the States he would avoid exposing them to the dangers of the journey as well avoid potential health problems in the unfamiliar surroundings of Paris.

However, three years later, while Jefferson was still in Paris, his baby daughter, Lucy II, died of whooping cough. Jefferson children's poor survival rate was, indeed, unusually high, even for the times.

## TOM, HARRIET I, BEVERLY, HARRIET II, MADISON, AND ESTON HEMINGS

Presumed illegitimate children of Thomas Jefferson and Sally Hemings

*Born:* Tom: 1790
   Harriet I: October 5, 1795
   Beverly : 1798
   Harriet II: May 1801
   Madison: January 1805
   Eston: May 21, 1808
*Birthplaces:* Tom: France
     Others: Monticello, Albemarle, Virginia.[17]
*Causes of Death:* Unknown
*Spouses:* Several married, as specified below, but times and names of mates are generally unknown.

---

Thomas Jefferson had been president of the United States for only a short time when the Washington rumor mill began hinting that several of the Jefferson slaves serving in the White House bore a strong resemblance to the president. The observations gave rise to a generally accepted love story alledged to have taken place between widower Thomas Jefferson and Sally Hemings, a Jefferson slave.

Sally Hemings, born to Betty Hemings, a household slave of Thomas Jefferson's father-in-law from a supposed union between Betty Hemings and her master, became a Jefferson slave upon the death of his father-in-law. Nine-year-old Sally, described as pretty and almost white, moved with her mother to the Jefferson home. Both she and her mother were given the duties of caring for Jefferson's dying wife, Martha Wayles Skelton Jefferson. Sally became a runner for the sickroom, while her mother cared for the rapidly failing Martha. Running to the sound of a "tinkling silver bell," Sally carried messages throughout the household. (The bell, handed down through four generations of Hemingses, was presented to Howard University in the 1960s.)[18]

A physically mature fourteen-year-old Sally accompanied Jefferson's youngest daughter, Polly, when she traveled to join her father and sister in France following the death of her small sister, Lucy Elizabeth II, in Virginia. Two years later, Sally returned to the United States with an infant son.[19] Shortly thereafter Jefferson also returned to the States.

The Jefferson "Farm Book" records the births of four children as follows: Beverly, 1798; Harriet, 1801; Madison, 1805; and Eston, 1808. There is some question whether a fifth child, recorded "Harriet" ambiguously, belonged to Sally Hemings. The case for the parentage of these children by Jefferson rests on the following points:

1. The "Farm Book" does not mention the father. Identification of slave sires was common practice, by Jefferson as well as other slaveholders.
2. Harriet I was born October 5, 1795, during a period of two years (1794–1796) that Jefferson spent at Monticello.
3. Harriet II was born in May 1801, and Eston was born in May 1808, both nine months after Jefferson's regular August vacation at Monticello.
4. Madison was born in 1805, just nine months after Jefferson attended the Monticello funeral of his daughter, Polly.

Madison and Eston were made carpenter apprentices to Sally's brother, John, who was Jefferson's chief carpenter at Monticello. Harriet II became a favorite household slave. When Jefferson died in 1826 he freed Madison, Eston, and Sally's brother, John Hemings. Sally, fifty-three at the time of Jefferson's 1826 death, disappears completely from all records.

After being freed, Madison, supposed son of Jefferson, claimed that his mother came home from France and gave birth to a son by Thomas Jefferson. Also, "She gave birth to four others and Jefferson was the father of all of them. Their names were Beverly, Harriet, Madison (myself), and Eston. We all became freed because of a treaty entered into by our parents before we were born."[20]

Madison married the daughter of a slave and worked in Ohio, where he became a respected member of the community. Sister and brother Harriet and Beverly moved to Washington, D.C., married whites, and lived as members of the white community. Brother Eston married a black woman, produced three children, and died shortly after moving to Wisconsin, according to Madison.[21]

Such is the story of Jefferson's children by Sally Hemings. Whether all or any of the Jefferson/Hemings story is true cannot definitely be proven. However, as the story continues to be debated among historians, it is included for clarification in this section on Jefferson's children.

## FOR FURTHER READING

Brodie, Fawn M. *Thomas Jefferson: An Intimate History.* New York: W. W. Norton, 1974.

Burnham, Sophy. *The Landed Gentry: Passions and Personalities inside America's Propertied Class.* New York: G. P. Putnam's Sons, 1978.

Dabney, Virginius. *Jefferson Scandals: Rebuttal.* New York: Dodd, Mead, 1971.

McDonald, Forrest. *Presidency of Thomas Jefferson.* Lawrence: University Press of Kansas, 1976.

Malone, Dumas. *Sage of Monticello: Jefferson and His Time.* Vol. 6. Boston: Little, Brown, 1981.

Mapp, Alf, Jr. *Thomas Jefferson: A Strange Case of Mistaken Identity.* Lanham, Md.: Madison Books, 1987.

———. *Thomas Jefferson: Passionate Pilgrim: The Presidency, the Founding of the University, and the Private Battles.* Lanham, Md.: Madison Books, 1991.

Miller, Hope Ridings. *Scandals in the Highest Office.* New York: Random House, 1973.

Randolph, Saval Nicholas. *Domestic Life of Thomas Jefferson.* Charlottesville: University of Virginia Press, 1978.

Schachner, Nathan. *Thomas Jefferson: A Biography.* New York: Appleton-Century Crofts, 1951.

Smith, Page. *Jefferson: A Revealing Biography.* New York: American Heritage Publishing, 1976.

Sullivan, Michael John. *Presidential Passions—From Washington and Jefferson to Kennedy and Johnson.* New York: Shapolsky Publishers, 1991.

# 4  JAMES MONROE'S CHILDREN

## ELIZA KORTRIGHT MONROE HAY

First child of James Monroe and Elizabeth Kortright
*Born:* December 1786      *Birthplace:* Virginia
*Died:* 1835      *Age at Death:* 49 years
*Cause of Death:* Unknown
*Education:* Madame Campan's School for Girls in Paris, France
*Profession:* Housewife, mother, White House hostess
*Spouse:* George Hay      *Number of Children:* 1, at least

Eliza Monroe, a tall, glossy-haired, black-eyed beauty, received her education in Europe. At the age of seven, when her father was minister to France, she entered Madame Campan's renowned school for girls on the outskirts of Paris. It was there that she established a lifelong friendship with Hortense Beauharnais, the daughter of Josephine Bonaparte, the future Queen of Holland and mother of Napoleon III of France. So intense was this long-lasting friendship that Eliza named her daughter Hortense, in honor of her royal friend.

In 1817, when James Monroe entered the White House, Eliza was married to George Hay, a prominent attorney noted for his role as prosecutor in the infamous treason trial of Aaron Burr. Her role as wife was interrupted frequently by the necessity of substituting for her mother as hostess at the White House because her mother, Elizabeth, could not tolerate the ordeal of being the White House mistress. At the White House, Eliza is primarily remembered for her domineering style and insistence that every iota of protocol be followed. While Eliza served as hostess, her husband George became secretary to her father, President James Monroe.

Following Monroe's presidency, Eliza and her family moved to a new Virginia home. The home, whose rough plans had been drawn by her father and Thomas Jefferson, was the site of family gatherings. Life was comfortable for the Hays, and the family's income was assured when John Quincy Adams, successor to Monroe as president, repaid debts to the family by appointing Eliza's husband as judge for Virginia's eastern court.

When James Monroe died, Eliza returned to France to visit her friend Hortense. The two traveled to Rome, where Eliza was converted to Catholicism by Pope Gregory XVI. Eliza died in Paris, where she is buried.

## J. S. MONROE

Second child, only son of James Monroe and Elizabeth Kortright
*Born:* May 1799     *Birthplace:* Unknown     *Died:* September 28, 1801
*Age at Death:* 2 years, 4 months     *Cause of Death:* Unknown

---

In the Monroe family burial plot there is a gravestone bearing the initials "J.S.M." which are believed to be those of James Monroe's only son.[22] It is assumed that the initials represent James, after his father, and Spence, after Monroe's father and brother, though it is only speculation as almost nothing is known about the Monroe boy.

The little boy suffered from "a series of childhood diseases," as Monroe informed Thomas Jefferson by letter.[23] Apparently Mrs. Monroe traveled far from the family's Virginia home in search of a healthy place to revitalize their sickly son but to no avail; "J. S." Monroe died shortly after his second birthday.

## MARIA HESTER MONROE GOUVENEUR

Third child, second daughter of James Monroe and Elizabeth Kortright
*Born:* 1803     *Birthplace:* Paris, France     *Died:* 1850
*Age at Death:* 47 years     *Cause of Death:* Unknown
*Education:* Private schools in Washington, D.C.
*Profession:* Housewife, mother

*Spouse:* Samuel Lawrence Gouveneur
*Number of Children:* 3

Born in Paris, France, the daughter of the future president of the United States, Maria did not see her parents' homeland until she was four-and-one-half years old. Her arrival in America sparked a new fashion fad. Little Maria wore "pants." The pants, more properly known as "pantalettes," represented haute couture on the Continent.

Attending schools in Washington, D.C., where her father was very active in the politics of the city, young Maria became known as a fashion pacesetter and was very popular with the younger set of the city's elite. When she was fourteen yeas old, her father was elected to the presidency.

Shortly after her father's term began, he employed Samuel Lawrence Gouveneur to work for him as a junior secretary in the White House. For Maria, it was love at first sight, and she immediately set her cap for him. The couple was married in 1820 in the first White House wedding.

When Monroe's second term in office ended in 1825, Maria and her husband moved to his hometown of New York City. Samuel was appointed as postmaster of New York City by Monroe's successor to the presidency, John Quincy Adams. In this way Adams further repaid political debts owed her father. Thus, Maria, Samuel, and their three children were able to live comfortably. However, by the late 1820s, Maria's father was in financial difficulties and he turned to Maria and Samuel for help. He sold his Virginia home and moved to New York City to live his final years with his daughter.

## FOR FURTHER READING

Cresson, William Penn. *James Monroe.* New York: Archon Books, 1971.

Kane, Joseph Nathan. *Facts about the Presidents.* 4th ed. New York: H. W Wilson, 1981.

Klapthor, Margaret Brown. *First Ladies.* Washington, D.C.: White House Historical Association, 1979.

Richardson, James D. *A Compilation of the Messages and Papers of the Presidents, 1789–1897.* Washington, D.C.: n.p., 1897.

Whitney, David C. *The American Presidents.* 4th ed. Garden City, New York: Doubleday, 1978.

# 5 JOHN QUINCY ADAMS'S CHILDREN

## GEORGE WASHINGTON ADAMS

First child of John Quincy Adams and Louisa Catherine Johnson
*Born:* April 13, 1801     *Birthplace:* Berlin, Germany
*Died:* April 30, 1829     *Age at Death:* 28 years
*Cause of Death:* Drowning
*Education:* Tutors, preparatory schools, Harvard University
*Profession:* Lawyer     *Spouse:* None     *Number of Children:* 1

George Washington Adams, born in Berlin, Germany, where his father was serving as America's minister to Prussia, was named after George Washington, whose death had occurred only a year earlier. His birth followed several miscarriages and was extremely difficult for his mother, Louisa. Perhaps the difficult birth can be seen as setting the tone of George Washington Adams's difficulty in living up to the desires of his father as they are reflected by the selection of this almost awesome name for his first son. The task of living up to both his name and his father's expectations would prove to be more than the young man could manage.

In early childhood, George showed signs of brilliance, but, as his grandfather, John Adams, second president of the United States, warned, "George is a treasure of diamonds. He has genius equal to anything; but like all other genius requires the most delicate management to keep it from running into eccentricities."[24] Characterized as sensitive, with a strong interest in art and music, he never experienced the "delicate management" prescribed by his grandfather. On the contrary, his entire life was spent with his father's scoldings, commandments, and periodic tirades raining down upon him.

Acknowledged by his family as a nervous, overgrown boy of unsteady health, George was privately tutored in preparation for his admission to Harvard. Once at Harvard, George received directions by mail from his father on how to conduct every aspect of his private life. His father told him when to work, at which times of the day to play, and reminded the young man that he was an Adams and he must recognize that, "[My] sons have not only their honor but that of two preceding generations to sustain."[25] John Quincy thought that George's aspirations toward poetry and literature were inappropriate to the family's name. As if to confirm his father's opinion, George became involved in a student riot at Harvard and, as was later discovered, led a double life. Nonetheless, George graduated from Harvard, was admitted to the Massachusetts bar in 1824, and practiced law in Boston. In 1825 George reached the zenith of his achievements when he was elected to the Massachusetts state legislature. During this short period of success, George seemed to be on the road to fulfilling his father's ambitions for him. As much of the Adamses' property was in Boston, George took over management of the family finances, earning a short-lived acceptance by the family.

George traveled frequently to Washington, D.C., when his father occupied the White House. It was during these trips that he fell in love with his cousin, Mary Catherine, who, along with several other orphaned children of his mother's sister, stayed at the White House during John Quincy Adams's administration. As John Quincy was Mary Catherine's guardian, George approached his father about marriage to her. Both father and son agreed that it would be better if George developed his law practice for four or five years, and, then, possibly the marriage could be considered. George returned to Boston to work.

In his absence, Mary Catherine became attracted to George's younger brother, John II, who also lived at the White House. Eventually Mary Catherine broke the engagement in order to marry John II. Thereafter, George's apparent devotion to his family and career began to dissipate. He began to neglect his law practice, to acquire numerous debts, and to stay out late drinking.

In the summer of 1827, his mother visited Boston during one of George's periodic illnesses to nurse him back to health. She wrote to John Quincy, describing George as "the same old exaggerated conceited timid enthusiastic negligent cold and eccentric being that he had been since he was born."[26] John Quincy asked that George send him his diary for evaluation. Later that year, the president traveled to Boston to visit his eldest son, whom he decribed as "dutiful and affectionate, and wants nothing but a firm purpose to be all that I could wish."[27]

In the spring of 1829, George traveled to Washington for a visit with his family. Those who saw him recognized that something was seriously wrong. His appearance and actions showed physical and mental degeneration. Returning home by way of New York City, George left Washington on April 29, 1829, complaining of a very bad headache.

During his return from Washington he told fellow passengers on the ship that he heard voices of people who were spying on him. At 3 A.M. on April 30, George went to the ship's captain and demanded the ship be stopped so he could get off, and, after giving these clearly disturbed orders to the captain, George disappeared. Later, his hat was seen off the stern of the ship. Within two weeks, George's body was discovered near City Island in New York. It was determined in the investigation only that George had fallen or jumped overboard. His body was returned to the family's Braintree County home for burial.

Soon after his death it was discovered that George had been leading a double life. Papers were found in which George acknowledged his parenting of a child by a maid of the Adamses' Boston doctor. The affair was known in the Boston area, but it was a surprise to the Adams family. A blackmailer entered the scene. To keep the family's sordid secret quiet, the blackmailer demanded payment. On behalf of the family, Charles Francis Adams, George's younger brother, refused to pay to suppress the scandal. In anger the blackmailer published and circulated a forty-four-page pamphlet intended to embarrass the Adams family. George's mother always maintained that her eldest son was a sacrifice to the political ambitions of the Adams family. Charles Francis later observed of his brother, "Poor fellow, he had wound himself nearly up in his own web."[28]

## JOHN ADAMS II

Second child, second son of John Quincy Adams and Louisa Catherine Johnson
*Born:* July 4, 1803      *Birthplace:* Boston, Massachusetts
*Died:* October 23, 1834      *Age at Death:* 31 years, 3 months
*Cause of Death:* Alcoholism
*Education:* Preparatory schools, Harvard University
*Profession:* Secretary, presidential aide, gristmill manager
*Spouse:* Mary Catherine Hellen      *Number of Children:* 2

It was his mother who frequently observed, following the early death of John Adams II, that he was yet another sacrificial lamb on the doorstep of the Adams family ambition for political power.

As a young man, John and his brother George accompanied their father to England, while he served in his third major diplomatic post. At this stage of his life, John Adams II was outgoing and eager. In 1817 the family returned to the United States. In the manner accepted for prominent families of the time, John was educated in preparatory schools and was admitted to Harvard in 1819. He excelled in sports but was only a fair scholar.

When he found out that John II stood only forty-fifth in his Harvard class of eighty-five, his father refused John permission to return home for Christmas vacation. The senior Adams stated his position in a characteristically harsh letter: "I could feel nothing but sorrow and shame in your presence."[29] Spurred on by his father's anger, John managed to move his standing up to twenty-fourth in his class, but it was not good enough for his father. He informed John that he would not attend his graduation ceremonies unless he stood fifth or better. However, his father's warnings were not tested. In 1823, just before his graduation, John became involved in a student rebellion and he and forty-two other students were expelled from Harvard.

When he left Harvard, his father brought John II to join the family in the White House while he served what would be his single term as president of the United States. John became his father's secretary. In a White House wedding, John married his cousin, Mary Catherine, who had earlier been engaged to his older brother George. In a letter Louisa Adams wrote to her youngest son, Charles Francis, she observed that John looked as if "the cares of the world lay on his shoulders and my heart tells me there is much to fear."[30] It was a prophetic observation.

John and Mary lived at the White House during their first years of marriage, and their first child was born in the White House. It was a time of family entertainment, such as playing musical instruments and taking part in family theatricals, as well as presidential duties and the politics of government. But their tranquility was short-lived.

During the 1828 New Year's Eve celebration held at the White House, the president insulted a guest, Russell Jarvis, in front of other guests, as well as in the presence of John II. Since the president was not liable to challenge because he was the president, Jarvis challenged John II to a duel. Jarvis then sent a letter to John II demanding a duel, but he received no response. Not to respond to such a challenge was thought cowardly by many Americans. To further humiliate the president through his son, Jarvis felt it necessary to provoke an incident. Jarvis intercepted John II in the rotunda of the capitol as he carried a message from his father's office to Congress. Jarvis yanked

John's nose and slapped his face, all standard and approved provocations for a duel. Again, John did not respond. However, John Quincy's disapproval of dueling was made evident when he responded for his son by sending a message to Congress that "his secretary" had been waylaid and assaulted by "a person," requesting that Congress provide funds to secure the way between the president's office and Congress so that future incidents could be prevented. The press had a time with the "nose-pulling" episode, and Congress went so far as to investigate by calling both John II and Russell Jarvis before it for examination. John's mother always maintained that the humiliation of the nose-pulling incident ruined her son's career.

John moved from the White House to take over management of a family-owned gristmill. The business had never been successful, and under John's management it began to go broke. John began to drink heavily. By the late 1820s, John Quincy observed that "my dear son has been in declining and drooping state of health."[31]

Losing his bid for a second term as president, John Quincy returned to the family home near Quincy, Massachusetts. John II remained at the gristmill near Washington, D.C., his health steadily deteriorating. In late October 1834, John Quincy received notice that his thirty-one-year-old son was gravely ill. He rushed to his son's bedside, arriving only four hours before John II died.

John's death was a cause for heightened tensions within the family. Louisa accused John Quincy of sacrificing another son to political ambition. Whether or not mother Louisa's accusation was justified, it is certain that John Quincy's treatment of his son lacked parental warmth and affection. It was not easy to be a member of the Adams family, and more particularly the son of John Quincy Adams.

## CHARLES FRANCIS ADAMS

Third child, third son of John Quincy Adams and Louisa Catherine Johnson
*Born:* August 18, 1807     *Birthplace:* Boston, Massachusetts
*Died:* November 21, 1886     *Age at Death:* 79 years, 3 months
*Cause of Death:* Stroke
*Education:* Tutors, private schools, Harvard University
*Profession:* Writer, politician
*Spouse:* Abigail Brown Brooks     *Number of Children:* 6

Educated through travel with his family on trips to Russia and England during John Quincy Adams's service in the diplomatic corps, Charles spoke fluent French, German, and Russian at a very young age. Following attendance at several European schools, as well as the Boston Latin School, Charles graduated from Harvard College in 1825. From Harvard, Charles went to apprentice in law under the tutelage of the famous Daniel Webster. Yet, even with this excellent beginning, he was never to practice law.

At the age of twenty-two, Charles married Abigail Brown Brooks, daughter of Peter Brooks, at the time the wealthiest citizen of Boston. Following his marriage, Charles turned from law to writing, editing, and publishing family documents, as well as writing on subjects such as economics and foreign policy, often taking controversial stands on political issues of the time. Charles championed the radical position of abolishing slavery, and he even went so far in his assistance to the blacks' cause as to initiate Boston laws to prevent discrimination on public conveyances.

With the death of his wife's father, Charles inherited a huge estate, enabling him to pursue politics without monetary concerns. In 1841 Charles became his father's and grandfather's successor apparent when he was elected to the Massachusetts state legislature. By 1848 he had become a spokesman for the abolitionist movement, first as a delegate and then when he chaired the state's convention seeking to end slavery. The convention was part of the separatist movement that split from the Democratic party and was renamed the Free-Soil party. Former president Martin Van Buren was selected to head the new party's national ticket, and Charles Francis Adams was chosen as the vice presidential candidate. But the time was not yet ripe. Van Buren, an abolitionist, and Adams were soundly defeated by the Whigs' southern candidate, Zachary Taylor.

Elected to the House of Representatives in 1858, Charles was strangely silent on his abolitionist stand, causing the nickname "Silent Charles" to be hurled at him by his detractors. Following in the tradition of his grandfather and father, Charles was appointed as minister to Great Britain, where he served with a high level of popularity.[32] "This scion of the Adams clan was 'to the manner born' so that his family prestige and the wealth of his wife paved the way into the inner circles of British society."[33] It was said that "though he had his father's name, he lacked personal magnetism."[34]

In 1872 and again in 1876 Charles's name was placed in nomination at the Republican convention as candidate for president of the United States. Charles advocated civil service reform and control of business—much in advance of his peers. Neither convention concluded with Charles as the party's contender for the presidency.

Charles retired to Boston, concluding his public life. He was free to devote time to his continuing scholarly work on the Adams family, an undertaking which extended to ten volumes. Charles died on November 21, 1886. According to newspaper accounts, "he had not been well for some time, and suffered more or less for the past five years from some brain troubles, the result of overwork."[35]

But for his championing of the right causes at the wrong time, there is reason to believe that Charles might well have been the third in a dynasty of American presidents.

## LOUISA CATHERINE ADAMS

Fourth child, only daughter of John Quincy Adams and Louisa Catherine Johnson

*Born:* 1811    *Birthplace:* St. Petersburg, Russia    *Died:* 1812
*Age at Death:* 1 year    *Cause of Death:* Unknown

Louisa Catherine, conceived and born in St. Petersburg, Russia, lived only a short time. While John Quincy Adams was serving as U.S. minister to Russia, his last child was born. When ordered, by Madison, to Paris to negotiate the Treaty of Ghent in 1814, ending the War of 1812, his wife's major concern was "that the baby would be left behind in Russia's inhospitable clime."[36]

How did the infant Louisa Catherine die? There is no known record of the cause. She may have been the victim of the high infant mortality rate characteristic of the time, or the rigors of the Russian winter may have been responsible for her early demise. Even her exact birth and death dates are unknown.

Somewhere in Russia's St. Petersburg rest the remains of a child of the eighth president of the United States.

### FOR FURTHER READING

See list following the chapter about John Adams's family.

# 6 MARTIN VAN BUREN'S CHILDREN

## ABRAHAM VAN BUREN

First of four sons of Martin Van Buren and Hannah Hoes
*Born:* November 27, 1807      *Birthplace:* Kinderhook, New York
*Died:* March 15, 1873     *Age at Death:* 65 years, 3 months
*Cause of Death:* Unknown      *Education:* West Point
*Profession:* Soldier, presidential secretary
*Spouse:* Angelica Singleton      *Number of Children:* 3

Perhaps the best description for the first of Martin Van Buren's four sons is that of steady head and hand constantly in attendance to his father's needs. So much is this true that it seems as if Abraham Van Buren had little life of his very own. As a young child, he identified only as his father's son; in adulthood, he came to be known as the husband of Angelica, his wife of many years.

Entering West Point when he was sixteen, Abraham graduated from the school in 1827 with a rank of second lieutenant in the army. Posted to an infantry regiment on the frontier for two years, he was promoted to the rank of first lieutenant after five years in the service, and then four years later was made a captain—a slow promotion rate in the military of the day, particularly given his father's political positions of the time. After serving in Congress, and as vice president to Andrew Jackson, Martin Van Buren was elected president in 1836. Abraham resigned his military commission to become his father's secretary.

The wife of James Madison, Dolley, introduced Abraham to her cousin, the beautiful and accomplished Angelica Singleton. Abraham married her in 1838, shortly after his father became president. Angelica, heir of a wealthy South Carolina family, spurned convention of the era that women of prominent families remain in the background, and she earned a lively reputation for herself when she acted as White House hostess during her father-in-law's term in office. It was claimed by Washington society that Angelica assumed airs!

With the outbreak of the Mexican War in 1846, Abraham was commissioned as a major and was actively involved in the campaign from Vera Cruz to Mexico City. Finally, in recognition of his service he was promoted to the rank of lieutenant colonel. Promoted at the same time was Robert E. Lee, who would command the southern forces in the Civil War. Abraham served in the army for a total of eighteen years, until his 1854 retirement.

Following retirement, he and Angelica earned a reputation for elegant and gracious hospitality. While the Van Burens thus appeared consumed with the social graces, Abraham was, in fact, busy editing and publishing Martin Van Buren's works.

It was said of Abraham that "he is very different from 'Prince' John, his younger brother, who resembles his father in using his fellow man as a ladder upon which to mount and when he is up he kicks it down and without scrupples [sic] of conscience denies he has had any aid."[37] Abraham not only did not kick the ladder down but, instead, served to steady his brother and father throughout his lifetime.

## JOHN VAN BUREN

Second of four sons of Martin Van Buren and Hannah Hoes
*Born:* February 18, 1810      *Birthplace:* Hudson, New York
*Died:* October 13, 1866      *Age at Death:* 56 years, 8 months
*Cause of Death:* Kidney failure
*Education:* Private studies, Yale University
*Profession:* Lawyer, politician
*Spouse:* Elizabeth VanderPoel      *Number of Children:* 1

John Van Buren is one of the most colorful of all presidential children. His life was marked by escapades as well as accomplishments, and he had equal numbers of followers and detractors. Perhaps, had he had less of an aversion to hard work and more ambition for public office, John Van Buren might have equaled his father's achievement and moved into the White House as president of the United States.

Tall, well built, with an unpretentious, personable quality, this son of a president was also described by contemporaries as extravagant, bold, notorious, and brilliant.

Reaching manhood in the 1830s, when young gentlemen were expected to have prowess in drinking, gambling, and lovemaking, John achieved notoriety and caused concern in the first two areas. After graduating from Yale in his late teens, John studied law in Albany, New York, and was admitted to the New York bar when barely twenty years old. He did not proceed directly to the practice of law because his father was named minister to England, and John accompanied his father as secretary to the American legation. He delighted in the elegant life of European nobility and was quickly accepted into high society. It was during this first Europeon journey that John developed close associations with influential Europeans that would be further cultivated in later years.

After spending two years in Europe, John returned to Albany, where he opened a law practice. Initially his law practice was highly successful and lucrative. However, habits acquired during college days, habits associated with drinking and gambling, soon made themselves known. News of John's notoriety reached the ears of his father, who had become president of the United States in 1837. The president wrote to his son expressing his concern: "What you may regard as an innocent and harmless indulgence will take you years to overcome in the public estimation." Further, "I was informed that you had been twice carried drunk from the race course."[38] What John needed, he suggested, was to reform with new habits and associations. He suggested a vacation in the London John so enjoyed, and John followed his father's suggestion.

To direct John on the right track in London, Martin Van Buren asked former President Jackson for letters of introduction to the Duke of Wellington—the British hero of Waterloo. Jackson complied with the request. Thus John was reintroduced to the most elite European society through the auspices of the conquerer of Napoleon, but it was to be this very elitism that would bring him difficulties in equality-loving America. John's name appeared on a guest list of a social event, with his name listed between royal titles as "John Van Buren, Son of the President of the United States."[39] An uproar appeared in the American press. A member of the U.S. House of Representatives stood "to denounce this flagrant departure from the ideals of equality for which the Founding Fathers fought against England."[40] Henceforth, in ridicule, John Van Buren became known to American people as "Prince John."

Notwithstanding the negative press, John engaged in some solid politicking among his constituents and was elected to Congress in 1840. Among his fellow representatives were former president John Quincy Adams and soon-to-be president Millard Fillmore, as well as James Roosevelt, the founding politico of two future presidents. Either despite his reputation for indulging in the bottle, or because of his prowess at imbibing, John was repeatedly reelected to the House of Representatives. Observations such as "John Van Buren is a rowdy, and the associate of rowdies" did him no harm in political contests.[41] On the burning issue of the day, slavery, John supported his northern colleagues, affirming, "I look with detestation upon the practice of buying and selling live bodies."[42] However he did not support slavery's abolition by proclamation, believing the method unconstitutional. Further, despite his abhorrence of slavery, John Van Buren did not support Abraham Lincoln's presidential bid, but instead supported the state's rights candidate John Breckenridge, the nominee of the southern faction of the Democratic party.

In his legal practice, John's most famous case was *Forrest v. Forrest* (1851–1852), a scandalous divorce action. The sordid details of infidelity by both parties made lurid headlines and advanced John's legal practice.

For the last few years of his life John was an invalid. For his health, as well as to see again places of pleasant memories, John went abroad in 1866. On the return journey, accompanied by his only child, John set sail aboard *The Scotia*, but he was never to see America again. John "Prince" Van Buren suffered complete kidney failure and died at sea.

John Van Buren, an American president's son, was actually called by a royal title, during his lifetime—though the title was in the form of ridicule which he overcame. Possessing the physical and mental characteristics and the proper associations, John had all the credentials for high achievement, possibly even the presidency itself. Yet, he sought only to taste the world, rather than to shape it.

## MARTIN (MAT) VAN BUREN, JR.

Third of four sons of Martin Van Buren and Hannah Hoes
*Born:* December 20, 1812    *Birthplace:* New York City, New York
*Died:* March 19, 1855    *Age at Death:* 42 years, 3 months
*Cause of Death:* Long-term illness    *Education:* Unknown
*Profession:* Presidential secretary    *Spouse:* None
*Number of Children:* None

Martin Van Buren, Jr., called Mat by family and friends, spent his entire life as a very sedate, controlled individual. Working as secretary to his father during Van Buren's presidency, he certainly was not the man to inspire either love or hate from those who knew him.

Described as very literary and not at all physical or robust in appearance, Mat developed his father's notes for the senior Van Buren's planned biography. However, by fall of 1849, Mat's lack of physical well-being took its toll and left him a very sick man. Though ill, he maintained a wide correspondence with his father's friends.

His seventy-year-old father was extremely worried about his son. He finally prevailed upon the failing Mat to seek help from Europeon doctors in Switzerland and England, as well as searching out the restorative powers offered by waters in France and Germany, but to no avail. "It had been the boast of Martin Van Buren that he had been the first president of the United States born under the American flag. It was the destiny of Van Buren, Jr., to be the first presidential son to die under a foreign flag."[43]

Mat Van Buren died in Paris while seeking relief from the illnesses that had plagued him all of his life.

## SMITH THOMPSON VAN BUREN

Fourth of four sons of Martin Van Buren and Hannah Hoes
*Born:* January 16, 1817     *Birthplace:* New York City, New York
*Died:* 1876     *Age at Death:* 59 years
*Cause of Death:* Unknown     *Education:* Unknown
*Profession:* Presidential aide, editor
*Spouses:* Ellen James, Henrietta Irving
*Number of Children:* Van Buren/James: 4; Van Buren/Irving: 3

Named after Van Buren's close friend and chief justice of the New York State Supreme Court, Smith Thompson Van Buren was raised in a sphere of political intrigue, compounded by controversy over the capabilities of his father, President Van Buren. Unlike his namesake, Smith avoided the judicial arena and spent most of his life defending his father and elder brother, John, who became known to the nation for his escapades in Europe. Occasionally, however, Smith Thompson, too, became the recipient of political attacks, particularly in reference to his reputation as being extremely tightfisted.

Never a candidate for public office himself, he did, however, attend numerous political gatherings, where his intensity on behalf of his father's political actions was well known. Considered knowledgeable about important people and issues of the day, the youngest Van Buren son worked constantly for his father during his presidency. Smith rendered real aid to his father by writing and preparing speeches and documents.

Little of Smith's private life is known. Though he married twice and sired seven children, his impact in history stems from his writings on the presidency of his father. Living fourteen years beyond his father, Smith completed and edited his father's treatise on the development of political parties.[44] Because of his invaluable contributions to our understanding of the Van Buren presidency, he may be credited with some responsibility for what there is of the senior Van Buren's mark on American history.

## FOR FURTHER READING

Kane, Joseph Nathan. *Facts about the Presidents*. 4th ed. New York: H. W. Wilson, 1981.

Whitney, David C. *The American Presidents*. Garden City, New York: Doubleday, 1978.

# 7 WILLIAM HENRY HARRISON'S CHILDREN

*AN INTRODUCTORY NOTE*

The ninth president of the United States, William Henry Harrison, was the nation's chief executive for only one month. The sixty-eight-year-old military hero of the War of 1812 came into the presidency following a hard-fought, vigorous campaign to win the office. On the day Harrison was inaugurated (March 4, 1841), the winds blew and there was a strong chill in the air. Harrison took an hour and one-half to read his inauguration address. His speech, combined with those of the other official speakers of the ceremonies, added up to a long exposure to chilly Washington, D.C., weather. Within days, the elderly man was suffering from pneumonia. He died thirty-two days later. Immediately succeeded by his vice president, John Tyler, it is almost as if William Henry Harrison never served as president of the United States. Today, about the only memory held of Harrison's presidency is the fact that he holds the record for the shortest presidential term in office, despite the fact that Harrison is well remembered by historians for his military leadership.

Perhaps because of his short service in the presidency, little is recorded about his children, although three of his sons achieved renown on their own, including one who would be the father of the twenty-third president of the United States, Benjamin Harrison. The others have received only the most perfunctory notes in history.

The lives of most of Harrison's ten children were short, ending while in their thirties. Most of the children preceded their father in death before, late in his life, he achieved his brief moment in the nation's highest office.

## ELIZABETH (BETSEY) BASSETT HARRISON SHORT

First child of William Henry Harrison and Anna Tuthill Symmes
*Born:* September 29, 1796
*Birthplace:* Fort Washington, Ohio Territory
*Died:* September 26, 1846    *Age at Death:* 50 years
*Cause of Death:* Unknown    *Education:* Unknown
*Profession:* Housewife    *Spouse:* John Cleves Short
*Number of Children:* Unknown

---

Born at Fort Washington, Ohio, only shortly after her father was given command of that fort, Elizabeth survived five years beyond her father's death.

She married her cousin, John Short, when she was eighteen years old, and the couple lived on a farm her father had given to them. Betsey's life ended a year after that of her youngest sister, Anna. The three younger Harrison daughters all died relatively early in life.

## JOHN CLEVES SYMMES HARRISON

Second child, first son of William Henry Harrison and Anna Tuthill Symmes
*Born:* October 28, 1798    *Birthplace:* Vincennes, Indiana Territory
*Died:* October 30, 1832    *Age at Death:* 34 years
*Cause of Death:* Unknown    *Education:* Unknown
*Profession:* Government employee    *Spouse:* Clarissa Pike
*Number of Children:* 6

---

Born in the new capital of the Indiana Territory, Vincennes, John Cleves Symmes, always referred to as Symmes, spent almost all of his short life in Indiana. Marrying the daughter of the famous General Zebulon Montgomery Pike, discoverer of Pike's Peak, Symmes fathered six children. To support his family he received an appointment arranged by his father, and he was assigned to the finance division of the government land office at Vincennes. It was a position of responsibility. Large sums of money regularly passed through his hands; at the time, the bureau in which he worked gave an expression to American slang; doing a land office business. For ten years, Symmes's honesty and integrity were unquestioned; however, Symmes was then accused of embezzlement.

Nearly $13,000 was missing from the government land office. The government took Symmes to court, and he was found guilty of embezzlement and commanded to make restitution of the missing money.

Since his father had posted surety for his son, he, as well as Symmes, was made responsible for repayment. Father and son did not share the financial burden of the judgment. Symmes died before the penalty was paid.

His father made restitution for the embezzlement, even while he grieved his son's death. Harrison also assumed responsibility for Symmes's widow, Clarissa, and the couple's six children. Ten years later, Harrison became president of the United States to serve for only thirty-two days.

## LUCY SINGLETON HARRISON ESTE

Third child, second daughter of William Henry Harrison and Anna Tuthill Symmes
*Born:* September 1800      *Birthplace:* Richmond, Virginia
*Died:* April 7, 1826      *Age at Death:* 26 years, 6 months
*Cause of Death:* Unknown      *Education:* Unknown
*Profession:* Housewife, mother      *Spouse:* David Este
*Number of Children:* 4

Married to David Este, a judge of the Superior Court of Ohio, Lucy Harrison gave birth to four children before her death at the age of twenty-six. When Lucy died, her father was a senator from the state of Ohio; it would be fifteen years before he became president.

## WILLIAM HENRY HARRISON, JR.

Fourth child, second son of William Henry Harrison and Anna Tuthill Symmes

*Born:* September 3, 1802  *Birthplace:* Vincennes, Indiana Territory
*Died:* February 6, 1838  *Age at Death:* 35 years, 5 months
*Cause of Death:* Alcoholism  *Education:* Transylvania College
*Profession:* Lawyer, politician, farmer  *Spouse:* Jane Findlay
*Number of Children:* Unknown

William, his father's namesake, showed little inclination toward the law career his father planned for him. The senior William had definite ideas about more than his son's career; he wanted his son to be his namesake in deed as well.

When he was seventeen years old, William was sent to school at Transylvania College in Lexington, Kentucky, despite the perpetual family financial difficulties. But the young man soon became homesick and discontented, complaining that he should be transferred to a college in Cincinnati so that he might be closer to the family. The family had moved to North Bend, Ohio, in 1814. The Harrison family rejected his pleas, and William completed his studies at Transylvania College, and though his grades were not particularly impressive, he earned a law degree. He began a short-lived Cincinnati law practice.

Within two years of William's graduation from law school, his father was appointed as minister to Mexico and secured the appointment of his son as his aide. During this period of international public service, William handled himself with the grace and skill of a political veteran, in contrast to his public behavior in later years.

Following this brief career in the diplomatic arena, William returned to Cincinnati and his law practice. He married Jane Findlay, daughter of his father's close friend, James Findlay. Their life together did not go well. By 1832 William was addicted to "demon rum." He abandoned his law practice because he could no longer cope with the demands of the profession. At his father's behest, William turned to farming, also unsuccessfully. Failure was again attributed to his alcoholism, which he never conquered. Eventually, his father took over support of William's family. In the end, William died from the effects of alcohol. When he buried his namesake the future president's dreams for his successor were ended. However, it was this son's wife, Jane, who served as White House hostess for her father-in-law's short-lived term as president of the United States.

# JOHN SCOTT HARRISON

Fifth child, third son of William Henry Harrison and Anna Tuthill Symmes
*Born:* October 4, 1804      *Birthplace:* Vincennes, Indiana Territory
*Died:* May 25, 1878      *Age at Death:* 73 years, 7 months
*Cause of Death:* Unknown      *Education:* Old Farmer's College
*Profession:* Farmer, politician
*Spouses:* Lucretia Knapp Johnson, Elizabeth Ramsey
*Number of Children:* Harrison/Johnson: 3; Harrison/Ramsey: 6

---

Son of a president and father of a president, John Scott Harrison served in the U.S. House of Representatives, although he never aspired to any elected office. John was a farmer for most of his seventy-three years, preferring his 400 fertile acres of land in North Bend, Ohio, to political intrigue. Nevertheless, the drama of political events followed him to his grave—and beyond.

John Scott, born in Vincennes, Indiana Territory, during his father's governorship of the territory, was educated at Old Farmer's College, where he studied law. Returning to the family lands, while his father was occupied with national politics and needed his son to run the farm, John Scott never practiced law. However, he was soon called upon by friends and neighbors to run for Congress. Successful, rather more for his popularity than for his political skill or interest, John served two terms in the Congress, but he was defeated in his third bid for the legislative seat.

After his political career ended, John Scott returned again to Hamilton County, Ohio, and to the farm where he was to live for the rest of his life. He tended his crops and watched the developing careers of his many children, among whom was Benjamin Harrison, who would become the twenty-third president of the United States.

On May 25, 1878, John Scott died of an unknown ailment. His death was followed by a bizarre succession of events which have never been satisfactorily explained.

Several days before his death, a young nephew, Devin, died and was buried in the Harrison family plot, but his corpse was stolen from the grave and disappeared. Taking no chance that such would occur to their father's body, John's children directed his grave be dug deep and a cement cover be used to protect it from would-be violators. Such was, supposedly, done.

A few days after John Scott's funeral, his son and several neighbors went to Cincinnati to search the medical school dissecting rooms for the body of

Devin, supposing that it had been sold to the school to be used in research.[45] The group searched all day but did not find the remains of Devin. However, as they prepared to leave the morgue, a body was discovered hanging in a shaft; the body's face was covered by a burlap bag. To the horror of John Scott's son, it was his father, John Scott Harrison, hanging in the shaft.

The newspapers had a field day with the grotesque details of the case. It was through this body-snatching that John Scott Harrison, a simple man known only in Ohio, became a national topic of conversation. When they buried John Scott Harrison again, in the family plot, his son and the future president, Benjamin Harrison, was standing by the grave. Some explained John Scott's disappearance as simply one of body theft for profit. Others found more devious reasons for the episode. It was suggested that Benjamin Harrison had made bitter and unforgiving enemies, who, not being able to triumph over Benjamin's Indiana political successes, had taken their vengeance out upon the unresisting corpse of his father.

Fame is a strange commodity. John Scott Harrison was both the son of a president and the father of a president and he served his country in Congress. Yet, though he is not well known in history, he is remembered primarily for the event that was surely one of the strangest incidents ever to befall a member of one of America's presidential families!

## BENJAMIN HARRISON

Sixth child, fourth son of William Henry Harrison and Anna Tuthill Symmes
*Born:* 1806     *Birthplace:* Vincennes, Indiana Territory
*Died:* June 9, 1840     *Age at Death:* 34 years
*Cause of Death:* Unknown     *Education:* Medical studies
*Profession:* Medical doctor
*Spouses:* Louisa Bonner, Mary Raney
*Number of Children:* Harrison/Bonner: 3; Harrison/Raney: 2

---

This, the first of the nation's Benjamin Harrisons, died while his nephew, who would be the twenty-third president of the United States, was but a small child. William Henry's son, Benjamin, accomplished much in his short life-span. Twice married, he fathered five children, three by his first wife and two by the second, and he completed medical studies, entering into a medical career—all before he was in his mid-thirties. Since his father had studied medicine, the only president to do so, it is not surprising that his son should follow his father's example.

In 1836, during the Texas/Mexico War that concluded with Texas becoming the Republic of Texas, this son of a future president was held as a prisoner by Mexican forces for a short period. Although the circumstances of his brief imprisonment are unknown, it may be assumed they were in conjunction with his education and career as a physician.

Benjamin died only months before his father was elected to the presidency. His name, however, was perpetuated when an older brother named his son in memory of his loved, admired, and accomplished brother, Benjamin.

## MARY SYMMES HARRISON THORNTON

Seventh child, third daughter of William Henry Harrison and Anna Tuthill Symmes
*Born:* January 22, 1809    *Birthplace:* Vincennes, Indiana Territory
*Died:* November 16, 1842    *Age at Death:* 33 years, 10 months
*Cause of Death:* Unknown    *Education:* Unknown
*Profession:* Housewife, mother
*Spouse:* John Henry Fitzhugh Thornton    *Number of Children:* 6

Carrying her mother's maiden name, Symmes, and representing a prominent family of the day, Mary Symmes Harrison married a physician when she was twenty years old. She soon had a large family of six children. Like so many of her siblings, this young woman too died at an early age, leaving little historical record of her short time as wife and mother.

## CARTER BASSETT HARRISON

Eighth child, fifth son of William Henry Harrison and Anna Tuthill Symmes
*Born:* October 26, 1811    *Birthplace:* Vincennes, Indiana Territory
*Died:* August 12, 1839    *Age at Death:* 27 years, 10 months
*Cause of Death:* Unknown    *Education:* Unknown
*Profession:* Lawyer    *Spouse:* Mary Anne Sutherland
*Number of Children:* 1

Only seventeen years old when his father was appointed by President John Quincy Adams to be minister to Colombia, Carter Bassett, named after his grandmother's family, accompanied his father on the trip to the South American continent. William Henry evidenced no concern that his son was completely unprepared for both the journey and the work. Instead, his father focused on the importance of proper attire for his staff, including the attire of his son: "a plain coat with the diplomatic buttons, which could only be got in Philadelphia, is all the uniform we require. . . . The button has an eagle with an olive branch in one talon, with a thunderbolt in the other."[46]

Almost immediately after arriving in Colombia, a revolution broke out. President John Quincy Adams recalled Harrison and his entire staff. He returned to the United States to wait until the end of the revolution, but William Henry Harrison was not reappointed to the ministry.

By the age of twenty-five, Carter Bassett had completed his education. He became an attorney, opened a small practice, married, fathered a child, and died. He, too, died slightly more than a year before his father was elected as the nation's chief executive.

## ANNA TUTHILL HARRISON TAYLOR

Ninth child, fourth daughter of William Henry Harrison and Anna Tuthill Symmes
*Born:* October 28, 1813      *Birthplace:* Cincinnati, Ohio
*Died:* July 5, 1845      *Age at Death:* 31 years, 9 months
*Cause of Death:* Unknown      *Education:* Unknown
*Profession:* Housewife      *Spouse:* William Henry Harrison Taylor
*Number of Children:* None

Anna Tuthill Harrison was born only four weeks after her father recaptured Detroit in the War of 1812, a battle that elevated William Henry Harrison to the status of one of the nation's great generals. Anna's birth took place in Cincinnati because her family was a victim of the war. They were forced to evacuate their Vincennes, Indiana, home to escape campaigns in which her father played such a prominent role.

Anna married her cousin. Her life was short. She died before her thirty-second birthday, less than two years after her father's death.

## JAMES FINDLAY HARRISON

Tenth child, sixth son of William Henry Harrison and Anna Tuthill Symmes
*Born:* 1814      *Birthplace:* North Bend, Ohio
*Died:* 1817      *Age at Death:* 3 years      *Cause of Death:* Unknown

---

The tenth and last child to be born to the William Henry Harrison family was born at the family home in North Bend, Ohio, only shortly after his father resigned from the army. Named for his father's close friend, James Findlay, he was the first of many Harrisons to die at a young age. He was also the first of two children to be associated with the prominent Ohio Findlay family; his brother, William Henry Harrison, Jr., married a Findlay daughter in later years.

The family mourned the death of this child, little knowing it was to be the first of many early deaths.

### FOR FURTHER READING

Beard, Charles. *Presidents in American History.* New York: Julian A. Messner, 1981.

DeGregorio, William A. *The Complete Book of U.S. Presidents.* 2d ed. New York: Dembner Books, 1989.

Donaldson, Norman, and Betty Donaldson. *How Did They Die?* New York: St. Martin's Press, 1980.

Kane, Joseph Nathan. *Facts about the Presidents.* 4th ed. New York: H. W. Wilson, 1981.

Whitney, David C. *The American Presidents.* 4th ed. Garden City, New York: Doubleday, 1978.

# 8  JOHN TYLER'S CHILDREN

## MARY TYLER JONES

First child of John Tyler and Letitia Christian
*Born:* April 15, 1815     *Birthplace:* Charles City County, Virginia
*Died:* June 17, 1848     *Age at Death:* 33 years, 2 months
*Cause of Death:* Unknown     *Education:* Unknown
*Profession:* Housewife, mother     *Spouse:* Henry Lightfoot Jones
*Number of Children:* 2

Mary was the first of eight children of Tyler and his first wife. Though her upbringing was strict, there was no lack of love in the family. Her father was intent that she grow up to be a proper lady. Commenting to her, when viewing her practicing her waltz dance lessons, she received his warning that the waltz was a dance "which I do not desire to see you dance. It is rather vulgar, I think."[47] Mary, observers claimed, blossomed from a little sylph to a woman with a fascinating way about her "who beguiled people of their senses."[48]

She married Henry Lightfoot Jones in December 1835 in an elaborate, expensive wedding that could little be afforded by her financially strapped, U.S. senator father. Jones was a tidewater planter of comfortable means who owned inherited lands in North Carolina.

Following her father's request, Mary moved with her son, Henry, Jr., to stay with her parents until her mother's death. Thus, Mary's second son, Robert, who would be promoted for gallantry in the Confederate Army for his service at Gettysburg, was born in the White House during this stay.

## ROBERT TYLER

Second child, first son of John Tyler and Letitia Christian
*Born:* September 9, 1816    *Birthplace:* Charles City County, Virginia
*Died:* December 3, 1877    *Age at Death:* 61 years, 3 months
*Cause of Death:* Unknown    *Education:* Private
*Profession:* Lawyer, politician, newspaper editor, presidential secretary
*Spouse:* Elizabeth Priscilla Cooper
*Number of Children:* 7

Robert Tyler, eldest son of Tyler's many children, was an extremely shy young man. His father, concerned for Robert's future, advised him to "learn to make yourself popular by accommodating yourself to the feelings, nay whims, of others; we are put into the world and it is our duty to use, while we abstain from abusing it."[49] Young Tyler learned, and by the time he was an adult he had trained himself not only to overcome his shyness, but also to charm and sway people.

Educated as a lawyer, although never working at anything before his father became president when Robert was just twenty-five, he began his working career as his father's White House private secretary. During this period of his life, his great romance and marriage took place. Seeing Elizabeth Priscilla Cooper, daughter of one of the nation's leading tragedians, Thomas Cooper, playing Desdemona, the young, tall, distinguished son of John and Letitia Tyler was smitten, and he soon married her. Young Robert, conveniently, had married in time for his elegant wife to take over the role of White House hostess, as the first lady was seriously ill and unable to perform the duties of White House hostess for her husband.

At the end of his father's term as president, Robert moved to Philadelphia where he successfully practiced law. But with the outbreak of the Mexican War in 1846, Robert heard the call of duty and raised a Pennsylvania volunteer regiment. So quickly victorious was the American army that Robert's troops were unneeded, and the U.S. Army declined to use his volunteers.

Robert's activities in forming the voluntary military contingent, in combination with the fact that he was the son of a president, brought him attention and an important role in Pennsylvania politics. Tyler became a champion of the poor, particularly of Irish immigrants, and he regularly served their causes. His work in the state's Democratic party brought him acclaim and also the chairmanship of the Democratic party's central committee, a position of great power, given the weight of Pennsylvania in the day's national politics. In recognition of his assistance in electing Democrat James Buchanan to the presidency in 1856, Buchanan offered Robert a clerkship in the U.S. District Court. Robert refused, saying, "I am distinctly my own master and no office seeker."[50] Indeed, an unusual statement for any politician.

With the outbreak of the Civil War, sectional animosity turned bitter. Pennsylvania was no place for a public figure with a well-known Southern heritage. Forced to flee for his life and losing all he and his family owned and treasured, Robert returned to Virginia in 1861. His abilities did not go unrecognized by the new Confederate government. He was immediately appointed registrar of the Confederate treasury, a position of great trust in the new nation.

Following the war, Robert did not return to the North but began a law practice in Montgomery, Alabama.

There, in a single upstairs room, unknown and without a single client, he resumed the practice of law. He cooked his own meals, washed his own clothes, scrubbed and cleaned his miserable habitation. James Buchanan, retired from the presidency, heard that Robert Tyler was in financial straits and sent him a $1,000 check, but he [Robert] declined to take it.[51]

Within ten years, Robert became Alabama Democratic state chairman and the editor of the leading Montgomery, Alabama, newspaper, *The Advisor*.

Upon his death, obituaries throughout his readopted Southern state observed that "no man was ever more unselfish. He devoted his time and talents to the cause of his people without reward or expectation of reward."[52] Truer words could only have been spoken if the obituary had added that this president's son not only did not expect reward, he completely refused it in order to remain his own man.

## JOHN TYLER, JR.

Third child, second son of John Tyler and Letitia Christian
*Born:* April 27, 1819    *Birthplace:* Charles City County, Virginia
*Died:* January 26, 1896    *Age at Death:* 76 years, 9 months
*Cause of Death:* Unknown    *Education:* College, law studies
*Profession:* Lawyer, politician, editor    *Spouse:* Martha Rochelle
*Number of Children:* 3

John Tyler, Jr., spent much of his life attempting to compete with the successes of his older brother and father. Though blessed with a gift for writing, John's pursuits in use of his inherent ability were limited.

Educated in law, John was his brother's assistant in dealing with the press on behalf of their father. It was in this capacity that his writing skills emerged. John wrote political tracts, some of which prompted anger by his father's detractors. However, his father was pleased with his son's writing, and he published some of them. On one occasion, an editor of a Richmond, Virginia, newspaper defamed the presidential father and his writer son in such a manner that John felt himself compelled to challenge the editor to a duel. Anticipating the duel, newspapers regularly seeking to undermine the president and his son suggested that John would play the coward and fail to appear at the appointed dueling hour. To the surprise and chagrin of the Tyler detractors, it was the paper's editor who failed to show. John survived this test of personal courage and maintained the family's honor.

The days of writing and the momentary fame gleaned from his show of strength in the dueling incident were, however, the high points of John's career. He spent the rest of his life recalling them, whenever he was not attempting to match the deeds of his brother. In one such attempt, after Robert had played a major role in the successful presidential election of James Buchanan, the new president acknowledged Robert's contributions. Attempting to emulate his brother, John sent Buchanan unsolicited advice; the president ignored him.

By 1857 the aging former president was alarmed at the lack of John's career progress. Attempting to reacquire some of the small successes he had experienced during his earlier days in Washington, D.C., John returned to the city. He took a short-lived position with the attorney general's office. In a short while, John left the job, although he remained in Washington, D.C.

In the last years of his life, John lived in difficult financial circumstances. He spent his later years talking to all who would listen as he told his tales of his influential role during his father's presidency.

## LETITIA TYLER SEMPLE

Fourth child, second daughter of John Tyler and Letitia Christian
*Born:* May 11, 1821     *Birthplace:* Charles City County, Virginia
*Died:* December 28, 1907     *Age at Death:* 86 years, 7 months
*Cause of Death:* Unknown     *Education:* Unknown
*Profession:* Housewife, mother, businesswoman, educator
*Spouse:* James A. Semple     *Number of Children:* None

The beautiful, high-spirited Letitia Tyler was already married to James A. Semple, the nephew and heir of a prominent Williamsburg judge, when her mother died. Periodically, while her husband worked as a purser on U.S. Navy ships, Letitia served as White House hostess, until her father married a much younger woman, Julia Gardiner. Thus, early in her life, two dominant themes were established: a husband who would increasingly become alienated from his wife and reality, and a mutual hatred between stepmother and Letitia that would end only with the death of one.

With the election of Abraham Lincoln as president of the United States in 1860, Letitia's husband resigned his commission from the U.S. Navy to support the Southern cause, as did all of the Tyler family and kin. During the war, Letitia's husband served the South as a member of the Confederate Navy. At war's end, unable to comprehend the South's disastrous defeat, James Semple became clearly deranged. He disguised himself so he could engage in espionage against the Union, even though the war had ended. While the forces of the Confederacy disbanded and returned to their homes, James continued to play at cloak and dagger in the year following the war. The entire family acknowledged James's mental disturbance. Letitia, forced into independence for most of their marriage, permanently separated from James. Moving to Baltimore, she opened a private school, the Eclectic Institute. Meanwhile, James continued his private war against the North until 1867, when he announced that he had been overcome.

In a strange relationship, Letitia's stepmother, Julia, widowed in 1862, became the confidante and benefactor of the deluded James. Letitia, for her part, was enraged, feeling that humiliation was being heaped upon her by her hated stepmother. She believed Julia's only motive for the involvement with Semple was to bring further scorn and derision upon Letitia. For his part, Semple fell in love with his wife's stepmother, and publicly he acknowledged his feelings for Julia. She, however, denied all rumors and refused his romantic attentions, but the public was never sure of the actual relationship. Semple then turned from his mother-in-law, as he had from his wife, to launch himself into a life of wine, women, and cards. Seeking to strike back at her stepmother, Letitia instituted a suit against Julia over possession of family portraits.

In 1907, at the age of eighty-six, Letitia died, a married woman without a husband, still locked in hatred for her father's second wife who had died many years before.

## ELIZABETH (LIZZIE) TYLER WALLER

Fifth child, third daughter of John Tyler and Letitia Christian
*Born:* July 11, 1823     *Birthplace:* Charles City County, Virginia
*Died:* June 1, 1850     *Age at Death:* 26 years, 11 months
*Cause of Death:* Childbirth complications     *Education:* Unknown
*Profession:* Housewife, mother     *Spouse:* William Nevison Waller
*Number of Children:* 5

---

Elizabeth, known as Lizzie, was eighteen when she was introduced to the White House social scene. Because of her mother's illness, she assisted her older sister, Letitia, in supervising domestic affairs of the mansion and acting as White House cohostess. In 1842 Lizzie married William Waller in a White House wedding. A surprise to all at the wedding was the appearance of her mother, who emerged this single time from her sickroom to be present at the union of her much loved daughter, Lizzie. Though Lizzie's husband was considered unsophisticated, he was known as both generous and honorable. Letitia Tyler's appearance at the union of these two in the White House was the last time she was seen in public, and she died only months later.

Lizzie, as was the case with her sister Letitia, would not at first acknowledge her father's marriage to a new, younger wife, Julia Gardiner. But, unlike Tyler's other children, Letitia and John, in time, Lizzie and Julia became friendly, and Lizzie even came to admire her stepmother.

In 1850 Lizzie died from complications arising from childbirth. Not yet twenty-seven years old, she died leaving five young children, including sons who later fought for the South in the Civil War.

## ANNE CONTESSE TYLER

Sixth child, fourth daughter of John Tyler and Letitia Christian
*Born:* April 1825     *Birthplace:* Charles City County, Virginia
*Died:* July 1825     *Age at Death:* 3 months     *Cause of Death:* Unknown

---

Anne Contesse lived but a few short months. Tyler, the epitome of American fatherhood, wrote a lament for his dead child:

O child of my love, thou wert born for a day;
And like morning's vision have vanished away.
Thine eye scarce had ope'd on the world's beaming light
Ere 'twas sealed up in death and enveloped in night.

O child of my love as a beautiful flower;
Thy blossom expanded a short fleeting hour.
The winter of death hath blighted thy bloom
And thou lyest alone in the cold dreary tomb.[53]

## ALICE TYLER DENISON

Seventh child, fifth daughter of John Tyler and Letitia Christian
*Born:* March 23, 1827    *Birthplace:* Charles City County, Virginia
*Died:* June 8, 1854    *Age at Death:* 27 years, 3 months
*Cause of Death:* Bilious colic    *Education:* Private school
*Profession:* Housewife, mother    *Spouse:* Henry Mandeville Denison
*Number of Children:* 2

Alice, described, perhaps a bit ungenerously, as "tall and fat" was fourteen when her father entered the White House. Under the wing of her sister-in-law, Priscilla, who acted as White House hostess for a short time, Alice received more attention than might have been expected from men, given the press's unkind physical description. Considering her teenage ungainliness, it was also observed that "her popularity was enhanced in some measure by her father's political position."[54]

Tyler married again, shortly after the death of Alice's mother. Julia, his new wife and former ward, was only six years older than Alice. Julia decided that Alice must attend a boarding school for her education. Thus, Alice was sent away despite her objections. Having a certain measure of the political acumen that had made her father president, Alice wrote such sweet and charming letters to her stepmother that Julia relented and brought Alice back to Washington for the social season.

Plunging into the social world, Alice received her share of marriage proposals although she rejected all suitors. When her father left office, Alice was still single; however, she had matured into a "tall and attractive young woman."[55]

In 1849, as friends and relatives of the twenty-one-year-old woman had just about given her up for an old maid, she met a tall, rugged ladies' man, Reverend Henry Mandeville Denison. Denison was the twenty-eight-year-old Episcopalian rector of the Williamsburg parish. Alice immediately set her cap for him, and by July of the next year she was his bride. It was a romantic union, as her husband had neither the economic nor the social status of Alice's previous suitors.

Alice gave birth to two children, only one of whom lived to adulthood. She died in 1854 of bilious colic leaving a grieving husband and a distraught father who had seen the death of three daughters in the space of seven years.

## TAZEWELL (TAZ) TYLER

Eighth child, third son of John Tyler and Letitia Christian
*Born:* December 6, 1830      *Birthplace:* Charles City County, Virginia
*Died:* January 8, 1874      *Age at Death:* 43 years, 1 month
*Cause of Death:* Alcoholism
*Education:* Philadelphia Medical College
*Profession:* Medical doctor      *Spouse:* Nannie Bridges
*Number of Children:* 2

The youngest of the eight children born to John and Letitia Christian Tyler, the first wife of John Tyler, was named by the older children after the Tyler family's close friend, Littleton W. Tazewell. Taz, as he came to be called, was fourteen when his father married for the second time. Father Tyler, an exceptional man to his many children, declared, "My children are my principal treasures," which may have made up for the frequent financial problems of the family.[56] Tyler's second wife lavished attention upon the young man as if he were her own child, frequently teasing him about his many lady friends, whom he pursued with all the vigor of his twenty years.

At the age of twenty, during the height of the California gold rush, Taz sought his family's acquiescence for his journey to that state so that he might begin a life of financial ease. But his father stopped him and for four years the hard-pressed family spent $700 a year on an expensive medical education, which finally ended when the talented young man studied under his uncle, Dr. Henry Curtis.

Little is known of his immediate beginnings in medical practice, but the Civil War found him in the Confederate Army serving in the medical corps. After the war, Taz practiced medicine in Virginia, then in Baltimore, Maryland; finally he reached his long-sought goal, California, when he moved to San Francisco.

Though Taz earned a measure of success in his field, by 1873 his wife, Nannie Bridges, whom he had married in 1857, had divorced him, citing "dissipation" as the cause.[57] The father of two children, neither of whom reached maturity, he died the year after the divorce at the age of forty-three. He left only the characterization in his obituary of "he was a genial gentleman."[58]

## DAVID GARDINER (GARDIE) TYLER

Ninth child of John Tyler; first child of John Tyler and Julia Gardiner
*Born:* July 12, 1846    *Birthplace:* Charles City County, Virginia
*Died:* September 5, 1927    *Age at Death:* 81 years, 2 months
*Cause of Death:* Unknown
*Education:* Private schools, Washington College
*Profession:* Lawyer, judge, politician    *Spouse:* Mary Morris Jones
*Number of Children:* 5

---

"Pooh," said President John Tyler, "I am just full in my prime," when privately and publicly he was criticized for his second marriage to a woman half his age.[59] He went on to prove his statement by fathering seven more children. The first of these children was David Gardiner Tyler, born one year after the 1845 summer marriage.

David, or Gardie as he was always called, was a sixteen-year-old student at Washington College at the outbreak of the Civil War. A loyal Southerner, as were all of the Tylers, Gardie left college and joined the Confederate Army, serving first in the infantry and then in the artillery. At war's end—his father died in 1862—his mother Julia sent Gardie and his brother John Alexander, to study in Germany. But Gardie, having difficulty with the German language and feeling an intense concern about the shape of the South as it struggled to emerge from defeat, returned to study at Washington College. He also read law and was admitted to the Virginia bar in 1870.

At the end of 1870, Gardie jumped enthusiastically into state politics, winning election to the position of attorney for Charles City County. Gardie rejected many of the changes being imposed on the South, but he was also strongly opposed to the white supremacy policies instituted by Southern reactionaries. His successful election was due to the combination of white and black votes. Surprisingly, his realistic position was not a barrier to further elected office or success in business. Gardie went on to the state's senate, to a circuit court judgeship, and finally into the U.S. Congress.

Marrying quite late in life, Gardie died having fathered five children. To the end of his days he was proud that, in his own way, and on his own terms, he was an unreconstructed Southerner.

## JOHN ALEXANDER TYLER

Tenth child of John Tyler; second child, second son of John Tyler and Julia Gardiner
*Born:* April 7, 1848      *Birthplace:* Charles City County, Virginia
*Died:* September 1, 1883      *Age at Death:* 35 years, 5 months
*Cause of Death:* Dysentery
*Education:* Private schools, Washington College
*Profession:* Surveyor, engineer      *Spouse:* Sarah Gardiner
*Number of Children:* 2

Born in the family home of Sherwood Forest, Virginia, Alex was the second child of John and Julia Tyler. Growing up as a "straight and strong and devilish child,"[60] Alex became known for his vivid imagination. Tyler hoped that his son's "imagination would be governed by discretion,"[61] but it was not to be.

At the age of fourteen, just after his father's death, Alex begged his mother to be allowed to go south from their home to "massacre Yankees." When his mother refused, Alex ran away to enlist in the Confederate Army at Baltimore. At that stage in the war the Confederacy seemed to be holding its own or better, so he was rejected as too young, and he was returned to his mother, where she and her children lived on Staten Island, New York. Later in the war, most assuredly, Alex would not have been rejected for such a reason.

But Alex would not give up in his attempt to fight for the South and eventually Julia consented to his wishes, provided he join the Confederate Navy, not the army. (The army suffered from an extremely high casualty rate in comparison with the navy.) Alex agreed, and he joined the Confederate Navy, only to be assigned to a ship that was quarantined because of yellow fever. Upon release from quarantine in the summer of 1864, Alex left the navy; joined his brother at Camp Lee, where he became a member of a prison guard unit; and, once again, was returned to his mother although this return was under the personal auspices of Jefferson Davis, president of the Confederacy. Constantly besieged by the Tyler family to leave the hated North, Julia moved to the South to join many of the Tyler family. She placed her son in Washington College, in Lexington, Kentucky. One of only twenty-two students in the school, he remained only three months and finally returned to the Confederate Army, just in time to witness the South's surrender at Appomattox Courthouse.

With the war over, Alex returned to the family home in Sherwood Forest to restore the estate to its original grandeur, but since the plantation had been thoroughly plundered, the task was beyond the young man's abilities. In the fall of 1865, his mother sent both Alex and his older brother, Gardie, to Germany to study. The costs entailed in this foreign education stretched Julia's finances to the limit, and each boy was allowed only twenty cents per week for necessities. Despite the frugality of his life, Alex was a good student. He mastered the German language rapidly, and finding that he had a flair for math and science, he set as his goal to become a mining engineer.

Given his experiences in the war, Alex was not to be denied a war, and the Germans thoughtfully provided one. At the outbreak of the Franco-Prussian War in 1870, Alex enlisted in the German army and served in France during its occupation for several months in 1871. For his services to the newly proclaimed German empire, the kaiser awarded Alex a ribbon for faithful service. Alex had enjoyed the war thoroughly, so much so that he had incurred large debts, which he and his family were unable to pay. In 1873 Alex returned to the United States.

Alex quickly found work in mining near Salt Lake City, but soon he was out of work because of a depression that year. For almost a year Alex could not find a job. When he did find work it was for the railroad, at a salary not beginning to equal his expenditures. Constantly on the run from creditors, and accused of laughing his way through life by his younger brother Lachlin, Alex finally appeared to settle down when he married a cousin, Sarah Gardiner. Both families approved of the match, as Sarah came from a monied family, though she lacked physical attributes that would inspire other suitors. Her family welcomed Alex's devotion to their daughter. Shortly after their marriage Alex was again unemployed, and so he remained for two years, though he did father two children during the period. Both the Tyler and the Gardiner families attempted to find the new father a suitable position.

The job that Alex finally took was that of surveyor of Indian lands in the Dakota territory, working as an experienced surveyor. Anticipating profits of at least $5,000, Alex bought into a surveyor partnership with funds provided by his mother. The venture was not a financial success. After 1879 Alex's wife rarely saw him. Appointed as an inspector and surveyor for the Department of Interior, Alex suddenly appeared at the governor's palace in Santa Fe, New Mexico, in 1883 after having been stranded in the desert without water. Half-crazed by the sun, Alex drank the desert's foul alkaline water, contracted dysentery, and died at the governor's palace, or so goes the story.

Alex's widow, Sarah, who lived on for many years, periodically heard from travelers a different version of her husband's end—that he had been murdered.

## JULIA TYLER SPENCER

Eleventh child of John Tyler; third child, first daughter of John Tyler and Julia Gardiner
*Born:* December 25, 1849      *Birthplace:* Charles City County, Virginia
*Died:* May 8, 1871      *Age at Death:* 21 years, 5 months
*Cause of Death:* Childbirth complications
*Education:* Tutors, convent school in Halifax, Nova Scotia, Canada
*Profession:* Housewife, mother      *Spouse:* William Spencer
*Number of Children:* 1

---

Julia Gardiner Tyler, named Julia after her mother, Tyler's second wife, was born on Christmas Day, 1849. While her mother immediately predicted a beautiful future for her firstborn daughter, her father expressed some concern about the baby's prominent nose, observing, "I hope that organ will rest awhile in its maturity, for its prominence is quite amusing."[62]

Julie, as she was called, began her education at a boarding school, but as finances deteriorated after her father's death, she was withdrawn from private school until more prosperous times. Tutored at home, with her schooling paid for by the sale of pelts captured on the family estate by the older boys, Julie remained at home until the end of the Civil War in 1865. The end of the war occurred just as Julie entered her teens. To her mother, Julie was a wild and flirtatious young woman. Concerned about her daughter's future, she sent Julie away to a convent school in Halifax, Nova Scotia. The school was chosen because it was far removed from the social world Julie knew; it was both restrictive and inexpensive, and it had an excellent reputation for its academics. But Julie was not long for the convent life. When the protestant Tylers received a letter from Julie telling them that the Catholic life in her school was leading her to consider becoming a nun, her Halifax education was ended.

In 1869 Julie married William Spencer. Though her family was elated that she was settling down to a proper life, Spencer was deeply in debt and had no economic prospects for the future. The newlyweds settled on Spencer's heavily mortgaged farm in upstate New York, where mother, daughter, and son-in-law spent much time together.

In the spring of 1871, Julie died giving birth to her daughter (also named Julia). Julie's mother's anguish was distracted by the requirements of caring for her granddaughter. William borrowed money from his mother-in-law to settle his long overdue debts, and then he disappeared. He surfaced briefly in Colorado's silver mines and in the California citrus groves, but then he disappeared from family records. Grandmother Julia raised Julie's daughter, hoping finally to build for this child the beautiful future she had so eagerly anticipated for her own daughter.

## LACHLIN TYLER

Twelfth child of John Tyler; fourth child, third son of John Tyler and Julia Gardiner
*Born:* December 2, 1851     *Birthplace:* Charles City County, Virginia
*Died:* January 25, 1902     *Age at Death:* 50 years, 1 month
*Cause of Death:* Unknown
*Education:* Private schools, medical school
*Profession:* Medical doctor     *Spouse:* Georgia Powell
*Number of Children:* None

Still a young boy when the Civil War erupted, Lachlin Tyler missed participating in the horrors of the nation's most costly war. Educated as a physician, he practiced medicine in the North, despite the Tyler family's Southern connection.

In 1877 Lachlin's analysis of his situation was that he had a few patients, yielding fewer dollars, and the expenses of a new wife. Therefore, he appealed to his mother to exert her influence, as a former first lady, to obtain a position for him as a police surgeon in Jersey City. But Julia was unable to help her son acquire the position. Lachlin then decided that Washington, D.C., offered opportunities for success. The couple had become so poor that Lachlin even considered letting his young wife, Georgia Powell, go to work in the Department of Agriculture, something simply not done by respectable women of the era.

Lachlin eventually found work in the medical division of the U.S. Navy, where he performed well. However he quickly became dissatisfied with the lack of interesting and responsible work. To advance to a position of surgeon, Lachlin would have to pass a battery of examinations, including grammar, geography, and history, disciplines in which Lachlin acknowledged his ineptitude. Writing to his mother he expressed the hope that he would be allowed to pass the examinations because "perhaps they modified things for those applicants who came forward highly recommended, or were undoubtedly gentlemen."[63] But he did not receive the appointment; the rejection notification simply stated "general debility," which, according to Lachlin, "means in the medical vocabulary everything or nothing."[64] He then began a body-building program, until 1879 when he again took the examination. On his second attempt, he passed both the academic and physical examinations and was certified a surgeon for the U.S. Navy. Lachlin also began a private medical practice.

In time Lachlin's private practice became very lucrative, and he relinquished his navy surgeonship to concentrate entirely on his private practice. At the age of fifty, childless, Lachlin died. He had, however, finally achieved some measure of the success he so desired.

## LYON GARDINER TYLER

Thirteenth child of John Tyler; fifth child, fourth son of John Tyler and Julia Gardiner

*Born:* August 1853     *Birthplace:* Charles City County, Virginia
*Died:* February 12, 1935     *Age at Death:* 81 years, 6 months
*Cause of Death:* Unknown     *Education:* University of Virginia

*Profession:* Teacher, administrator, lawyer, politician, author
*Spouses:* Anne Baker Tucker, Sue Ruffin
*Number of Children:* Tyler/Tucker: 3; Tyler/Ruffin: 2

---

Following the Civil War, Lyon Gardiner Tyler studied at the University of Virginia, receiving from that school both a bachelor of arts degree and a master of arts degree before taking up the study of law. When he found that the practice of law could not satisfy his quest for more information as well as the sheer joy of teaching, Lyon became a professor at the financially troubled William and Mary College in 1877. Then, for a brief period, he went to teach in a Memphis, Tennessee, high school.

Returning to Virginia, Lyon initiated his first and only substantial law practice, while he taught night school at a school he founded, the Richmond Mechanics Night School. Indeed, Lyon was so interested in teaching that when his school suffered financial reverses he managed to get state subsidies to continue the school. His law success also continued, and Lyon was elected to the state legislature. These early experiences were the foundation for the balance of Lyon's life.

The college of William and Mary had been forced to close in 1880, and the directors of the college now regarded the state legislator, and the school's former professor, Lyon Tyler, as a strategically placed man who could be interested in securing state funds to reopen the school. Their assumptions were correct. Lyon was both willing and able to come to the aid of education.

In grateful response, the directors of William and Mary College elected Tyler as president of the college. He held that position for thirty-one years. Lyon's administration of William and Mary was founded on the principles of academic excellence and financial security, and the school remained successful.

In 1919, after retiring from this presidential position and awarded the title of Professor Emeritus, Lyon devoted himself to historical research, specializing in genealogy and early Virginia history. Publishing frequently, Tyler made a name for himself in historical circles for his published works. He received honorary doctorates from Brown University, the University of Pittsburg, and Trinity College in Hartford, Connecticut.

In Lyon's later days he became a noted public speaker. As a historian of the South, he spoke with a definite point of view when the subject of the Civil War, or anything Southern, arose. At one time, speaking before

Confederate veterans, he referred to Abraham Lincoln as the "boss slacker" and insisted "that histories by northern writers should be barred from Virginia schools."[65] Lyon believed that Southerners were political slaves of the North, and "if through some cataclysm, the South should get control, the North would secede tomorrow."[66]

At the age of eighty-one, the distinguished historian, twice-married father of five died.

## ROBERT FITZWALTER (FITZ) TYLER

Fourteenth child of John Tyler; sixth child, fifth son of John Tyler and Julia Gardiner
*Born:* March 12, 1856     *Birthplace:* Charles City County, Virginia
*Died:* December 30, 1927     *Age at Death:* 71 years, 9 months
*Cause of Death:* Unknown
*Education:* Georgetown Academy, Georgetown University
*Profession:* Farmer     *Spouse:* Fannie Gluin     *Number of Children:* 3

Named Robert Fitzwalter in honor of Julia Tyler's ancestor of thirteenth-century England, he was the fourteenth Tyler child, and the sixth of the second wife to be born to this most prolific former president of the United States. His birth proved beyond all question that Tyler was correct when he said, upon his marriage to Julia, that he was yet "just full in his prime." Since his mother, Julia, converted to Catholicism after her husband's death, her son, Fitz, entered a Catholic school near Washington, D.C., at the age of fifteen. He continued his education at Georgetown College— now Georgetown University—near the nation's capitol. However, the family financial instability forced his withdrawal, and he never returned.

Instead of a professional career, Fitz turned to the land and became a Virginia farmer, initially on leased land near the Tyler family home, Sherwood Forest. Fitz was successful and remained a farmer for the rest of his life. He fathered three children by his one and only wife. His achievements, though highly desired by his mother, never matched the grandeur of his ancestral name, which had been carefully chosen to reflect the social aspirations of his ambitious mother.

# PEARL TYLER ELLIS

Fifteenth child of John Tyler; seventh child, second daughter of John
Tyler and Julia Gardiner
*Born:* June 20, 1860     *Birthplace:* Virginia
*Died:* June 30, 1947     *Age at Death:* 87 years
*Cause of Death:* Unknown
*Education:* Georgetown Academy, Sacred Heart Convent
*Profession:* Housewife, mother     *Spouse:* William Mumford Ellis
*Number of Children:* 8

---

Pearl Tyler Ellis, the last of the many Tyler children, was originally to be
named Margaret, but she was christened Pearl instead. She never knew her
father, who was seventy-two years old when she was born. With her
mother's conversion to Catholicism when she was about eleven, "Pearlie"
was sent with her brother, Fitz, to Georgetown Academy, a school run by
Catholic clergy. So intense were her convert mother's religious feelings and
concerns for her daughter's afterlife, that, when Pearlie fell ill, her mother
demanded that a bewildered priest rebaptize her daughter in order to ensure
that the rite had taken.

Later educated at the convent of the Sacred Heart in Washington, D.C.,
Pearlie married Major William Mumford Ellis in St. Peter's Cathedral. The
couple moved to Montgomery County, Virginia, where for more than fifty
years they lived in the upper end of Happy Valley near Roanoke. The mother
of eight was frequently visited by her own mother, Julia, and Julia's adopted
daughter, Julia III.

Of all the Tyler children, the youngest, Pearlie, lived a life most unaf-
fected by the power of her father's office or her mother's ambitions.

*FOR FURTHER READING*

Gerlinger, Irene. *Mistresses of the White House.* Freeport, N.Y.: Books for Librar-
    ies Press, 1950.
Klapthor, Margaret Brown. *First Ladies.* Washington, D.C.: White House Histori-
    cal Association, 1979.
Seager, Robert II. *And Tyler Too: A Biography of John and Julia Gardiner Tyler.*
    New York: McGraw-Hill, 1963.

Mary Elizabeth (Betty) Taylor (circa 1849–1850). Photo courtesy of the Library of Congress.

# 9 ZACHARY TAYLOR'S CHILDREN

## ANNE MARGARET MACKALL TAYLOR WOOD

First child of Zachary Taylor and Margaret Mackall Smith
*Born:* April 9, 1811    *Birthplace:* Jefferson County, Kentucky
*Died:* December 2, 1875    *Age at Death:* 64 years, 8 months
*Cause of Death:* Unknown    *Education:* Unknown
*Profession:* Housewife, mother
*Spouse:* Robert Crooke Wood    *Number of Children:* 4

The first of the Taylor children, Anne grew up on military posts as her father was transferred from one to another during his military career. As did her sister Sarah, Anne met her future husband, an army surgeon, at Fort Crawford, later known as Prairie du Chien, Wisconsin. Unlike her sister's husband, however, Anne's choice was accepted by the family. With Robert's career in the military, Anne changed from being a military child to living as a military wife and mother.

The Civil War split Anne's family. Robert, her husband, remained with the Union and served as surgeon general of the 14th Union Army. However, the couple's only sons, John and Bob, saw their duty in service to the Confederate States of America. Thus, father was pitted against sons. As the nation split, so too did Anne Taylor's family. By war's end, Anne was widowed.

Alone, Anne turned to her daughter for the emotional support and comfort so lacking in her life with her husband deceased. She then moved to Germany, where her daughter lived following her marriage to Baron

Guido von Grabow, of the German embassy staff, while the baron served his country in Washington, D.C. Anne remained in Germany, and she died there in 1875.

## SARAH KNOX TAYLOR DAVIS

Second child, second daughter of Zachary Taylor and Margaret Mackall Smith
*Born:* March 6, 1814   *Birthplace:* Fort Knox, Missouri Territory
*Died:* September 15, 1835   *Age at Death:* 21 years, 6 months
*Cause of Death:* Malaria   *Education:* Unknown
*Profession:* Housewife   *Spouse:* Jefferson Davis
*Number of Children:* None

---

Sarah Knox Taylor was called "Knox" throughout her life because she was named after the fort where her father was stationed at the time of her birth. She is described as very feminine, a typical image of Southern girls of the era, with blonde hair falling in ringlets to her shoulders and a sweetness that appealed to all who saw her.

When Knox was a teenager, her father was transferred to Fort Crawford, Wisconsin, later renamed Prairie du Chien. There, in 1832, she met her future husband, Jefferson Davis. The man who would become president of the Confederate States of America was a new West Point graduate, stationed at Fort Crawford. Knox and Davis were immediately attracted to each other, but her father, Zachary Taylor, disapproved entirely of young Davis, based on confrontations the two had over military matters. Davis, never known for his tact, had strongly expressed his opposition to superior officer Taylor's judgment. In rejecting Davis as his daughter's suitor, Taylor used the argument to her that as wife of a military man she would have to suffer many hardships. Davis was then transferred to a far-removed post, at St. Louis, Missouri. Sarah's father breathed a sigh of relief, having separated the young lovers. But the couple's love for each other grew despite the distance, and long and passionate letters were exchanged for two years.

In June 1835, Knox and Jefferson married, although they had not seen each other for the entire two years of their forced separation. The marriage, planned through the mail, took place in Louisville, Kentucky, at the home of one of Knox's aunts. Many of the Taylor family attended the wedding, although Zachary and his wife refused to sanction the marriage by their appearance. Davis, newly resigned from the army, took his young bride from Louisville to his brother's home, The Hurricane, in the deep South for their honeymoon. The couple then moved on to his sister's home in Louisiana. From there, exchanging letters with her reconciled parents, Sara wrote to her mother, "Do not make yourself uneasy about me, the country is quite healthy."[67] To her father she expressed appreciation for the money he had sent to her.

Ironically, shortly after her protestations of the healthiness of her new home, both she and her husband contracted malaria. Davis recovered, Sarah did not. Barely three months after their marriage she died.

The first wife of the thirty-years hence president of the Confederate States of America and daughter of a future president of the United States was buried in the Davis family graveyard on the banks of the Mississippi.

## OCTAVIA PANNEL AND MARGARET SMITH TAYLOR

Third and fourth children, third and fourth daughters of Zachary Taylor and Margaret Mackall Smith
*Born:* Octavia: August 16, 1816; Margaret: July 27, 1819
*Birthplace:* Jefferson County, Kentucky
*Died:* Octavia: July 8, 1820; Margaret: October 22, 1820
*Ages at Death:* Octavia: 3 years, 8 months; Margaret: 1 year, 3 months
*Cause of Death:* Probably yellow fever

The short lives of two Taylor daughters remind us of the ravages of disease common before the medical discoveries of the twentieth century. Both Octavia Pannel and Margaret Smith Taylor were victims of a fever whose origin was unknown at the time, but which especially attacked newcomers to the Mississippi Delta. Once infected, the small bodies of children were often helpless to evade the disease's onslaught, and the illness proceeded to death.

Zachary Taylor took his family, including the two little girls, to Bayou Sara, Louisiana, where he was engaged in the construction of a military road. Within months of their introduction to the region both girls became ill, and in July 1820, three-year-old Octavia died, followed by the death of her younger sister in October of the same year.

A third daughter, Sarah, only slightly older than the two small children, was yet strong enough to survive the illness. But Sarah was to tempt fate twice by returning to the Delta area following her marriage to Jefferson Davis; this time she did not survive the disease. Her mother's concern, expressed to Sarah upon her moving to the Delta with her new husband was founded in the deaths of her two small sisters, years earlier. Thus, three of Taylor's daughters died of the same disease in the same region of the nation, although the third death took place more than fifteen years after the first two.

## MARY ELIZABETH (BETTY) TAYLOR BLISS DANDRIDGE

Fifth child, fifth daughter of Zachary Taylor and Margaret Mackall Smith
*Born:* April 20, 1824      *Birthplace:* Jefferson County, Kentucky
*Died:* July 26, 1909      *Age at Death:* 85 years, 3 months
*Cause of Death:* Unknown      *Education:* Unknown
*Profession:* Housewife, White House hostess
*Spouses:* William Bliss, Philip Dandridge
*Number of Children:* None

Nicknamed "Betty," Mary Elizabeth Taylor, youngest of the Taylor daughters, was a beautiful and elegant woman. Possessing a natural poise and tact, she had large eyes, soft black hair, and a superb complexion.

Because Betty's mother opposed Zachary's acceptance of the nomination for president, when he was elected her mother refused to preside as White House hostess. Holding true to her threat, of necessity, "Miss Betty" took over the role as White House hostess in her mother's place. So well-suited was she to the position that a Washington, D.C., pundit observed she possessed "the artlessness of a rustic and the grace of a duchess."[68] Her charm attracted many suitors, but it was her father's adjutant general, Major William Bliss, who captured her heart.

Sixteen months after he became president, Zachary Taylor died. The family moved from the White House and from Washington, never to return.

In 1853 Bliss died, leaving Betty a childless widow. Several years later, Betty met and married Philip Dandridge, of Winchester, Virginia. Living to a ripe old age, Betty retained the charm that characterized her youth, and her home became known as the Salon of the Valley of Shenandoah.

## RICHARD (DICK) TAYLOR

Sixth child, only son of Zachary Taylor and Margaret Mackall Smith
*Born:* January 27, 1826      *Birthplace:* Louisville, Kentucky
*Died:* April 12, 1879      *Age at Death:* 53 years, 3 months
*Cause of Death:* Malaria
*Education:* European schools, Harvard University, Yale University
*Profession:* Soldier, plantation manager, politician, author
*Spouse:* Louise Marie Bringier      *Number of Children:* 5

The only son of General "Rough and Ready" Taylor, Richard spent his childhood at army camps watching military maneuvers and acquiring for himself, from the enlisted men, a vocabulary that could only be described as crude, and which remained with him throughout his life.

His mother, convinced that military posts were not the most suitable environments for the education of a gentleman, finally convinced his father to send young Dick to Edinburgh, Scotland, to study Latin and literature. After two years of education in Scotland, he was sent to France, where he studied for a year. When he returned to the United States he was privately tutored for a short time, to make up for certain deficiencies. In 1843 he was admitted as a junior to Harvard, but Harvard did not suit Dick and he moved to Yale, where he graduated when he was twenty-three years old.

When Dick graduated, the dispute over the Texas boundary with Mexico was about to flare into war with the United States. Dick joined his father, who was commanding the American troops in south Texas. He became his father's secretary and aide-de-camp, but he was soon stricken by fever. Leaving the army to recuperate, Dick traveled to Baton Rouge to the family's properties and worked on the sugar plantation until his father was elected to the presidency. Again he joined his father to become his secretary, though this time at the White House. Dick remained at his father's side until the president died, sixteen months after his inauguration.

Marrying well, Dick was elected to the Louisiana State Senate, and he remained for four years. Elected to the state convention that was established to decide the questions of secession from the United States of America, Dick opposed Louisiana's secession, but finally he went along with the majority. Dick, who saw through all the hoopla and careless wishful thinking of his fellow delegates, was later to reminisce, "At that secession time and since, I marveled at the joyous and careless temper in which men, much my superior in sagacity and experience, consummated these acts."[69]

When the war commenced, Dick Taylor became Colonel Taylor of the Confederate Army and commanded a regiment. Taylor and his men were on the march when the Battle of Bull Run was fought. He and his troops missed the combat, but the enemy of soldiers everywhere, disease, ravaged the troops' ranks. Taylor devoted himself to nursing his men back to health from the killer disease, measles. Then, he himself was felled by fever, and his commanding officer ordered Dick to take leave to recover his health. Nursed back to health and judged fit for military duty, he was promoted to the rank of brigadier general, though he protested the promotion as being undeserved. Taylor asked his one-time brother-in-law, Jefferson Davis, president of the Confederate States, to revoke his promotion. Davis did not.

During the war, Taylor became involved in two important initiatives on behalf of the Confederate government, although neither came to anything. Jefferson Davis, who trusted Taylor implicitly, gave him the mission of carrying communications from the Confederate government concerning a solution to the hostilities to the president of the United States, Abraham Lincoln. Taylor was also associated with General Robert E. Lee in an attempt to earn European support for the Confederacy. By 1864 General Taylor felt the South could not win the war but that he was honor-bound to continue fighting until the loss was unquestionable. Such was his commitment, that the man who had opposed secession was the last general to surrender his forces. Jefferson Davis, desperately trying to continue the struggle, even after Lee's surrender, understood that when Taylor finallly bowed to the North's superior force the cause was lost.

At war's end, Dick returned to his plantation, from which he had been almost constantly absent for four years. In his absence, his estate had been confiscated and sold. Out of pride, he refused to ask for reinstatement of his citizenship or for restitution for his property. He accepted the difficult times after the war as punishment for a failure that he had long foreseen.

Dick, admired and respected by leaders on both sides of the Mason-Dixon line, represented Louisiana, suffering from military occupation and reconstruction, in attempts to secure relief from the controlling Yankee government in Washington, D.C. In the capitol, even President Grant, who had served with Dick's father in antebellum days, accorded his former superior officer's son the respect due to the scion of a comrade-in-arms and former president. Of course, after America's most bloody war, there were those who could never forgive nor look above the battle to respect any individual's merit. Thus, some Northern newspapers, in reporting the movements of Dick Taylor, always reminded their readers of his diligence in the cause of rebellion.

In the last years of his life, Dick represented American business in Europe and authored his memoirs of the Civil War, titled *Destruction and Reconstruction*. Fighting malaria to the end, Dick lived long enough to finish his book and died in 1879, penniless though much honored and respected by former enemies and compatriots alike.

## FOR FURTHER READING

Beard, Charles. *Presidents in American History*. New York: Julian A. Messner, 1981.

Canfield, Cass. *The Iron Will of Jefferson Davis*. New York: Harcourt, Brace Jovanovich, 1978.

Hamilton, Holman. *Three Kentucky Presidents: Lincoln, Taylor, Davis*. Lexington: University of Kentucky Press, 1978.

# 10 MILLARD FILLMORE'S CHILDREN

## MILLARD POWERS FILLMORE

First child, only son of Millard Fillmore and Abigail Powers
*Born:* April 25, 1828     *Birthplace:* Aurora, New York
*Died:* November 15, 1889     *Age at Death:* 61 years, 6 months
*Cause of Death:* Apoplexy
*Education:* Tutors, Cambridge Law School
*Profession:* Lawyer, presidential secretary     *Spouse:* None
*Number of Children:* None

Was he trying to hide something? Or was it vengeance against his father
that made Millard Powers Fillmore destroy his father's correspondence?
What is certain is that his actions left a historical void in our knowledge of
the presidency of Millard Fillmore.

Called Powers throughout his life, Fillmore was educated in law, including training under his attorney father. Powers passed his New York bar, and
later he became his father's White House secretary. For a brief period,
Powers had a law office in Buffalo, New York, although he did not remain
in private practice for a long period. His work, its quality and quantity, his
associations, and his cases were lost forever in the same fire that consumed
his personal correspondence with his father and family. From private
practice, Powers moved to a federal court as a law clerk.

A clue to Powers's entire life may lie in his relationship to his mother.
An invalid, she died shortly after her husband had served his White
House term. His father remarried. Powers, a bachelor, did not accept his

father's new wife. Though in his will, his father requested that Powers and his second wife try to get along, the battle over inheritance was bitter. In his will, Fillmore left most of his belongings to his second wife. Powers sued to overturn the will and won. As soon as he could, Powers sold the inheritance—primarily wine, silver, and a major book collection.

From the time of his lawsuit and his victory until his death, Powers lived as a resident at the Tifft House, a Buffalo, New York, hotel. He spent his days talking with old cronies in the lobby of the hotel. Surviving his father by fifteen years, though in ill health for several years prior to his death, Powers died of apoplexy at the Tifft House. He left no known friends.

Powers's will, parts of which were printed in the *New York Times*, shocked society. In his will there was a strange commandment—for the son of a president. "I particularly request and direct my executor at the earliest practicable moment to burn or otherwise effectively destroy all correspondence or letters to or from my father, mother, sister, or me, and under his immediate supervision. I hope to be able to do this myself before my death."[70] That provision was carried out.

Why did Powers want to destroy his family documents? The nation speculated then, and we can only speculate now. There is not a clue to understanding his reasons. Perhaps the letters would have made very interesting reading, and, perhaps, that explains why they were destroyed.

Powers left bequests to some charitable institutions, the American Society for the Prevention of Cruelty to Animals, Young Women's Christian Association, and several churches and hospitals. He also left bequests to two aunts, as well as a sum of dollars to John Howcut, of Denver, whose relationship to Powers is not identified.

Powers was buried beside his father in Buffalo. But for the destruction of the papers it is possible to suggest that, perhaps, more could be said about the thirteenth president of the United States.

## MARY ABIGAIL (ABBY) FILLMORE

Second child, only daughter of Millard Fillmore and Abigail Powers
*Born:* March 27, 1832     *Birthplace:* Buffalo, New York
*Died:* July 26, 1854     *Age at Death:* 22 years, 3 months
*Cause of Death:* Cholera
*Education:* Sedgewick School, State Normal School, New York
*Profession:* White House hostess, teacher
*Spouse:* None     *Number of Children:* None

Mary Abigail, called Abby by family and friends, who spent her life "constantly thinking of some little surprise, some gift, some pleasure by which she could contribute to the happiness of others," is described as an extrovert and as gay, radiant, and charming.[71] Though never described as beautiful, her qualities attracted many people to her.

Her childhood interest was music, although her formal education was above that of her female contemporaries. In addition, Abby possessed her father's vitality and self-assuredness. Although she had prepared herself to become a teacher, it became necessary to fill her mother's duties as White House hostess, as Fillmore's wife, Abigail, spent most of her life as a semi-invalid.

In 1850, when vice president Fillmore became president after Zachary Taylor's death, teenaged Abby took over responsibilities as the White House hostess. In her new role, she was "as much at ease at the head of the presidential table as if she had been born a princess."[72] Abby, like her older brother, never married. Shortly after Fillmore's term ended in 1853, Abby's mother died, leaving Abby and her father to return to Buffalo where they buried Abigail. Abby began her teaching career.

Only a year after her mother's death, Abby, continuing her helpfulness, traveled to East Aurora, New York, to visit her grandfather and help him settle in a new home, despite the fact she had felt ill for days. Within twelve hours of her arrival at her grandfather's new home, Abby was dead of cholera.

Like a fairy princess, she entered life, touched all that knew her with kindness, and died in an act of caring.

## FOR FURTHER READING

Grayson, Benson Lee. *Unknown President: The Administration of Millard Fillmore*. New York: University Press of America, 1981.

Kane, Nathan Joseph. *Facts about the Presidents*. 4th ed. New York: H. W. Wilson, 1981.

Snyder, Charles M. *The Lady and the President: The Letters of Dorothea Dix and Millard Fillmore*. Lexington: University of Kentucky Press, 1975.

Taylor, Tim. *The Book of Presidents*. New York: Arno Press, 1972.

# 11 FRANKLIN PIERCE'S CHILDREN

## FRANKLIN AND FRANK ROBERT PIERCE

First and second children of Franklin Pierce and Jane Means Appleton
*Born:* Franklin: February 2, 1836; Frank Robert: August 27, 1839
*Birthplace:* Franklin: Hillsborough, New Hampshire; Frank Robert: Concord, New Hampshire
*Died:* Franklin: February 5, 1836; Frank Robert: November 14, 1843
*Ages at Death:* Franklin: 3 days; Frank Robert: 4 years, 3 months
*Causes of Death:* Unknown

Almost nothing is known of the first two sons born to Franklin and Jane Pierce. But it is understood that it was the early deaths of these two sons that contributed to the mental instability that eventually convinced Jane that the Pierces must never again become involved in Washington, D.C., politics.

But all of Jane's precautions were for naught since the second of these two boys died, even though Jane had convinced her husband to resign his Senate seat and return to New Hampshire and supposed safety. With the death of the two boys, the grieving Jane was left with their only remaining child, son Benny.

When her last son, Benny, died in a terrible railroad accident, Jane's precarious mental stability snapped. She was unable to comprehend the deaths of all of her children, and she spent her days as the nation's first lady communing with her dead children. For the most part, she confined herself to a White House sitting room and did not involve herself in her husband's hated politics.

## BENJAMIN (BENNY) PIERCE

Third child, third son of Franklin Pierce and Jane Means Appleton
*Born:* April 13, 1841    *Birthplace:* Concord, New Hampshire
*Died:* January 6, 1853    *Age at Death:* 11 years, 8 months
*Cause of Death:* Railroad accident

---

Benjamin, the third son and last child of the Pierces, was their only child to survive beyond early childhood. The deaths of his brothers had, understandably, instilled fear for Benny's life in his mother. Indeed, Pierce's family life came to revolve around concern for the life of their last son. Yet, despite all of their precautions, their last child was not spared, and he died in a terrible train wreck.

Shortly before the death of Benjamin's brother, Frank, Jane Pierce convinced her senator husband to leave Washington because "Washington is tainted by the evils of politics."[73] To placate his wife, Pierce resigned his Senate seat in 1842 and moved from Washington, D.C., back to Concord, New Hampshire, where he practiced law. While the quiet life of Concord suited Jane and her children, Pierce was never content away from the excitement and challenge of public life. Jane's contentment was, however, destroyed when in 1843 their second son, Frank Robert, died in Concord.

Pierce sought and found an escape. The outbreak of the Mexican War offered him the perfect opportunity to leave Concord. He joined the army, was made a brigadier general, and took an active part in the war. Jane and her remaining son, Benny, remained at home in New Hampshire, until Pierce returned from the war in 1848 to, again, begin the quiet life in New Hampshire.

But when Pierce was nominated as the Democratic-Republican presidential candidate in 1852, he leapt at the chance to reenter politics. Jane, on the other hand, prayed for his defeat. She detested politics and, even more, feared Washington, D.C. Unfortunately for Jane and Benny, Pierce won the election.

Defeated by her husband's victory, Jane made peace with her husband and decided to accept the situation. To celebrate the election and Christmas, 1852, the small family set out by train for a Boston respite before presidential politics would be entered with his Washington, D.C., inauguration.

After the vacation, when the returning train neared their Concord, New Hampshire, home, an axle broke and the train jumped the track and went over a fifteen-foot embankment.[74] Franklin and Jane were only slightly bruised, but when the train's cars settled, they saw their only surviving son, Benny, crushed beneath the railroad car. He was the only passenger killed in the accident.

Jane Pierce never recovered from the loss of her third son in such a tragic accident. She, having fought so hard to keep her husband from returning to politics, was convinced "that Benny's fate was a divine punishment meted out for Pierce's political ambition."[75]

The shadow of Benny's death hung over the Pierce White House. Jane Pierce came to the White House only to spend most of her time in the sitting room, scribbling notes to her dead Benny. Jane Pierce eventually retreated completely into a fantasy world, where she talked and played with her three dead sons.

## FOR FURTHER READING

Bell, Carl Irving. *They Knew Franklin Pierce (and Others Thought They Did): A Sampling of Opinions about the 14th United States President Drawn from His Contemporaries.* Springfield, Vt.: April Hill, 1980.

Gerlinger, Irene. *Mistresses of the White House.* Freeport, N.Y.: Books for Libraries Press, 1950.

Moses, John B., and Wilbur Cross. *Presidential Courage.* New York: W. W. Norton, 1980.

(Left to right) Mrs. Abraham (Mary) Lincoln, Robert Todd, Thomas (Tad), and Abraham Lincoln (circa 1863–1865). Photo courtesy of the Library of Congress.

# 12 ABRAHAM LINCOLN'S CHILDREN

## ROBERT (BOB) TODD LINCOLN

First child, first of four sons of Abraham Lincoln and Mary Todd
*Born:* August 1, 1843    *Birthplace:* Springfield, Illinois
*Died:* July 25, 1926    *Age at Death:* 82 years, 9 months
*Cause of Death:* Unknown
*Education:* Public schools, Phillips Exeter Academy, Harvard University
*Profession:* Lawyer, business executive, politician
*Spouse:* Mary Harlan    *Number of Children:* 3

Robert Todd Lincoln perhaps best personifies the character of an individual born into a family that would become an American legend. The many opportunities available to few of his generation came to Robert by virture of his birth; nevertheless, Robert was quite simply his own man—perhaps destined to lead by genetic programming, but certainly not to be underestimated in his own right for the successes he experienced on a path both very similar in leadership skills, but quite different from that of his father.

Born in Springfield, Illinois, Bob Lincoln lived in the home his father had purchased and enlarged during Bob's first sixteen years of life. He showed no exceptional ability in scholarship, which was a matter of concern to his father, who observed of his son, "He is quite smart enough. I sometimes fear that he is one of those little 'rare-ripe' sort that are smarter at about five than ever after."[76] His observation was shown to be accurate when Robert attempted to enter Harvard College. He failed in sixteen of the seventeen subjects in which he was examined. Following his failure, he was enrolled in Phillips Academy in Exeter, New Hampshire. After a year of study, he was admitted to Harvard. Years later, Bob observed that upon announcing that he would study law, his father gave him the only advice about his career that he was ever to receive from him: "You should learn more than I ever did, but you will never have time."[77] During his Harvard schooling, Bob took a short leave to attend his father's inauguration as president of the United States.

Almost immediately upon assumption of his term as president, Lincoln was faced with the inevitability of the Civil War. He called for 75,000 volunteers to protect properties of the Union, but a celebrated missing volunteer was his son, Bob. Though students and scholars left colleges en masse throughout the North, Lincoln's oldest son steadfastly continued his studies. There is a great deal of opinion about his reason for not enlisting: he did not do so in deference to his mentally disturbed mother, Abraham Lincoln did not want his son in the army, or simply that Bob felt no obligation to enter the army merely because his father had declared the war.

However, when Bob graduated from Harvard in 1864, Lincoln interceded and requested that General Grant find a position for his twenty-one-year-old son, saying, "having graduated from Harvard, [he] wishes to see something of the war before it ends. I do not wish to put him in the ranks, nor yet give him a commission, to which those who have already served are better entitled and better qualified to hold."[78] Grant responded by giving his commander-in-chief's son the rank of captain. Lincoln then immediately appointed Bob as assistant adjutant general of the army. He, therefore, "did manage to be at a camp around Petersburg, and at Appomattox to witness the surrender of Robert E. Lee."[79] Because Bob never actually served in any battle of the Civil War, there is a certain irony when later Northern newspapers wrote of "Robert Lincoln's distinguished service as an Army officer."[80]

On the fateful evening of Lincoln's assassination, Bob was in Washington in the White House. (On a certain note of irony, he would also be nearby both Garfield's and McKinley's assassinations.) Following his father's funeral, he immediately returned to his home state, Illinois, to enter a leading law firm, though he was not formally admitted to the Illinois bar until 1867. Quickly, his law practice flourished, and he married Mary Harlan, the only daughter of Iowa's senator, in a small ceremony. The small wedding was due, in large measure, to his mother's erratic behavior.[81]

Continuing his law practice in Chicago, in 1876 Bob was elected to the only public office he ever held through election—Supervisor of the Southern Section of Chicago.[82] Between 1876 and 1881, his law practice brought him in close contact with many Chicago-based major corporations, including the infamous Pullman Palace Car Company, for which he acted as chief counsel.[83]

In 1881 Robert Lincoln was appointed to Garfield's cabinet as secretary of war, a position he continued through Garfield's successor, Chester A. Arthur.[84] Robert then became an "almost ran" addition to presidential candidates. Three times he was mentioned for nomination as the Republican candidate for president. In 1880 his name was even submitted at the Republican party convention, where he received four votes. In both 1884 and 1888 he was again named by Republicans hoping to entice support from his long-deceased father's public image. However, as it was observed in 1884, "[N]o one claims that young Lincoln ever uttered a word or formed a solitary act showing superior ability, character or fitness to entitle him to the chief magistracy of the Republic."[85] Lincoln continued as secretary of war until the only Democratic president between Lincoln's administration and Woodrow Wilson's, Grover Cleveland, was elected to the presidency.

Robert returned to law practice until Republican president Benjamin Harrison was elected. Harrison then appointed him as minister to Great Britain, where he served until the end of Harrison's term in 1893.

Yet again, Robert returned to practice law, which had already made him a wealthy man. From his associations with the Pullman Palace Car Company, for which Robert had acted as chief counsel during the heyday of railroads—and during the Haymarket Square riots—Robert became president of the Pullman Company. With this change in his business career, Robert entered the arena for which he earned his own, personal, fame.

Robert became a major influence in industry, and he is associated with responsibility for a business that covered almost all railway development. With passengers numbering almost 10 million each year, Robert Todd Lincoln's influence was so strong that he was catered to, even by foreign dignitaries, as an "emperor of business."[86] He held this "imperial" position until his 1911 retirement.

Robert's death in 1926 furthered the Lincoln family legend, even mysteries. This oldest son of one of the nation's most-loved presidents requested that his personal collection of his father's papers not be opened until after 1947.

The contrast in characters between father and son is evident. While his father suffered and achieved heroic stature through the sheer force of will and intellect, Robert attained wealth and fame without the intellect, but through dogged determination. However, his own contributions were neglected and memories of his father influenced even those who wrote his last notices, after Robert's death.

Without risking the dangers of the battlefield, without service or exertion he became Assistant Adjutant General of the Army. Without completing his law studies, he obtained membership in an outstanding law firm. Without experience in military science he was appointed Secretary of War. Without any knowledge of diplomacy he became Minister to Great Britain.[87]

Yet, no notice of his extended leadership of one of the nation's major transportation firms was ever given.

No matter what this son had accomplished, he was not allowed to replicate his father's status and position as one of the nation's foremost heros. Robert's obituary demonstrates that the public did not allow him to stand beside his father.

## EDWARD BAKER LINCOLN

Second child, second of four sons of Abraham Lincoln and Mary Todd
*Born:* March 10, 1846     *Birthplace:* Springfield, Illinois
*Died:* February 1, 1850     *Age at Death:* 3 years, 11 months
*Cause of Death:* Unknown

The second of four Lincoln sons, Edward Baker, who was named after his father's close personal and political associate, Edward D. Baker of Illinois, did not survive childhood.

Edward was born when Abraham Lincoln was struggling to earn a living as a perambulating attorney in the Eighth Judicial Court District of Illinois. Riding "circuit" from September to December each year, and then again from February to June, his father was absent from the family home in Springfield for most of Edward's few years of life. Describing his son to a friend, Lincoln wrote that Edward was not much like his elder brother, Bob, because Eddie was "rather of a longer order."[88]

When Edward died Lincoln wrote to his stepbrother, "We lost our little boy. It was not our first, but our second child. We miss him very much."[89] According to Lincoln, his son lay dying for fully two days. The love that Lincoln would shower on his other three sons can, perhaps, be better understood by the early loss of his second child, Eddie.

# WILLIAM (WILLIE) WALLACE LINCOLN

Third child, third of four sons of Abraham Lincoln and Mary Todd
*Born:* December 21, 1850    *Birthplace:* Springfield, Illinois
*Died:* February 20, 1862    *Age at Death:* 11 years, 2 months
*Cause of Death:* Pneumonia

Willie Lincoln, believed to be his father's favorite child, was ten years old when his father was elected president of the United States. To Willie and his brother, Tad, the White House offered increased opportunity for the fun and games that characterized the lives of these two close brothers. Willie's boyish pranks kept the White House constantly in an uproar. For example, there was the occasion when he and his brother drove a goat through the drawing room, to the astonishment of the assembled visitors. Yet there was also a serious side to this Lincoln son, for he was particularly fond of drawing and writing poetry, some of which was published in newspapers.

Less than a year after the beginning of the Civil War, with newspapers announcing in headlines the battles as they took place, there was also the announcement that "the president's son, William, aged ten or eleven years, died [this evening] of pneumonia."[90] Young Willie's untimely death was yet another burden to the Lincolns, who were caught in the midst of the nation's tragedy. Lincoln and his wife were utterly distraught. Mary Todd Lincoln never again entered the White House room where her son had died, nor even where his coffin had rested. So great was Lincoln's grief that it was a popular belief that Lincoln had Willie's body disinterred twice so that he might view it. Willie's remains were placed in a vault, in a Washington, D.C., cemetery, where they remained until his father's assassination.

Upon his father's assassination, Willie's body was removed from its resting place and put in the same funeral car with Lincoln's body, which then traveled across the country to the martyred president's interment in Springfield, Illinois. Of the over $7,000 expended for the funeral for the fallen president, $10 was spent so that Willie could accompany his father on their last trip. The last public record of Lincoln was that of the undertaker who noted the cost of his service as "removing the remains of Willie $10."[91]

## THOMAS (TAD) LINCOLN

Fourth child, fourth son of Abraham Lincoln and Mary Todd
*Born:* April 4, 1853    *Birthplace:* Springfield, Illinois
*Died:* July 15, 1871    *Age at Death:* 18 years, 3 months
*Cause of Death:* Diphtheria    *Education:* Private schools

---

Eight years old when his father became the first Republican president of the United States, young Tad, as he was called, spent his first years in Springfield, Illinois. It was during his last summer spent in Springfield that Tad contracted scarlet fever, and although it is only an assumption made by historians, it may have been the extremes of fever that caused the young man a great deal of difficulty in speaking, noted as "an unusual impediment in little Tad's speech [that] made it extremely difficult for him to pronounce certain words, and really impossible for him to ennunciate a name like Smith, for instance."[92] His impediment, whatever its cause, combined with the death of Lincoln's much loved Willie, endeared little Tad even more to his father.

Lincoln was not alone in his adoration of the small boy; secretaries within the White House loved him, constantly deferring to him with affection. Described as merry, warm-blooded, and kindly, the little boy was, however, perfectly lawless. He ran freely throughout the White House, interrupting whatever struck his fancy. The president, catering to the little boy, would often let him play until he fell asleep, and then pick him up and carry him to bed.

On one occasion, young Tad, inspired by the war talk that filled the White House, was commissioned a second lieutenant in the army by Secretary of War Edwin Stanton. Tad believed the commission was real—not an unnatural assumption for a boy of his age and circumstances. The president did nothing to discourage the young boy's fantasy. Acting out the accepted fantasy, Lieutenant Tad overcame the night guards defending the White House in Civil War times, relieved them of their weapons, and mustered the gardeners and servants as his own guard, turning over the borrowed weapons to his troops. When Tad tired of being a lieutenant, his father promoted him to the rank of colonel. To enhance the credibility of the appointment, Lincoln ordered official stationery prepared with "Colonel Lincoln" printed upon it. Tad even sent telegrams signed Colonel Lincoln. In the course of carrying out his "colonel" duties, Tad found himself forced to sentence a doll to the death penalty, but the boy could not stomach the idea of actually carrying out the sentence. Appealing to his father to intervene to spare the life of the guilty doll, Tad called upon his father as president of the United States to exercise his constitutional power of pardon. With all solemnity, Lincoln heard the case and wrote, "The doll Jack is pardoned by order of the President. Signed, A. Lincoln."[93]

Upon Lincoln's assassination, Tad came entirely under the care of his mother, Mary Todd Lincoln, who, throughout her life, suffered from mental problems. His mother became obsessed that she and her little boy were abandoned in the world and that they were poverty stricken. She took Tad with her to stay with her eldest son, Robert, but her erratic behavior soon disturbed his family. After a short stay with Robert, Mrs. Lincoln took Tad to Europe, where she alternately put him into private schools and then removed him, for no apparent reason. Throughout the European travels, she insisted on lodging in the cheapest accommodations available. With no apparent plan, mother and son returned to Chicago. Shortly after returning, Tad contracted diphtheria and died.

Mary Todd Lincoln, utterly devastated by the loss of her third son, became even further removed from reality, and her only remaining child, Robert, was forced to commit her to a mental institution.

## FOR FURTHER READING

Baker, Jean H. *Mary Todd Lincoln: A Biography*. New York: W. W. Norton, 1987.

Bruce, David K. *Sixteen American Presidents*. New York: Bobbs-Merrill, 1962.

DeGregorio, Wiliam A. *The Complete Book of U.S. Presidents*. 2d ed. New York: Dembner Books, 1989.

Johannsen, Robert, ed. *The Letters of Stephan A. Douglas*. Urbana: University of Illinois Press, 1961.

Oates, Stephan B. *With Malice Toward None: The Life of Abraham Lincoln*. New York: Harper & Row, 1977.

Perling, Joseph J. *Presidents' Sons: The Prestige of Name in a Democracy*. New York: Odyssey Press, 1947; Freeport, New York: Books for Libraries Press, 1971.

Sandburg, Carl. *Abraham Lincoln: The War Years III*. New York: Harcourt, Brace and World, 1939.

Semone, Hattie. *Duel with Destiny*. Radford, Va.: Commonwealth Press, 1976.

# 13 ANDREW JOHNSON'S CHILDREN

## MARTHA JOHNSON PATTERSON

First child of Andrew Johnson and Eliza McCardle
*Born:* October 25, 1828     *Birthplace:* Greenville, Tennessee
*Died:* July 10, 1901     *Age at Death:* 72 years, 8 months
*Cause of Death:* Unknown     *Education:* Unknown
*Profession:* White House hostess, housewife, mother
*Spouse:* David Trotter Patterson
*Number of Children:* 2

She left her mark in history and on White House tradition when she filled the role of mistress of the White House, following the chaos of the Civil War years. Like several other daughters of presidents, Martha Johnson Patterson inherited the position of White House hostess because her mother was unable and unwilling to serve in that capacity. Unlike others who preceded her, Martha converted the jumbled White House of war years into the symbol of American elegance that continues since her intervention.

When Andrew Johnson took over the presidency following Lincoln's assassination in April 1865, the mansion showed the war's impact, as well as prior years of neglect and misuse. Civil War soldiers had wandered unchallenged throughout the entire White House, with the result that the furnishings were dirty and broken. Soldiers spat on floors, they slept throughout the mansion, and, quite literally, crowds trampled the rugs to tatters.

Despite her father's difficulties with Congress, which eventually led to impeachment proceedings, Martha was able to convince influential congressmen that the White House deserved renovation. Congress appropriated $30,000 for interior redecoration. Despite the fact that this was a niggardly sum even in 1866, Martha accomplished such substantial renovations that visitors were amazed. Everybody said that never before had the presidential home been so simply and yet so beautifully appointed! In addition to her pleasure in refurbishing the executive mansion, Martha felt great pride in the White House dairy, with prize cows grazing on what is today the White House lawn.

Possessing nervous energy much like her father's, as well as an extremely strong will, Martha accomplished much with very little. Raised by her mother in Tennessee, she once remarked, "We are just plain people from the mountains of Tennessee, placed in this great tragedy. We have no desire to put on airs."[94]

When Lincoln was assassinated, Martha was married with two lively children. Her husband, a senator from Tennessee, was a devoted husband and son-in-law, though known as a heavy drinker. The White House parties for the children and entertainment gained for the Johnsons a reputation for graciousness and elegance. Assisted by her sister, Mary, they gave to the White house a character never before seen in the presidential home.

Present day expectations for the quality of the White House were initiated by the activities of this daughter turned hostess to the nation's first family's home. Though she described herself as "just plain people," ironically, she is most responsible for the world-renowned image of the White House as the fashionable home of the nation's first families.[95]

## CHARLES JOHNSON

Second child, first son of Andrew Johnson and Eliza McCardle
*Born:* February 19, 1830     *Birthplace:* Greenville, Tennessee
*Died:* April 4, 1863     *Age at Death:* 33 years, 2 months
*Cause of Death:* Riding accident—deliberate or accidental?
*Education:* Unknown
*Profession:* Medical doctor, pharmacist, soldier
*Spouse:* None     *Number of Children:* None

Charles Johnson, the eldest of three Johnson sons, was educated in medicine in accordance with the method of the day—serving an internship. He became a physician as well as a partner in a drug store in Tennessee before the Civil

War. As a political activist, opposed to Tennessee's secession from the Union, Charles put his medical skills to the Union's service at the outbreak of the Civil War. He joined the First Middle Tennessee Infantry as a surgeon.

In 1863 the son of Tennessee's governor and future president of the United States died in a riding accident; some of his contemporaries believed the fatal accident was brought about by Charles's own choice. The much-loved son of Andrew, described as "his own worst enemy," was unable to face the struggle between the states; completely exhausted, and addicted to stimulants, he ended his own life.[96] (This conclusion is both accepted and rejected by historians. Most often this son's death is attributed to a riding accident.)

Charles's funeral cortege was escorted by his own infantry regiment, as well as by the cavalry regiment commanded by his younger brother, Robert. Charles, an easygoing, personable man until his Civil War involvement, was the first of three Johnson sons to come to an early end. His obituary was buried among headlines that spoke of the greater sorrow of the day—"General Grant Preparing to Bombard the City" (Vicksburg, Mississippi).[97] Thousands of other fathers would also mourn their losses before the final act would be played in the greatest tragedy America has known.

## MARY JOHNSON STOVER BROWN

Third child, second daughter of Andrew Johnson and Eliza McCardle
*Born:* May 8, 1832      *Birthplace:* Greenville, Tennessee
*Died:* April 19, 1883      *Age at death:* 50 years, 11 months
*Cause of Death:* Unknown      *Education:* Unknown
*Profession:* Housewife, mother
*Spouses:* Daniel Stover, William Brown
*Number of Children:* Johnson/Stover: 3; Johnson/Brown: None

Mary, the younger of the two Johnson girls, was a complete contrast to her sister Martha. While Martha was a dark-haired, grave child and woman, much like her father, Mary, fair and cheerful, had a volatile temperament. The mother of three children before her father became president of the United States, she lived with her husband Daniel Stover, an east Tennessean with a spread of land in Watuga Valley, Tennessee. Her married life was thus spent in a home close to her birthplace.

During the Civil War the Stover home became the center for the entire Johnson clan. For part of the war, Mary's mother lived with the Stovers, and Mary spent much of her time catering to her mother's fears for her husband, Andrew. Mary's husband Daniel, like the Johnsons, a Southerner by birth, fought in the Union's cause as a scout. Daniel died from disease, the scourge of armies before twentieth-century medicine, leaving Mary a widow when her father entered the White House in 1865.

When Mary's father became president following the assassination of Abraham Lincoln, Mary was called upon to serve, with her sister Martha, as White House hostess. Their mother was ill and unable to act in this capacity. The White House reverberated with the noises of the daughters' children during Johnson's administration.

At the conclusion of Johnson's presidency, he moved back to Tennessee with his daughters. Mary remarried in 1869. She made her home near her parents in order to be ever present to see to their needs. Mary and her new husband, William Brown, spent their summers at the Stover farm Mary had inherited from her first husband.

Mary, a constantly dutiful daughter, continued as a pillar of strength and pleasure to her family. She shared with millions the tragedy of the Civil War, and then she further suffered the singular misfortune of the bitter presidency of Andrew Johnson.

## ROBERT JOHNSON

Fourth child, second son of Andrew Johnson and Eliza McCardle
*Born:* February 22, 1834     *Birthplace:* Greenville, Tennessee
*Died:* April 22, 1869     *Age at Death:* 35 years, 2 months
*Cause of Death:* Alcoholism     *Education:* Unknown
*Profession:* Lawyer, soldier, presidential secretary
*Spouse:* None     *Number of Children:* None

Robert Johnson, a Southerner by birth and upbringing, fought for the Northern cause in the Civil War. As a member of the Tennessee legislature, while his father was military governor, Robert spoke against secession from the Union.

Going beyond words in his defense of the united Union, Robert organized an infantry regiment of Tennessee volunteers to fight to preserve the Union. Commissioned a colonel, Robert not only led his men but also fought side by side with them. Because of his character, expressed through very real concern for his troops, Robert Johnson earned a measure of respect accorded few commanding officers.

Following Lincoln's assassination, Robert's father became president of the United States, and Robert immediately went to Washington, D.C., to become his father's private secretary. By all accounts Robert's work was exemplary; however, early in 1866, Robert's social drinking had definitely become serious drinking. Alcohol had become such an obvious problem for Robert that his father sought ways to remedy his illness by removing access to drink.

Devising a scheme in which Robert would take a long sea voyage, supposedly to investigate the slave trade on the African coast, the president planned that his son would abstain during the long trip. But national politics intervened and almost cost Andrew Johnson his office through impeachment. The trip was delayed over and over again because of the acute conflict between Robert's father and the Congress over reconstruction of the conquered South. When President Johnson had the time to turn his mind to his son's dilemma and finalize the projected sea voyage, his son refused to go.

Robert, a highly eligible bachelor, loose in Washington's society, nevertheless remained unmarried throughout his life. After his father's term as president, all of the Johnsons returned to Tennessee. The elder Johnson, far from removing himself from politics after his brush with impeachment, became a popular public speaker. It was during one of his speaking tours that Andrew Johnson was summoned back to Nashville, with news that his son Robert had died.

This respected, honorable man, who fought for his principles, became the object of passions that could not touch his father. Many of the obituaries for Robert were really arrows aimed at Lincoln's successor. Said one paper, "[T]he devil came for the old man and not finding him took the son."[98]

## ANDREW JOHNSON, JR.

Fifth child, third son of Andrew Johnson and Eliza McCardle
*Born:* August 6, 1852    *Birthplace:* Greenville, Tennessee
*Died:* March 12, 1879    *Age at Death:* 26 years, 7 months
*Cause of Death:* Unknown    *Education:* Unknown
*Profession:* Journalist    *Spouse:* Bessie May Kumbaugh
*Number of Children:* None

Little is known of the youngest of the Johnson children, the namesake of his father. He was raised in the protected atmosphere of his Tennessee home, cared for by his mother, rarely seeing his politician father who only infrequently visited his home. Suddenly, the assassination of President Lincoln hurled his father into the presidency and changed the life of Andy, Jr. Thus, the only time the impressionable boy had an opportunity to know his father was when he was the most powerful man in the nation.

After completing his schooling, following the end of his father's term as president, Andy entered a career in journalism. He organized a newspaper, the *Greenville Intelligencer*, when he was only twenty-one years old. Quickly, he acquired 800 subscribers, a sizeable number for the day, but the paper failed. Perhaps its failure was due in part to the paper's excessive concentration on his father's activities and accomplishments. Thus, the *Intelligencer* began well, but ended rapidly.

At the age of twenty-six Andy, Jr., died, surviving his father by only four years. Though he was married, he left no surviving children.

## FOR FURTHER READING

Castel, Albert. *Presidency of Andrew Johnson*. Lawrence: Regents Press of Kansas, 1979.

Miller, Hope Ridings. *Scandals in the Highest Office*. New York: Random House, 1973.

Thomas, Lately. *The First President Johnson*. New York: William Morrow, 1968.

Williams, Frank B., Jr. *Tennessee's President*. Knoxville: University of Tennessee Press, 1981.

# 14 ULYSSES SIMPSON GRANT'S CHILDREN

## FREDERICK DENT GRANT

First child of Ulysses Simpson Grant and Julia Boggs Dent
*Born:* May 30, 1850 *Birthplace:* St. Louis, Missouri
*Died:* April 11, 1912 *Age at Death:* 61 years, 11 months
*Cause of Death:* Cancer *Education:* West Point
*Profession:* Soldier, politician, police commissioner
*Spouse:* Ida Honore *Number of Children:* 2

By the time he was thirteen years old, Frederick Dent Grant had shown his preference for a military career. His experiences were not common to other thirteen-year-old boys, for Frederick's father was commander of the Union Army at the battle of Vicksburg, and the boy accompanied his father on the campaign. When Grant took Jackson, Mississippi, it was his son who would, years later, lay claim to the honor of the capture. Running ahead of his father's troops, young Frederick halted only at the sight of Confederate troops on the outskirts of the city. There he lay in wait for the Union soldiers. When his father's troops arrived, he proclaimed that he had been there first and to him was due the honor of laying siege to the city.

Entering West Point at fourteen with inadequate scholastic preparation, it took Frederick five years to complete the normal four-year course. Graduating as a second lieutenant, Frederick was assigned to the cavalry on patrol at the Mexican border. From this rather mundane assignment, nineteen-year-old Frederick was next transferred to General Philip Sheridan's command as his aide. The popular understanding was that he had

(Left to right, standing) Mrs. Frederick (Ida) Grant, Frederick Grant, unidentified person, Mrs. Jesse (Elizabeth) Grant, Jesse Grant. (Left to right, seated) Frederick Grant's children, with Mrs. Ulysses S. (Julia) Grant, Ulysses S. Grant, and Jesse's daughter (circa 1885). Photo courtesy of the Library of Congress.

received his new position because his father had just recently become president of the United States. He served with Sheridan until the general's death. In 1889 Frederick resigned from the army to accept President Benjamin Harrison's appointment as minister to Austria. In 1894 Frederick became New York City's police commissioner and held that position for four years.

But the call of the trumpet enticed him back into military service. The Spanish-American War began in 1898, and Frederick, by virtue of his experience, quickly became Colonel Grant of the Fourteenth New York Infantry. From colonel, Frederick advanced to the rank of brigadier general, commanding the volunteers. At war's end he retained his rank, though in the regular army. In 1906 he was promoted to major general. His peacetime service included two tours of duty as commander of Governor's Island, New York, as well as holding the command of the Department of the Great Lakes.

Frederick's return to the military continued the path of his boyhood experiences. During one brief period, it seemed as if he would follow the pattern of his father, from the army to politics. In 1887 the Republican president nominated him for the cabinet position of secretary of state, but the Senate refused to confirm the nomination, agreeing with the newspapers' editorials that "the nomination of Colonel Grant would never have been had he not been his father's son"[99] and that "everyone knows that it is only as the son of his father that he was given the place."[100] Thus quickly began and ended the political potential of President Grant's son Frederick.

By 1912 Grant held the second highest military position in the United States, outranked only by Major General Leonard Wood, Washington, D.C., chief of staff. Returning to New York City from inspecting posts under his command at Portland, Maine, and as far south as Galveston, Texas, Frederick took a leave of absence to spend some time with his wife, or so the press was informed.

Instead, Frederick underwent surgery for cancer, but the nature of his illness was kept secret. Ever since his father's terrible death from throat cancer, Frederick had lived in fear that he too would suffer the same death. His fearful premonition was correct.

Seeking to evade possible publicity, Frederick and his wife registered under a false name in a New York hotel. On the evening of April 11, 1912, only hours after he had arrived at the hotel, the general began to choke. Doctors were called, but it was too late.

The press announced that Frederick had died of heart failure, complicated by diabetes and intestinal disorders, but the news of his illness was not long kept secret. General Frederick Dent Grant was accorded a military funeral with all honors. Services were attended by thousands, including

PresidentTaft, the nation's vice president, the mayor of New York, and most of the highest ranking officers of the regular army and the National Guard. A military caisson drawn by six horses escorted his coffin to its West Point burial ground. In the style of military funerals, his favorite horse, Pet, was led along the way of the procession, with the general's boots reversed in the saddle's stirrups. A final thirteen-gun salute ended the ceremonies of one of the nation's leading military men, the army's second General Grant.

## ULYSSES SIMPSON (BUCK) GRANT II

Second child, second son of Ulysses Simpson Grant and Julia Boggs Dent
*Born:* July 22, 1852     *Birthplace:* Bethel, Ohio
*Died:* September 25, 1929     *Age at Death:* 77 years, 2 months
*Cause of Death:* Unknown
*Education:* Phillips Exeter Academy, University of Gottingen, Harvard University
*Profession:* Lawyer, presidential secretary, businessman
*Spouses:* Josephine Chaffee, America Workman Wills
*Number of Children:* Grant/Chaffee: 5; Grant/Wills: None

Born in Ohio and called Buck for most of his life because of his birthplace in the Buckeye State, Ulysses Grant II was but sixteen when his father went to the White House. But this Buck who was Ulysses Simpson Grant II, was, in fact, the first Ulysses of the Grants. As Buck himself would later relate, his father's name was Hiram Grant until his West Point entrance, when a clerk mistakenly wrote a "U" initial rather than an "H," and thus rechristened Hiram S. Grant as U.S. Grant, the Ulysses being Grant's personal choice, given the limitation of the letter "U." However, the credibility of Buck's explanation is questioned by some authorities.

Buck graduated in 1874 from Harvard, having previously studied at Phillips Exeter Academy and the University of Gottingen, Germany. Admitted to the bar, Buck did not practice law but rather served as his father's presidential secretary.

After Ulysses, Senior, left the White House, Buck became a junior partner in a large law firm, a remarkable achievement for so young and inexperienced a man. But despite the auspicious beginning, Buck's practice did not develop, and he rapidly became disenchanted with the law. Buck shifted westward with his marriage to Josephine Chaffee, daughter of Colorado Senator Jerome B. Chaffee. He married Josephine, fathered five children, and prospered in mining and land development. His Western interests proved imminently successful.

Following his wife's 1913 death, sixty-one-year-old Grant married America Workman Wills, a widow in her thirties. Both children and friends opposed the marriage, but Grant, once rather shy and retiring, flaunted his new wife. He announced that the bulk of his estate would be hers upon his death. The Grants traveled the world, often socializing with nobility while U.S. II developed ideas of his own political future.

Returning to California, Buck began work to gain the nomination for U.S. senator from California. His goal was reasonable, given his political heritage, but his political career was scuttled when it was proven that he had been involved in bribery schemes.

At one time, U. S. Grant II became the largest taxpayer in San Diego County, after he built a major hotel as a memorial to his father—the U. S. Grant Hotel. Cynics observed it was the only dividend-paying "memorial" ever erected to a president's memory.

When Buck died, his big talk, flamboyancy, and facade of wealth, all of which had developed in his later years, crumbled. His great fortune, upon which he had based all of his later years' schemes, was found to be no more than $10,000.

## ELLEN (NELLIE) WRENSHALL GRANT SARTORIS JONES

Third child, only daughter of Ulysses Simpson Grant and Julia Boggs Dent
*Born:* July 4, 1855     *Birthplace:* Wistonwisch, Missouri
*Died:* August 30, 1922     *Age at Death:* 67 years, 2 months
*Cause of Death:* Paralysis/stroke?     *Education:* Unknown
*Profession:* Housewife, mother
*Spouses:* Algernon Charles Frederick Sartoris, Franklin Hatch Jones
*Number of Children:* Grant/Sartoris: 4; Grant/Jones: None

Ellen Grant, nicknamed Nellie, was General Grant's only daughter. At the age of thirteen, when her father entered the White House, Nellie moved into the elite circle of Washington, D.C., teenagers. It was in the atmosphere of international Washington that seventeen-year-old Nellie met and married

British diplomat Algernon Sartoris. The couple married in the White House, in a ceremony described by contemporaries as an extravaganza. The romantic story of a president's daughter and a distinguished diplomat and the splash of a White House wedding captured the public's imagination. Newspapers detailed her life from the wedding onward. When the couple moved to Britain, English newspapers took up the story with the added twist that, from the British perspective, Nellie was the president's daughter. "America's royalty" intrigued British readers.

Four children were born to the couple, but shortly after the birth of their fourth, Sartoris died. Nellie was left as a British subject, a status she acquired by her marriage to a British subject. Far from home and family, Nellie wanted to return to the country of her birth. She petitioned the U.S. Congress for renewal of her citizenship. Congress complied. An American citizen once again, Nellie returned to the United States as a financially comfortable widow.

Nellie married Franklin Hatch Jones in 1912. Jones had been first assistant postmaster general during Grover Cleveland's administration, and he became head of the Illinois division of the Woodrow Wilson Foundation, an organization devoted to the support of scholarship. The couple were married in Nellie's summer home in Ontario, Canada. However, only months after the marriage, she became seriously ill from a disease that was never identified to the public. During the last seven years of her life she was paralyzed and was unable to take part in social activities. Her active life was replaced by illness for the remaining years of her life.

## JESSE ROOT GRANT

Fourth child, third son of Ulysses Simpson Grant and Julia Boggs Dent
*Born:* February 6, 1858    *Birthplace:* St. Louis, Missouri
*Died:* June 8, 1934    *Age at Death:* 76 years, 4 months
*Cause of Death:* Unknown
*Education:* Cornell University, Columbia University
*Profession:* Engineer, author
*Spouses:* Elizabeth Chapman, Lillian Burns Wilkins
*Number of Children:* Grant/Chapman: 2; Grant/Wilkins: None

Jesse Root Grant, the last of the four Grant children, chose a life very different from that of his father. Selecting engineering as his career, Jesse studied at Cornell, although, for a short time, he had considered entering law when he studied at Columbia Law School. Perhaps the trip Jesse took with his father around the world, following Grant's second presidential term, evoked a wanderlust in young Jesse. Earning a engineering degree, Jesse traveled the world constantly as a freelance mining engineer.

Though he married and fathered two children, he never settled down to a regular family relationship, preferring traveling and spending little time at home. Ironically, in 1914, Jesse filed divorce proceedings in Nevada, on grounds of desertion by his wife. His wife, Elizabeth, had the divorce set aside. But four years later Jesse tried again, and this time he was successful in obtaining his divorce on the grounds his wife had deserted him. One week after the second divorce was granted, Jesse married a widow, nineteen years his junior. He outlived her by ten years.

In opposition to his father, Jesse was a Democrat. From his college days he took an active interest in politics, although he never attempted to seek office until 1908.

Returning to New York City from a speaking tour in the South and West, Jesse astonishingly announced his candidacy for the Democratic nomination for the presidency of the United States. Clearly, his ambitions were waylaid, as the party nominated William Jennings Bryan who was soundly defeated by Republican William Howard Taft.

Jesse's final days were spent writing about his father. In his book, *In the Days of My Father, General Grant*, published in 1925, Jesse presents an image of President Grant as "the kindest, most thoughtful and most abstemious man I ever knew."[101] The Grant image that emerges from Jesse's memoir is not the man known to history. Most Grant historians portray him as steel-hard, a raucous high-liver, and a drunk. Clearly, his son's image adds a different character to his father president. Surviving years beyond his brothers and sister, Jesse publicly defended his father, perhaps in truth touched by the sentimentality of age.

## FOR FURTHER READING

Faber, Doris. *Presidents' Mothers*. New York: St. Martin's Press, 1978.

Long, E. B., ed. New introduction by William S. McFeely. *The Personal Memoirs of U.S. Grant*. New York: DeCapo Press, 1982, reprint.

McFeely, William S. *Grant: A Biography*. New York: W. W. Norton, 1974.

*New York Times*, August 31, 1922, 5:4.

*New York Times*, September 27, 1929, 27:3.

Sadler, Christine. *Children in the White House*. New York: G. P. Putnam's Sons, 1967.

# 15 RUTHERFORD BIRCHARD HAYES'S CHILDREN

## SARDIS (BIRCHARD) AUSTIN HAYES

First child of Rutherford Birchard Hayes and Lucy Ware Webb
*Born:* November 4, 1853    *Birthplace:* Cincinnati, Ohio
*Died:* January 24, 1926    *Age at Death:* 72 years, 2 months
*Cause of Death:* Unknown
*Education:* University of Michigan, Cornell University, Harvard University
*Profession:* Lawyer    *Spouse:* Mary Nancy Sherman
*Number of Children:* 5

An Army "brat" for the first ten years of his life, and called Birchard throughout his life, he was sent to live with his uncle in Fremont, Ohio, so that he might prepare for entry into higher education. Undecided as to which college to attend, Birchard first went to school in Michigan and then, dissatisfied, he chose Cornell after lengthy consultations with his father.

Birchard's college education was uneventful. His father explained that his son's lack of academic distinction was because "his diffidence has kept him from improving his opportunity to learn to speak. He is an accurate, thorough student, not fond of books as I was, with an unusual fondness for statistics, especially for the preparation of tabular information."[102]

It was entirely fitting, therefore, that with this background and natural bent Birchard entered Harvard Law School, graduating in 1877, shortly after his father had become president of the United States.

Though he began his law career in New York with a leading firm, within two years Birchard moved to Toledo, Ohio, and began a law practice specializing in taxation and real estate law. He continued his practice for twenty-six years. In 1926 Birchard died.

## JAMES WEBB (WEBB COOK) HAYES

Second child, second son of Rutherford Birchard Hayes and Lucy Ware Webb
*Born:* March 20, 1856     *Birthplace:* Cincinnati, Ohio
*Died:* July 26, 1934     *Age at Death:* 78 years, 4 months
*Cause of Death:* Unknown     *Education:* Cornell University
*Profession:* Presidential secretary, businessman, soldier
*Spouse:* Mary Otis Miller     *Number of Children:* None

James Webb Hayes, who inexplicably later changed his name to Webb Cook Hayes, was educated at Cornell inspite of the fact that he was not a particularly good student. However, his father did employ him as his confidential secretary during his presidency from 1877 until 1881.

After his service in the White House, Webb moved from the political world to business and became an officer in a small business. In time, under Webb's direction, the small firm reorganized, expanded, and absorbed numerous other businesses. The small enterprise became the giant multinational Union Carbide Corporation. Webb became rich—even a bit more than merely rich—and he found himself able to indulge in his passion: war.

In 1898 Webb was commissioned a major in the U.S. Army, and he led troops against the Spaniards in Cuba and Puerto Rico during the Spanish-American War. Wounded in action, he was awarded the Congressional Medal of Honor and promoted to the rank of lieutenant colonel. But the all too brief Spanish-American War had only whetted Webb's appetite for adventure.

In 1900 Webb was in China fighting in the Boxer Rebellion. In both 1911 and 1913 he was on the Mexican border, fighting bandits. When he was fifty-eight years old, Webb joined British and French brigades in Italy fighting in the battles before the United States was drawn into the carnage of World War I. When America did enter the war, Webb transferred to the U.S. Army. He was decorated for his service in both France and Africa.

Webb survived and clearly enjoyed his phenomenal business success, which allowed him, at a mature age, to engage in the excitement and patriotism of three wars and numerous adventures before his 1934 death.

# RUTHERFORD PLATT HAYES

Third child, third son of Rutherford Birchard Hayes and Lucy Ware Webb
*Born:* June 24, 1858    *Birthplace:* Cincinnati, Ohio
*Died:* July 31, 1931    *Age at Death:* 70 years, 11 months
*Cause of Death:* Long-term illness
*Education:* University of Michigan, Cornell University, Boston Institute
of Technology    *Profession:* Businessman, librarian
*Spouse:* Lucy Hayes Platt    *Number of Children:* 3

---

Rutherford, characterized by his father as "the mild," was a tall, slender youth, who, at sixteen, was considered unfit for future hard work or hard study. However, proving to the contrary, Rutherford overcame early estimations of him and developed into a bright, jovial, and handsome man.

While his father was president of the United States, Rutherford studied at both the University of Michigan and Cornell University, completing his undergraduate work in 1880. He continued graduate studies at the Boston Institute of Technology until 1882. Returning to the family home in Fremont, Ohio, Rutherford became a cashier in a savings bank, a position of much higher status in those days than today. When the bank panic of 1892 hit, Rutherford is credited with guiding his bank through the difficult period.

Because a rich uncle had founded the Birchard Library, Rutherford became a trustee for that library. In that fashion, quite by chance, Rutherford stumbled onto an avocation that was to become his passion—libraries. In 1895 he was a major founder of the American Library Association (ALA), today, with thousands of members, considered the major professional library association in the United States.

In creating what he called "mobile libraries" to bring books from libraries to the public, Hayes anticipated the bookmobiles of today's public library systems. It was also Rutherford who began the first reading room especially designed for children, an innovation which has become an American library standard.

In his own quiet way, the "mild" Rutherford made contributions to the American system of education and learning which would be exceeded, perhaps, only by another man of Rutherford's time and passion—Andrew Carnegie, called the father of the American library system.

## JOSEPH THOMPSON HAYES

Fourth child, fourth son of Rutherford Birchard Hayes and Lucy
Ware Webb
*Born:* December 21, 1861     *Birthplace:* Cincinnati, Ohio
*Died:* June 24, 1863     *Age at Death:* 1 year, 6 months
*Cause of Death:* Dysentery

---

Joseph Hayes was born just before Christmas in the year the Civil War
began. His father, stationed at Camp White, near Charleston, Virginia, in
the part of Virginia that stayed loyal to the Union, was not present at his
birth and did not see his son until the boy was almost eighteen months old,
when the family arrived at their father's camp from their Cincinnati home.

Within a few short days of the family's arrival, the baby, already a sickly child,
became further weakened by dysentery and died. The cottage that Rutherford
Hayes had taken, planning a happy family reunion, became a funeral parlor when
the little boy's body was placed on the table used as a makeshift bier.

Though his father had scarcely known the boy, he observed that "he was
afflicted with some kind of mental disorder . . . that the boy's brain was
excessively developed and that death had prevented further greater suffering."[103] (From Hayes's description, it appears likely that the child suffered
from hydroencephalitis; today, of course, the illness could be cured.)

## GEORGE CROOK HAYES

Fifth child, fifth son of Rutherford Birchard Hayes and Lucy Ware Webb
*Born:* September 29, 1864     *Birthplace:* Chillicothe, Ohio
*Died:* May 4, 1866     *Age at Death:* 1 year, 8 months
*Cause of Death:* Scarlet fever

---

Very little is recorded of the birth and death of the namesake of General George
Crook, who was so much admired by little George's father. The boy was born
only shortly after his father's hero was credited with winning a major Civil
War battle, although later history would credit Philip Sheridan with the
victory. George, the second of the Hayes's children to be born during war

years, lived only slightly past the great war's end, when he succumbed to the dreaded disease, scarlet fever.

## FRANCES (FANNY) HAYES SMITH

Sixth child, only daughter of Rutherford Birchard Hayes and Lucy Ware Webb
*Born:* September 2, 1867     *Birthplace:* Cincinnati, Ohio
*Died:* March 18, 1950     *Age at Death:* 82 years, 6 months
*Cause of Death:* Unknown     *Education:* Tutors, finishing school
*Profession:* Housewife, mother     *Spouse:* Harry Eaton Smith
*Number of Children:* 1

The only daughter among seven brothers, Fanny's earliest years were spent in Ohio where her father was the state's governor. Named after Hayes's much-loved sister, she was constantly pampered and catered to by all of the family, as well as by her father's associates. On one occasion a huge dollhouse was presented to the little girl. When it was later carted to the White House, all who saw it knew immediately that an important small child had taken up residence in the White House.

Only nine years old when her father became the nation's president, Fanny traveled frequently with her mother, her aunts, and her father throughout the nation. But Hayes, the consummate father, saw to it that his daughter took all the lessons essential to make her a fine and proper lady. Both swimming and dancing lessons were part of propriety for a young woman of her generation. Fanny attended school during their days in Ohio with her close friend, another president-to-be's child, Molly Garfield. Later she completed her education in Connecticut at a finishing school.

Following the end of the Hayes' presidency in 1881, Hayes returned to the Ohio family home to live a gentleman's life, involving himself and his family in hobbies as well as keeping abreast of national affairs. Fanny was still at home when her mother died in 1889. Hayes was distraught at the loss of his wife, and the young daughter replaced her mother by filling the duties of hostess and travel companion, even accompanying her father to Bermuda in 1890.

Fanny's life changed following her father's death. She married Harry Eaton Smith and bore one child. After her husband's death, she changed her name back to Hayes.

## SCOTT RUSSELL HAYES

Seventh child, sixth son of Rutherford Birchard Hayes and Lucy Ware Webb
*Born:* February 8, 1871      *Birthplace:* Columbus, Ohio
*Died:* May 6, 1923      *Age at Death:* 52 years, 3 months
*Cause of Death:* Cancer      *Education:* Unknown
*Profession:* Businessman      *Spouse:* Maude Anderson
*Number of Children:* Unknown

Only five years old when his father became president of the United States in 1877, Scott was described by his father as "our handsomest. Interesting, too honest to joke, or to comprehend a joke readily. He talks with some hesitation when excited and has many pretty ways. He says many queer things. He is fond of animals."[104] His father also described Scott as an "adventurer," though this quality apparently left him before he reached adulthood.

After Scott completed his education, he became an executive for a railroad spring and airbrake manufacturing company, eventually achieving financial success. Scott showed no interest in politics, but nevertheless was the closest to his father of all the Hayes sons. Indeed, it was to Scott that the former president wrote his last letter.

At the age of fifty-two, Scott Hayes entered the hospital for an operation on a brain tumor, but he died before the operation took place. Scott left his widow, but there were no children to follow him to his burial site in Fremont, Ohio.

## MANNING FORCE HAYES

Eighth child, seventh son of Rutherford Birchard Hayes and Lucy Ware Webb
*Born:* August 1, 1873      *Birthplace:* Fremont, Ohio
*Died:* August 28, 1874      *Age at Death:* 1 year
*Cause of Death:* Childhood disease

The last-born child and seventh son of Rutherford Hayes, Manning Force survived only long enough to celebrate his first birthday, and then his life was suddenly cut short by a childhood disease.

Named after the son of Hayes's friend, Peter Force, with whom Hayes had attended Harvard, Manning was born only shortly after his mother's two brothers had died. Manning brought some joy into an otherwise sorrowful time for the family, although, with his death, he became one of three Hayes sons to die in infancy.

## FOR FURTHER READING

Davison, Kenneth E. *The Presidency of Rutherford B. Hayes.* Westport, Conn.: Greenwood Press, 1972.

Eckenrode, H. J. *Rutherford B. Hayes.* New York: Kennikat Press, 1963.

Geer, Emily. *First Lady: The Life of Lucy Webb Hayes.* Kent, Ohio: Kent State University Press, 1984.

*New York Times*, July 27, 1934, 17:4.

*New York Times*, August 1, 1934, 19:4.

Whitney, David C. *The American Presidents.* 4th ed. Garden City, New York: Doubleday, 1978.

Williams, T. Harry. *Hayes of the Twenty-Third: The Civil War Volunteer Officer.* New York: Alfred A. Knopf, 1965.

(Left to right) Mary (Molly) Garfield, Harry, James, Irvin, and Abe (circa 1881–1883). Photo courtesy of the Library of Congress.

# 16 JAMES ABRAM GARFIELD'S CHILDREN

## ELIZA (TROT) ARABELLA GARFIELD

First child of James Abram Garfield and Lucretia Rudolph
*Born:* July 3, 1860  *Birthplace:* Hiram, Ohio
*Died:* December 3, 1863  *Age at Death:* 3 years, 5 months
*Cause of Death:* Diphtheria

Eliza, the first of seven Garfield children, became her father's pride and joy. Garfield, who had experienced some trepidation at the prospect of fatherhood, came to adore his firstborn, whom he dubbed "Trot" after a literary character from a Dickens novel.

Despite Garfield's undoubted affection for the girl, the press of his military and political duties allowed him little time to express that affection. Thus, Trot was usually under the care of her mother, as they lived with Trot's grandparents.

Constantly in motion, demanding and giving affection freely, Trot completed Garfield's image of an ideal family: a husband, wife, and child. To house this ideal family, Garfield purchased the first family home for $825. Though the house badly needed repairs, it represented to Garfield the solid foundation of family life he had earlier found difficult to imagine for himself. Soon after the move into the family home, a second child, Harry, was born.

But tragedy quickly intruded into the Garfield home. The joy of Garfield's election to Congress from Ohio was followed by Trot's death from diphtheria. During her illness, Garfield sat beside her. He later wrote, "We buried her . . . on the 3rd day of December, at the very hour she would have lived the fifth month of her fourth year. . . . It seems as if the fabric of my life were torn to atoms and scattered to the winds."[105] It was with his mind tormented by the death of his daughter that Garfield left for Washington, D.C., to begin his national political career.

## HARRY (HAL) AUGUSTUS GARFIELD

Second child, first son of James Abram Garfield and Lucretia Rudolph
*Born:* October 11, 1863     *Birthplace:* Hiram, Ohio
*Died:* December 12, 1942     *Age at Death:* 79 years, 2 months
*Cause of Death:* Long-term illness
*Education:* Williams College, Columbia University, Oxford University, England
*Profession:* Lawyer, teacher, politician, businessman
*Spouse:* Belle Hartford Mason     *Number of Children:* 4

Born at the height of the Civil War, Harry, nicknamed Hal, entered Williams College about the time his father became president of the United States in 1881. Hal graduated with a bachelor's degree in 1885 and went on to study law at both Columbia, in New York, and Oxford, in England. After completing his education, Harry opened a law office with his younger brother, James, in Cleveland, Ohio. Displaying a particularly strong aptitude for business, Hal became the vice president of the Cleveland Trust Company. While in that position, he also developed other business interests, such as a coal syndicate to develop mines in Ohio.

Notwithstanding his involvement in business, it was the law that dominated Hal's career. He became professor of contract law at Western Reserve College (later renamed Case Western Reserve University) near his Cleveland home. From Western Reserve, Hal moved to Princeton University, where, as a president's son, he taught politics. There he became friends with Princeton's president and a future president of the United States, Woodrow Wilson. Williams College selected its former student as its president. Hal accepted and remained at Williams College as its president until America's entry into World War I.

War brought the need for organizing America's industrial power. President Woodrow Wilson called upon his old friend, Hal Garfield, to head the newly created Fuel Administration, which would control both the supply and distribution of the nation's energy resources. Although Hal's innovations increased the production of coal, his authoritarian attitude brought national protests and earned Hal the unflattering title, "Dictator of the nation's fuel resources." However, at the war's end, Garfield was awarded the Distinguished Service Medal.

After the war, Hal returned to Williams College where he resumed his presidency of the school, and where he developed the Institute for Human Relations as a major resource for the study of international politics. He retired from his position in 1934.

Hal's life ended in 1942 at the age of seventy-nine, and although he was involved primarily in academics for a major portion of his life, this presidential son was a major contributor to the first major regimentation and governmental control of American life, prompted by the emergency needs of World War I.

## JAMES RUDOLPH GARFIELD

Third child, second son of James Abram Garfield and Lucretia Rudolph
*Born:* October 17, 1865     *Birthplace:* Hiram, Ohio
*Died:* March 24, 1950     *Age at Death:* 84 years, 5 months
*Cause of Death:* Pneumonia     *Education:* Columbia University
*Profession:* Lawyer, politician     *Spouse:* Helen Newell
*Number of Children:* 4

Fifteen-year-old James Garfield was with his father, traveling to meet his mother at the New Jersey seashore, when a man stepped from the crowd at the railroad station and shot the elder Garfield, the second American president to be assassinated.

As Jimmy grew he developed an interest in sports. Lawn tennis and the newly invented game of baseball were his favorites. Perhaps because of his close association with his brother Hal, he also became fascinated by the law. Graduating from Columbia Law School in 1888, Jimmy married the daughter of a railroad president. The couple moved to a large Ohio home, where Jim raised cattle, but he continued his interest in the law and entered a partership with his older brother, Hal.

Perhaps because of his name, James Garfield was elected to the state senate before his thirtieth birthday, thus beginning a career in politics. President McKinley, who also was fated to be assassinated, appointed James to the newly established United States Civil Service Commission, which was assigned responsibility to oversee and assess federal jobs newly removed from partisanship of the spoils system. James was also appointed to a post in the Department of Commerce and Labor. Later, under Teddy Roosevelt, Jim headed investigations of monopolistic practices and controls of such industries as meat, oil, and coal. His investigative skills led Roosevelt to appoint him as Secretary of the Interior, a position he held until the end of Roosevelt's 1909 term.

Teddy and James developed a mutual respect for each other that extended their friendship after Roosevelt's presidency ended. When Roosevelt decided to buck the Republican organization and develop his own political party, the Bull Moose party, Jim helped manage the vigorous campaign. The defeat of the Bull Moose party ended Roosevelt's political activism, and Jim's as well.

In later years, Jim contributed his organizational abilities to the Red Cross effort in World War I. He later lent his support to Herbert Hoover in his 1932 second-term run for the presidency against Franklin Delano Roosevelt, which, despite Jim's help, Hoover lost.

Dying in 1950, Jim's life spanned momentous changes in world history: from the end of the Civil War to the Korean War, from the railway to rocketry, and through Roosevelt to Roosevelt. Indeed, a life filled with qualities the nation would miss upon his death.

## MARY (MOLLY) GARFIELD STANLEY-BROWN

Fourth child, second daughter of James Abram Garfield and Lucretia Rudolph
*Born:* January 16, 1867    *Birthplace:* Washington, D.C.
*Died:* December 30, 1947    *Age at Death:* 80 years, 11 months
*Cause of Death:* Unknown    *Education:* Private schools
*Profession:* Housewife, mother
*Spouse:* Joseph Stanley-Brown    *Number of Children:* 3

Mary, the only Garfield daughter to survive beyond early childhood, was always called Molly. Born while her father was an Ohio congressman,

Molly went to private schools in her hometown of Washington, D.C. Educated far beyond women of her day, her scholastic abilities were a source of pride to her father.

Upon his election to the presidency, Garfield selected Joseph Stanley-Brown to serve as his private secretary (the name Stanley-Brown came when he added the hyphen between his middle and last names, in the style of British aristocracy). Molly immediately developed a crush on her father's secretary. Fate seemed to conspire against the young girl, twice. On his way to join Molly and her mother at the New Jersey seashore, where Mrs. Garfield was recovering from malaria, a bullet struck her father, ending his life. The same bullet appeared also to end her romantic dreams. When the Garfield administration ended, Molly and Joseph were separated, but the couple continued to correspond and develop their relationship.

In 1888 Joseph and Molly married and lived in New York where their three children were born. Molly was well suited to the role of homemaker to a man of prestige, which her husband became following graduation from Yale after their marriage. He became involved with geological studies, and eventually he added to his success, becoming involved in both banking and railroads.

Joseph died in 1941 and she in 1947, having lived together long enough to celebrate their golden wedding anniversary.

## IRVIN MCDOWELL GARFIELD

Fifth child, third son of James Abram Garfield and Lucretia Rudolph
*Born:* August 3, 1870      *Birthplace:* Hiram, Ohio
*Died:* July 18, 1951      *Age at Death:* 80 years, 11 months
*Cause of Death:* Unknown      *Education:* Williams College, Law School
*Profession:* Lawyer      *Spouse:* Susan Emmons      *Number of Children:* 3

The terror of the White House, Irvin McDowell Garfield well deserved his reputation. "In bad weather he would ride high-wheeled bicycles indoors and careen down the staircase and through the corridors, gouging chunks from the historic wainscotting and scattering the lines of office-seekers waiting for an office with his father."[106] But his White House experience was short-lived, for his father was assassinated when Irvin was only eleven years old.

Irvin graduated from Williams College and continued on to law school, as did his older brothers. But, unlike both Jim and Hal, who set up practice in Cleveland, Irvin went to Boston to begin his law practice. His clientele grew, and in time Irvin argued his cases before the Massachusetts Supreme Court, commanding astronomical fees for his services.

Surviving until the ripe old age of eighty, Irvin took part in charitable organizations as well as alumni activities of his old alma mater, Williams College, until only shortly before his death.

## ABRAM GARFIELD

Sixth child, fourth son of James Abram Garfield and Lucretia Rudolph
*Born:* November 21, 1872     *Birthplace:* Washington, D.C.
*Died:* October 16, 1958     *Age at Death:* 85 years, 11 months
*Cause of Death:* Long-term illness
*Education:* Tutors, Williams College, Massachusetts Institute of Techology     *Profession:* Architect
*Spouses:* Sarah Granger, Helen Grannis Mathews
*Number of Children:* Garfield/Granger: 2; Garfield/Mathews: None

Born in Washington, D.C., Abram was still a small boy when his father was assassinated, yet it was his father's strong beliefs concerning education that influenced the course of Abram's life. Garfield had come to the conclusion that the public schools were not adequate: "My faith in our public schools is steadily diminishing . . . the course of study is unnatural and the children miss a solid health growth."[107] In keeping with his father's beliefs, Abram was tutored by a young Englishman and eventually both Abram and his elder brothers received private tutoring from Dr. Hawkes, who was imported from the Montana Territory.

Whether private instruction proved better in the end, it certainly did not hinder the boy's academic advancement, for young Abram graduated from Williams College and took postgraduate studies at the Massachusetts Institute of Technology and graduated in 1896. Upon graduating, Abram set out to make a grand tour of Europe with the object of studying, at first hand, the great architectural achievements of Western civilization. With this tour, he capped his academic education in architecture and prepared himself to his own satisfaction for a career as an architect.

With the establishment of his own architectural firm in Cleveland, Ohio, Abram's professional career coincided with the great age of American architecture. Abram's architectural design credits include Hiram and Kenyon Colleges, Cleveland's Babies Hospital, offices, and many homes of Cleveland's elite. He was elected a fellow in the American Institute of Architecture, and he served two terms as the organization's director.

Having achieved national recognition, Abram was appointed by Teddy Roosevelt to the National Council of Fine Arts in 1909. Later, President Coolidge named him to serve on the National Fine Arts Commission in 1925.

Abram once observed that "achievement and success will bring about desirable personal publicity but personal publicity may hardly be depended upon to bring achievement and success."[108] At the age of seventy-five, Abram remarried a much younger woman and lived for another ten years.

## EDWARD GARFIELD

Seventh child, fifth son of James Abram Garfield and Lucretia Rudolph
*Born:* December 25, 1874     *Birthplace:* Hiram, Ohio
*Died:* October 25, 1876     *Age at Death:* 1 year, 10 months
*Cause of Death:* Whooping cough

The last of the Garfield children was destined to a short life. The family had been hoping for a girl. Instead, Edward, the third successive male, appeared to the initial disappointment of all, especially young Molly Garfield, who had anticipated a little sister's birth. Garfield, straining at wit observed, "We receive not when we ask amiss."[109]

It was during Garfield's campaigning in New Jersey that he was informed that his young son, "Neddie," as young Edward was called, was seriously ill. Garfield immediately rushed back to his Ohio home to be at his side, but Neddie was already unconscious from the ravages of whooping cough by the time his father returned home. For four days the parents prayed for the recovery of their son. His brothers knew that Neddie had died when they returned home from school to find white crepe on the door, symbolizing a death in the family.[110]

Garfield, deeply pained at the death of his young son, tried to teach his remaining children a philosophical view of death, never suspecting they would have need for such consolation when their father was assassinated a few years later.

Neddie was buried next to his sister, Trot, on Hiram Hill in Ohio.

## FOR FURTHER READING

Doenecke, Justus D. *Presidencies of James A. Garfield and Chester A. Arthur.* Lawrence: Regents Press of Kansas, 1981.

Leech, Margaret, and Harry Brown. *The Garfield Orbit.* New York: Harper & Row, 1978.

*New York Times*, December 13, 1942, 73:1; March 25, 1950, 13:3; July 20, 1951, 21:5; October 17, 1958, 30:1.

Peskin, Allan. *Garfield.* Kent, Ohio: Kent State University Press, 1978.

# 17 CHESTER ALAN ARTHUR'S CHILDREN

## WILLIAM LEWIS ARTHUR

First child of Chester Alan Arthur and Ellen Lewis Herndon
*Born:* December 10, 1860    *Birthplace:* New York City, New York
*Died:* July 7, 1863    *Age at Death:* 2 years, 7 months
*Cause of Death:* Convulsions

Born in late 1860 while his father was in the military, William Lewis Arthur was the first of three children to be born to Nell and Chester. The young couple and their child lived in "a plushly furnished family hotel, near Twenty-second and Broadway," in New York City.[111] It would have been strange if the young couple, she from a Southern family and he a regular soldier in the U.S. Army, soon to become the Union Army, had not felt the rising tensions from their different heritages—tensions that culminated in the nation's Civil War.

When the boy died at the age of two-and-one-half, the couple were "prostrated with grief."[112] Chester wrote to his brother, and the child's namesake, of the boy's death saying,

We have sad, sad news to tell you. We have lost our darling boy. He died yesterday morning at Englewood—where we were staying for a few weeks— from convulsions, brought on by some affection of the brain. It came upon us so unexpectedly and suddenly, Nell is broken-hearted. I fear much for her health. You know how her heart was wrapped up in her dear boy.[113]

His fears for his wife's health were justified, and though two other children were born to the couple, Arthur would enter the presidency as a widower with two young children.

The young parents, convinced they had pushed their firstborn too hard, and had demanded so much from him that his young brain was taxed, bore the blame for their first son's death. William's early death—though childhood deaths were not uncommon at all to the era—caused a great deal of pampering of the next child, also a boy, for fear that another young death might occur.

## CHESTER ALAN ARTHUR II

Second child, second son of Chester Alan Arthur and Ellen Lewis Herndon
*Born:* July 25, 1864    *Birthplace:* New York City, New York
*Died:* July 17, 1937    *Age at Death:* 73 years
*Cause of Death:* Heart attack
*Education:* Princeton University, Columbia University
*Profession:* Playboy
*Spouses:* Myra Townsend Fithian Andrews, Rowena Dashwood Graves
*Number of Children:* Arthur/Andrews: 1; Arthur/Graves: None

Born in New York City, just before the closing battles of the Civil War, Chester Alan Arthur II led a life that closely resembled that of European royalty. His father was on the staff of the governor of New York. His mother, who died shortly before her husband became president, was the daughter of a U.S. Navy officer, Captain William Lewis Herndon, who was the discoverer of the source of the Amazon River's headwaters and who came from a socially prominent background. Even as a young man, Chester Alan was accustomed to the life of a gentleman.

During his father's presidency, Alan, as the young man was called, was a student at Princeton. He disdained the simple life, reveling in luxuries available to him as the president's son. Thus, Alan often used both the president's yacht and his influence. The president, himself fond of titles and wealth, transmitted these characteristics to his children. In an era that often confused stilted formality with elegance, Alan conformed to the popular expectations of a rake, earning for himself the nickname, "Prince of Washington."

In accordance with his father's wishes, Alan pursued law studies at Columbia University in order that he might eventually take over his father's New York City law firm.

Attending his father during his father's final days, Alan earned himself an additional title of "presidential papers destroyer." Following his father's instructions, Alan filled three garbage cans with official papers and began to burn them. He began the complete destruction of all his father's papers, but before finishing his assigned job, he was stopped by the intercession of others.

After his father's death, Alan did not return to Columbia, but took a six-month break in Europe. In Europe, the six-foot, four-inch American rapidly became associated with the Prince of Wales set, the jet set of the time. Alan took to European high society as if he had been born to it. Not hesitating to trade on his father's name, because he was a deceased president's son, Alan enjoyed all the benefits normally reserved for European royalty. The attractions of life in the capitals of Europe proved irresistable, and Alan never returned to Columbia to complete studies that would have concluded in his career as his father had envisioned. In a sense, Alan's European trip, begun as an extended mourning period for his father, was not to end until his own death. Alan maintained residences throughout his life on both the Continent and in the United States.

Twice-married, the father of one child, Alan's career was the playboy life of polo, parties, and art. In later years, Alan made his home in Colorado, but even there, in the heart of America, he brought Europe with him. Alan established the game of polo in the city of Cheyenne, Wyoming!

Chester Alan Arthur II died in 1937 at the age of seventy-three, having thoroughly enjoyed a lifelong romp with wine, women, and song.

## ELLEN (NELL) HERNDON ARTHUR PINKERTON

Third child, only daughter of Chester Alan Arthur and Ellen Lewis Herndon
*Born:* November 21, 1871     *Birthplace:* New York City, New York
*Died:* September 6, 1915     *Age at Death:* 43 years, 10 months
*Cause of Death:* Surgical complications
*Education:* Unknown
*Profession:* Housewife     *Spouse:* Charles Pinkerton
*Number of Children:* Unknown

Not yet ten years old when her father unexpectedly became president of the United States, following Garfield's assassination, Ellen, called Nell, entered the White House under the care of her aunt, who served as White House hostess to the widowed president. Nell's life, prior to White House days, was one of a young girl growing up in a cozy, comfortable, upper-middle-class home during the depression-ridden 1870s. There was nothing of note in her pre–White House days, and her father insisted that his child's life remain private. Arthur, socially prominent, as well as extraordinarily hand-some, was protective of his children, stating, on one occasion at least, "Madame, I may be the President of the United States, but my private life is nobody's damned business."[114] Nell, because of this insistence on privacy, never became the object of massive press attention, and rarely was she even photographed.

Nell married Charles Pinkerton, and the couple, as best is known, lived their married life in upstate New York. Nell's death in 1915 was noted primarily for the highly unusual (for the day) medical treatment of using blood transfusions to save her life, although the developing technology failed and did not save her life.

When Nell Arthur Pinkerton died, she left a sizable estate of $175,000, most of which went to her husband. However, her will also included a bequest of $2,000 to her brother, Chester Alan Arthur II and his son. So ended the life of a most private presidential child.

### FOR FURTHER READING

Doenecke, Justus D. *Presidencies of James A. Garfield and Chester A. Arthur.* Lawrence: Regents Press of Kansas, 1981.

Kane, Joseph Nathan. *Facts about the Presidents.* 4th ed. New York: H. W. Wilson, 1981.

*New York Times,* July, 19, 1937, 16:2; September 29, 1937, 9:4.

Reeves, Thomas C. *Gentleman Boss: The Life of Chester Alan Arthur.* New York: Alfred A. Knopf, 1975.

# 18 GROVER CLEVELAND'S CHILDREN

## RUTH CLEVELAND

First child of Grover Cleveland and Frances Folsom
*Born:* October 3, 1891    *Birthplace:* New York City, New York
*Died:* January 7, 1904    *Age at Death:* 12 years, 3 months
*Cause of Death:* Diphtheria
*Education:* Miss Mary Fine's Private School

Ruth Cleveland, the darling of the nation, bounced through the White House during her father's second term as president. Grover Cleveland was reelected president after a break of four years. When a third child was born to the Clevelands in the White House, Ruth became eldest of Cleveland's three children to live in the White House.

Ruth's every move captured the attention of the nation. Her blonde babyness was reported regularly in the press, earning for her the nickname of "Baby Ruth." When Cleveland's second term ended in 1897, the family moved back to Princeton, New Jersey, where Ruth attended Miss Mary Fine's Private School, but the nation continued its fascination with the young girl—not unlike the experiences of the Kennedy children long after their father's assassination.

In the first days of January 1904, the "nation's sweetheart" developed "a mild attack of diphtheria." She was ill for only four days, and her illness was not diagnosed as serious. But "a sudden weakness of the heart, brought on by the diphtheria caused a rapid sinking spell."[115] Almost before her parents and the family doctor realized the critical nature of her illness, she was dead.

Mrs. Grover (Frances) Cleveland and (Baby) Ruth Cleveland (circa 1893). Photo courtesy of the Library of Congress.

Ruth's obituary, carried in the *New York Times*, contained a list of her toys, including a pony and a tan go-cart and a bicycle. Further descriptions told of "rollicking good times" in the White House, as well as the physical strength of her sister, who had fought a serious attack of diptheria the previous year.[116]

Ruth's burial was simple and immediate, "owing to the contagious nature of the disease."[117] Miss Mary Fine's Private School closed for the balance of the week in honor of a much-loved student. There are no photographs of Baby Ruth from the later years of her short life because the Clevelands feared that potential harm might come to their children through public recognition. However, Ruth, "Americas sweetheart," was not to be forgotten.

As the result of a 1921 Curtiss Candy Company employee contest, Ruth's nickname became immortalized throughout the world as the name of the Baby Ruth candy bar. The candy, originally named Candy Cake, was renamed Baby Ruth for promotional purposes in a sweet tribute to "America's sweetheart," Cleveland's eldest daughter, Baby Ruth Cleveland.[118]

In another coincidence of history, at the time the candy bar Baby Ruth was marketed, one of the nation's most famous sport's heroes was making his mark as the homerun king with the New York Yankees. Believing the name to be an illegal use of his nickname, Babe Ruth instituted suit for damages. He was quickly silenced when the source of the candy bar's name was found to be that of a president's daughter.

## ESTHER CLEVELAND BOSANQUET

Second child, second daughter of Grover Cleveland and Frances Folsom
*Born:* September 9, 1893    *Birthplace:* New York City, New York
*Died:* June 26, 1980    *Age at Death:* 86 years, 9 months
*Cause of Death:* Brief illness
*Education:* Unknown    *Profession:* Housewife, mother
*Spouse:* William Sydney Bence Bosanquet    *Number of Children:* 2

---

Esther, the second of Cleveland's daughters, was born shortly after her father entered the White House for his second term. Her father was a bachelor the first time he was elected to the presidency. In the four years intervening between his first term as president and his second term as president, Cleveland had married and sired a daughter and became the father of a second girl just after his second term began. The nation was delighted that Cleveland had fulfilled himself as a family man.

In 1918 Esther married England's Captain William Sydney Bence Bosanquet, the son of Sir Albert Bosanquet, whose family long represented prominence in British high society. Though they had met briefly in Switzerland, prior to the war years, their acquaintance was reestablished when Esther served in England before America's entry into World War I. Shortly after meeting again, they were married in Westminster Abbey.

Esther and Bosanquet produced two children. No record of social or political prominence concerning this branch of the Bosanquet family is known, other than that Esther's husband died in 1966, leaving a very sizable estate to the family.

Esther returned to the United States after his death and lived in Tamworth, New Hampshire.

## MARION CLEVELAND DELL AMEN

Third child, third daughter of Grover Cleveland and Frances Folsom
*Born:* July 7, 1895      *Birthplace:* Buzzards Bay, Massachusetts
*Died:* June 18, 1977      *Age at Death:* 81 years, 11 months
*Cause of Death:* Long-term illness
*Education:* Westover School, Columbia University Teacher's College
*Profession:* Housewife, mother, social leader
*Spouses:* William Stanley Dell, John Harlan Amen
*Number of Children:* Cleveland/Dell: 1; Cleveland/Amen: None

Eighty-one years old when she died in New York City, Marion Cleveland, youngest daughter of Grover Cleveland, was involved in so many activities in the city that she acquired an admirable reputation as one of that city's major social leaders and charity fund-raisers.

After graduating from Westover School in 1916, Marion spent two years at Columbia University Teacher's College. Her first marriage was to Stanley Dell, by whom she had one child, a daughter. In 1926 she married again, this time to a man who soon became one of New York's most colorful personalities, John Harlan Amen. Though not flamboyant, and described as a bit absentminded, Amen became the city's leading "crime buster" from

1928 to 1942, as special assistant to the U.S. attorney. It was Amen who began to apply antitrust laws to such diverse interests as corporations and gangsters. Marion's husband continued his public service when, after World War II, he served on the U.S. legal staff at the Nuremburg war crimes trials in Germany.

Marion died at eighty-one years, having outlived her second husband by almost an entire generation. Finally, after being known only as Amen's wife and as a president's daughter, Marion managed to gain some fame in her own name for her work and her support of many charities.

## RICHARD (DICK) FOLSOM CLEVELAND

Fourth child, first son of Grover Cleveland and Frances Folsom
*Born:* October 28, 1897     *Birthplace:* Princeton, New Jersey
*Died:* January 10, 1974     *Age at Death:* 76 years, 3 months
*Cause of Death:* Unknown, found dead in his apartment
*Education:* Phillips Exeter Academy, Princeton University, Harvard Law School     *Profession:* Lawyer
*Spouses:* Ellen Douglas Gailor, Jessie Maxwell Black
*Number of Children:* Cleveland/Gailor: 6; Cleveland/Black: None

Richard Folsom Cleveland, Grover Cleveland's first son, was born after his father left the White House, while Grover was a Princeton professor. The nation, which had been captivated by the little Cleveland girls during his term in office, expected the son would be named after his prestigious father. In the same expectation, the press announced that Grover Cleveland, Jr., had been born. Fooling everybody, Cleveland had always felt that the name "Grover" was a bother, and he refused to inflict the name on his newborn son. Despite Grover's best intentions the boy was often referred to in newspapers as Grover, Jr.

Dick, as he was called by friends and family, attended college preparatory school at Exeter before he studied at Princeton University. Following her husband's death, his mother married a Princeton professor, and he became Dick's stepfather.

At college, Dick played football and participated in track events and was an extremely popular student. But Dick also had a serious side which emerged when he took part in the movement against the exclusive club system at Princeton, a battle which soon brought fame to Woodrow Wilson, then president of Princeton.

In June 1917, with the United States at war with the central powers, Dick left college to enlist in the Marine Corps, where he rose through the ranks to first lieutenant. After the war, he returned to Princeton and graduated with a bachelor's degree in 1919 and earned a master's degree in 1921.

Tracking along the normal path of a well-to-do man provided the pattern for Dick when he took a vacation in Europe and met and married a socially acceptable bride, Ellen Gailor, a graduate of both Vassar and Columbia. Dick then studied law at Harvard, was admitted to the Maryland bar, and soon became associated with a large Baltimore law firm.

Dick was often mentioned as a possible mayoral candidate for Baltimore, or for a position as a U.S. attorney. He was even suggested for the vice presidency, simply on the basis of his name. He refused all such suggestions, preferring to work for the Democratic party, although periodically he accepted appointments to Maryland state offices. Though he supported Franklin Delano Roosevelt for the presidency in 1932, by 1936 Dick had changed his mind and vigorously opposed the reelection of Roosevelt and the continuation of the New Deal. Despite his opposition to Roosevelt, Dick and the party leaders were reconciled in time. He received various appointments to government commissions dealing with the problems of young people, especially juvenile delinquency and education.

Dick, who died in 1974, is remembered today as a successful man, a good father, and a leader in his Baltimore, Maryland, community.

## FRANCIS GROVER CLEVELAND

Fifth child, second son of Grover Cleveland and Frances Folsom
*Born:* July 18, 1903      *Birthplace:* Buzzards Bay, Massachusetts
*Died:* Unknown      *Age at Death:* Unknown
*Cause of Death:* Unknown
*Education:* Phillips Exeter Academy, Harvard University
*Profession:* Teacher, actor      *Spouse:* Alice Erdman
*Number of Children:* 1

Born in Buzzards Bay, Massachusetts, the last of five Cleveland children, his father was sixty years old and had already left the White House when he was born. Francis was only five years old when his father died. Francis grew up under the direction of his mother's second husband, Thomas J. Preston, Jr., a Princeton professor.

As a young man Francis attended Exeter Academy and then Harvard with the class of 1925, and though he did not graduate that year he did marry. Francis studied drama, and though he taught at a private school, drama was his real love. His passion eventually led him to the stage, where he became a self-described actor, even appearing in a New York stage show. At this juncture, entering what would seem the most public time of his life, Francis is lost to press coverage.

## OSCAR CLEVELAND

Supposed illegitimate son of Grover Cleveland and Maria Crofts Halpin
*Born:* September 1874     *Birthplace:* Buffalo, New York
*Note:* Little is definitively reportable about this alleged child of a president, but the story has been so well publicized and mentioned in books and other reports, that the authors determined it appropriate for inclusion in this report on Cleveland's children.

---

The legitimacy of Oscar Cleveland, his parentage, and the conditions of his birth became a major topic in the 1884 presidential election of Democrat Grover Cleveland. Grover Cleveland, a bachelor, was accused of fathering an illegitimate child.

The story began when Grover, a sheriff in New York State, met thirty-five-year-old widow Maria Crofts Halpin from New Jersey. He and his friends, the self-styled "rowdy reefers" (so-named in reference to their frequent fishing trips to the nearby Great Lakes), established a relationship with Maria, newly arrived in Buffalo. What the exact nature of the relationship was became a matter of discussion when Maria claimed that Grover was the father of her baby boy; she even gave the child the last name of Cleveland to indicate paternity. Maria demanded that Grover marry her and legitimize her son. Grover did consider marriage, but, according to his own later explanations, he was not sure the child was his, though he did not deny paternity and did periodically contribute to the support of both child and mother.

Within a year of the birth of her child, Maria became a heavy drinker and was committed to an asylum for a short time. Grover decided that, given the condition of Maria, the boy's future was questionable. What was needed was a normal family setting, and so Grover contributed $5 per week for the boy's care to an orphanage until such time as the boy was adopted. Sometime between 1875 and 1876 the boy was adopted by a prosperous Buffalo, New York, family who promised to educate the boy into a professional career.

When she was released from the asylum, Maria turned to Grover for money. She recognized that he had the potential for power and she felt he had a duty to compensate her. She requested that he set her up in business by loaning her $500. He did. Maria's business failed. Maria is alleged to have remarried and settled in upstate New York, only to reappear again after Grover Cleveland was elected to his first term as president.

During Cleveland's first campaign for the presidency, the relationship of Grover and Maria emerged as a major issue. Cleveland was held up to ridicule by his opponent, Republican Maine Senator James Blaine, as the father of an illegitimate child. To question Cleveland's morality, Blaine's supporters invented the ditty, "Ma, Ma, where's my pa? Gone to the White House . . . ha ha ha!"

Two years before the end of his first term, Cleveland was confronted by Maria, who demanded money and threatened otherwise to reveal more embarrassing facts to the public, thus ruining his future in public life. Cleveland ignored the threat.

Oscar Cleveland's place in history is at the center of one of the nation's most degrading presidential campaigns. But, in this instance, the mud-slinging did not work. Cleveland was elected despite the dirt hurled by opponents, and he would return to office after one term away—he was the only president to serve in two separated terms.

Though unsubstantiated, periodic stories have stated that the supposed illegitimate son of Grover Cleveland died while in his late twenties; unable to face the shame of his birth he turned to the security of the bottle.

## FOR FURTHER READING

DeGregorio, William A. *The Complete Book of U.S. Presidents*, 2d ed. New York: Dembner Books, 1989.

Leitch, Alexander. *Princeton Companion*. Princeton, N.J.: Princeton University Press, 1978.

Miller, Hope Ridings. *Scandals in the Highest Office*. New York: Random House, 1973.

*New York Times*, March 8, 1966, 30:2; June 18, 1977, 22:1.

Wallace, Irving. *Intimate Sex Lives of Famous People*. New York: Delacorte Press, 1981.

# 19 BENJAMIN HARRISON'S CHILDREN

## RUSSELL BENJAMIN HARRISON

First child of Benjamin Harrison and Caroline Lavinia Scott
*Born:* August 12, 1854    *Birthplace:* Oxford, Ohio
*Died:* December 13, 1936    *Age at Death:* 82 years, 4 months
*Cause of Death:* Unknown
*Education:* Military school, Lafayette College
*Profession:* Businessman, engineer, politician, lawyer
*Spouse:* Mary Angeline Saunders    *Number of Children:* 2

Russell Benjamin Harrison, born in Oxford, Ohio, the son of an army officer, was six years old when the Civil War began, and he observed later that "I was too young to know the causes which led to the war, and the great forces which were the factors in the intellectual struggle which preceded it, but I was in the Army [in later years] for a time, and I know what it all meant."[119] Russell's early schooling was at a military academy, and he completed his education at Lafayette College, in Easton, Pennsylvania, where he received an engineering degree at the age of twenty-three.

After graduation Russell traveled to his family's Indiana home, where he obtained a job as an engineer with the local gas and light company. After a brief time, Russell was appointed as assistant assayer of the U.S. Mint at New Orleans. He married the daughter of the influential Republican Senator Saunders, Mary (called Mamie), and the newlyweds moved to Helena, Montana. Russell was appointed to the position of assistant U.S. treasurer, a position he held for eight years. Becoming involved in the cattle business in

Mary (Mamie) Scott Harrison (circa 1882–1884). Photo courtesy of the Library of Congress.

his adopted state, Montana, Russell was appointed as secretary of that state's Board of Stock Commissioners, and he acquired a financial interest in a cattle journal, eventually becoming its executive officer. But Russell's association with the journal brought more problems than credit, when the publication was sued for libel over a number of articles. Criticism of his handling of the journal largely revolved around his inexpertise. Inexperience also characterized Russell's ventures into stock and feed, as well as his new publishing venture, the *Helena Daily Journal*. None of his ventures was a financial success.

In 1889 Russell's father was inaugurated as president of the United States. During periodic visits to his father at the White House, Russell established a lasting friendship with a developing political figure, Teddy Roosevelt. The friendship was based on their mutual love of the West. It was a relationship that would stand Russell in good stead in future years. In 1890 Russell moved permanently to Washington, D.C., to become his father's White House aide and then his secretary. Russell's wife, Mamie, took over direction of White House social affairs because the president's wife was seriously ill. There was talk that his new financial success, coinciding with his Washington appointment, was not entirely due to shrewd econonic management. Clearly, his business ventures prior to the move had not demonstrated a high level of business acumen. Nevertheless, in 1891, Russell became a major stockholder of a railroad, holding more than $500,000 worth of stock. The *New York Times* suggested that some fraud was involved in the president's son's finances, but the accusations were dropped when no evidence was brought forward to prove that he had received stock in return for presidential favors.

With new money, the Harrisons' lifestyle changed, and they sported a wardrobe that became the talk of the social set. "Where did the money come from?" questioned the press. Defenders said it was natural for Russell to acquire information that allowed him to make judicious investments. Russell added that he was not aware that certain men of property were investing in his name. Thus, he claimed, he received stocks without direct involvement in the financial affairs.

Russell's wife continued as the White House hostess during President Harrison's term; Harrison's wife died of her lingering illness before his term ended. During Harrison's unsuccessful election bid for a second term in office, the president, Russell, and his wife, as well as the president's wife's niece, set out on a campaign swing. On the trip a fondness between niece-in-law and Harrison blossomed. Eventually, Benjamin Harrison married the young woman, and father and son became estranged over both the speed and the circumstances of the marriage.

From presidential secretary Russell became president of a street car company in Terre Haute, Indiana, where he stayed until the onset of the

Spanish-American War in 1898. Commissioned as a major, Russell's most important command was in the suburbs of Havana, Cuba, supervising the evacuation of the Spanish troops after the war. Promoted to the rank of lieutenant colonel, Russell was made inspector general of the territory surrounding Santiago, Cuba. He was discharged in 1899 following a bout with yellow fever.

Russell, educated in engineering, drawn to journalism, and thrust into politics and business by his father's position, switched to the practice of law in Indiana after the end of his father's term. Among his clients was the Mexican government, and he became counsel for Mexico in Indiana. He maintained the position and relationship with Mexico for twenty years, while he carried on all of his other business interests, as well as during his membership in the Indiana state legislature. Serving in both the House and the Senate of the Indiana legislature, his service also included chairmanship of the judiciary committees.

Extending a helpful hand to fellow veterans of the Spanish-American War, Russell was responsible for the appropriation of $1,000 for the organization of Spanish-American War veterans to stage an encampment. He later discovered that one-third of the $1,000 had been used to purchase jeweled medals for past commanders of the veterans' group. Outraged, Russell charged the veterans' organization with misappropriation of funds. For their part, the officials responded by calling him to appear before them to uphold his charges. Russell was able to defend his outrage when he appeared, but, in reality, Russell lost the cause because he offended many of the state's leading citizens. For the rest of his life he would suffer the social ostracism America reserves for those who offend upstanding members of society.

Russell's death at age eighty-two was barely noticed, as it coincided with the hoopla attached to the resignation of the British king, who left the throne for the love of a divorced American woman.

## MARY SCOTT (MAMIE) HARRISON MCKEE

Second child, only daughter of Benjamin Harrison and Caroline Lavinia Scott
*Born:* April 3, 1858     *Birthplace:* Indianapolis, Indiana
*Died:* October 28, 1930     *Age at Death:* 72 years, 6 months
*Cause of Death:* Cancer     *Education:* Private school, college
*Profession:* Housewife, mother     *Spouse:* James Robert McKee
*Number of Children:* 2

The beauty of Mary Scott Harrison McKee, elder daughter of Benjamin Harrison, was said to rival that of other noted White House beauties: Dolley Madison, Lucy Hayes, and Frances Folsom Cleveland. Mary came to the White House as a widow with two children to take the place of her mother during her illness and subsequently after her mother died while her father was president. She became one of the nation's most celebrated hostesses.

It was Mary, called Mamie, who introduced the tradition of a White House Christmas tree. She wanted to introduce a homelike atmosphere into the mansion for her children's sake, and so she initiated the tradition which continues today.

Mamie began her life in Indianapolis. Her father, who was in his twenties when she was born, had to struggle to support not only his own children, but also his four younger brothers and sisters. Under the strain of tending to all his burdens, Benjamin Harrison suffered a brief mental and physical collapse. However, her father's illness did not hinder Mary's education, for she remained in private school, regardless of cost, and even took private dancing lessons at home.

Entering college just as her father was coming into national prominence in the Republican party, Mamie's first introduction to the White House was as a guest of President Hayes, who invited the Harrison family to visit as an expression of gratitude for Benjamin's support for his presidency. In 1881 Harrison became a Republican senator from Indiana, from which position he moved to the White House. When the family moved to Washington, D.C., Mamie was her mother's constant companion during the illness from which she never recovered.

While in Washington, D.C., during her father's term as senator, Mamie maintained contact with her "boyfriend," James McKee, in Indiana. They married in 1884. Her father was elated when she gave birth to a boy named Ben in honor of his grandfather.

By the time her father was elected to the presidency in 1888, Mamie was a widow. She moved to the White House with her two children to act as White House hostess. Victorian elegance and pretension were well-mated to the explosive industrialization of this era in America. Mamie, her children, and the White House sparkled even in this most glittering, gaudy, and arrogant high society.

In his second campaign for the presidency, the widowed Harrison took his daughter with him on his campaign tour. The Harrison group included her brother, and various other campaign associates, as well as Harrison's ward and Mamie's cousin, recently widowed Mary Scott Lord Dimmick, the woman who would take the place of Mamie's mother—much to Mamie's chagrin.

Mamie's disapproval of her father's second marriage in 1894 never ended. Years later her relationship with both stepmother and stepsister were, at best, cursory. Mamie's stepmother outlived her by eighteen years.

## ELIZABETH HARRISON WALKER

Third child of Benjamin Harrison, only child of Benjamin Harrison and Mary Scott Lord Dimmick
*Born:* February 21, 1897     *Birthplace:* Indianapolis, Indiana
*Died:* December 26, 1955     *Age at Death:* 58 years, 10 months
*Cause of Death:* Short-term illness
*Education:* Westover School, New York University Law School
*Profession:* Lawyer, writer, businesswoman, television and radio personality
*Spouse:* James Blaine Walker     *Number of Children:* Unknown

Born in Indianapolis following her father's second marriage to his young niece, Elizabeth was the couple's only child. However, she knew little about her father since he died before she was five years old. Her mother, Mary Scott Lord Dimmick, her husband's former ward, was still a young woman, and when her husband died she took Elizabeth on travels throughout Europe until she remarried.

Elizabeth acquired an education that was exceptional even for males of the day. Graduating from Westover School, she earned a bachelor's degree in both science and law, as well as a law degree from New York University Law School; eventually she became a member of state bars in both New York and Indiana, all by 1919. In 1921 Elizabeth married the grandnephew of her father's secretary of state, James Blaine Walker. The couple became prominent members of high society.

Elizabeth, a forerunner of today's liberated women, founded a monthly news service for women, "Cues on the News," which gave economic advice and investment tips to women. Elizabeth's reputation grew and brought her an appointment to a national, all-male commission for economic development. Toward the end of her life Elizabeth was seen and heard frequently on television and radio, dispensing advice and commentary on economic issues, particularly those that affected women.

Only fifty-eight years old when she died in 1955, this president's daughter may well be ranked with such women as Eleanor Roosevelt, Helen Taft

Manning, and Margaret Chase Smith, whose accumulated efforts formed a practical foundation for the modern American women's feminist movement.

## FOR FURTHER READING

Beard, Charles. *Presidents in American History*. New York: Julian A. Messner, 1981.

Kane, Joseph Nathan. *Facts about the Presidents*. 4th ed. New York. H. W. Wilson, 1981.

*New York Times*, October 23, 1930, 16:3; October 28, 1930, 25:4; December 26, 1955, 19:3; April 7, 1967, 37:4.

Van Steenwyk, Elizabeth. *Presidents at Home*. New York: Julian A. Messner, 1980.

# 20 WILLIAM MCKINLEY'S CHILDREN

## KATHERINE AND IDA MCKINLEY

Only two children of William McKinley and Ida Saxton
*Born:* Katherine: December 25, 1871; Ida: April 1, 1873
*Birthplace:* Canton, Ohio
*Died:* Katherine: June 25, 1875; Ida: August 22, 1873
*Ages at Death:* Katherine: 3 years, 6 months; Ida: 5 months
*Cause of Death:* Katherine: Typhoid fever; Ida: Unhealthy at birth

The lives of the only two children of President William McKinley and his wife are so closely entwined that to speak of one is also to speak of the other.

The elder of the two daughters, Katherine, was born on Christmas Day when her father was a Canton, Ohio, lawyer. "Katie," as she was called, soon became the apple of her daddy's eye. In return Katie worshipped her father. But it was her mother, Ida, who smothered her with love until the birth of a second McKinley daughter.

The second McKinley girl, named Ida after her mother, was born in the spring of 1873 following a difficult delivery. The difficulty of the birth left a physical imprint on the mother who suffered for the rest of her life with phlebitis and a nervous illness, as well as epilepsy. Little Ida died after only five months. Her mother was so disturbed by the death that she was never again the same.

After the infant Ida's death, the mother lavished on Katherine an all-consuming love reflected in her protectiveness and jealousy. Spending days in bed, in a state of depression, Ida wondered why God had placed such punishment upon her. She demanded that both her husband and her daughter constantly shower her with displays of love and affection. Such was the extent of the mother's psychological needs that her husband and daughter had to guard against displays of mutual affection, so the mother would not become jealous. Above all, Ida feared the loss of her firstborn. As in a melodrama of the period, the fear that haunted Ida came true. At three and one half, Katie died of typhoid fever.

Ida McKinley was shattered mentally and physically. Invalided for the rest of her life, she came to devote her entire being to her husband. McKinley lavished upon her the devotion, concern, and solicitude that might otherwise have been shared by his children. McKinley's displays of affection for his wife, which so much endeared him to the American public, in large measure resulted from the death of Ida McKinley, the daughter who died so young.

Thus, it was the deaths of the McKinleys' only two children that brought the husband and wife closer together. And, it was the public's perception of the loving couple that was the source of so much of the approval of this American president.

But the happy ending so often resolving the problems in a melodrama was not to be. Ida's husband William McKinley was assassinated. His chronically ill wife survived her husband by almost six years. Despite the heights to which William McKinley had risen, underlying all was the tragedy of childhood illnesses and deaths.

## FOR FURTHER READING

Gould, Lewis L. *Presidency of William McKinley*. Lawrence: Regents Press of Kansas, 1980.

Morgan, H. Wayne. *McKinley and His America*. Syracuse, N.Y.: Syracuse University Press, 1963.

Moses, John B., and Wilbur Cross. *Presidential Courage*. New York: W. W. Norton, 1980.

Whitney, David C. *The American Presidents*. 4th ed. Garden City, New York: Doubleday, 1978.

# 21 THEODORE ROOSEVELT'S CHILDREN

## ALICE LEE ROOSEVELT LONGWORTH

Only child of Theodore Roosevelt and Alice Lee Hathaway
*Born:* February 12, 1884    *Birthplace:* New York City, New York
*Died:* February 20, 1980    *Age at Death:* 96 years
*Cause of Death:* Pneumonia    *Education:* Private tutors
*Profession:* Housewife, mother    *Spouse:* Nicholas Longworth
*Number of Children:* 1

The woman who became the "grande dame" of Washington, D.C., society was born in New York City to Teddy Roosevelt and his first wife, Alice Hathaway. Because her mother died soon after Alice's birth, Alice was brought up by her father's second wife, Edith. Alice was seventeen years old when her father became president of the United States following the assassination of President McKinley in 1901.

Alice, a female version of the "man about town," was far in advance of her time. Independent, enthusiastic, and always in search of the new, Alice established herself in the public eye with such acts as her regular appearance in an open touring car, watching practice takeoffs of the new "aeroplane" and dispensing alcoholic drinks to companions and to whomever struck her fancy.

Unwilling to play second fiddle to her father, Alice, who married the thirty-six-year-old Ohio congressman, Nicholas Longworth, refused to have a traditional White House wedding. Dressed in her blue wedding gown, dramatically cutting the wedding cake with a sweep of a sword, Alice

(Left to right) Archie, Teddy Roosevelt, and Quentin (circa 1904). Photo courtesy of the Library of Congress.

would not allow her father to upstage her at her own wedding, proclaiming, "My father always wants to be the corpse at every funeral, the bride at every wedding, and the baby at every christening."[120]

As the wife of a congressman who became a powerful speaker of the House of Representatives, Alice became a leader of Washington, D.C., society. Even after her husband's 1936 death, she continued her residence in Washington. Alice also continued to capture the imagination of the public and press. She was more than a mere party giver, she was an acknowledged wit—a wit that became ever more sharp as her penetrating barbs were long remembered and often were so accurate as to remain stuck to her target. Thus, Alice, who met every president between the late 1880s president, Benjamin Harrison, and the 1980 president-elect, Ronald Reagan, colorfully described Harding, Coolidge, and the 1940s presidential candidate, Thomas Dewey. Fielding questions from the press on her eightieth birthday, Alice took full credit for calling them as she saw them. "I'm just a kindly amiable old thing. . . . If anyone takes that seriously, hah. . . . My specialty is detached malevolence."[121] One of her more famous remarks was, "If you haven't got anything nice to say about anybody, come, sit next to me."[122] Shortly before her health began to fade, well into advanced age, Alice said during an interview, "I don't think I'm insensitive or cruel. I laugh. I have a sense of humor. I like to tease. I must admit a sense of mischief does get hold of me from time to time. I'm a hedonist. I have an appetite for being entertained. Isn't it strange how that upsets people?"[123]

A widow of more than forty years, whose only daughter died at the age of thirty-one, Alice was survived by her granddaughter, who was her close and constant companion in later years. The ninety-six-year-old Alice was a charmer to the end. Her barbs mostly hurt those whose skin was too thin and those whose wit was too dull.

## THEODORE ROOSEVELT, JR.

Second child of Theodore Roosevelt; first child of Theodore Roosevelt and Edith Carow
*Born:* September 13, 1887      *Birthplace:* Oyster Bay, New York
*Died:* July 12, 1944      *Age at Death:* 56 years, 10 months
*Cause of Death:* Heart attack
*Education:* Groton Preparatory School, Harvard University
*Profession:* Businessman, politician, soldier, author
*Spouse:* Eleanor Butler Alexander      *Number of Children:* Unknown

As a father, Teddy Roosevelt was as equally demanding of his sons as he was of himself. Thus, it was that after sending his eldest son to Groton, the traditional Roosevelt preparatory school, and to Harvard University, Teddy sent Teddy, Jr., to learn business from the ground up. Like any other workman carrying his dinner pail, Teddy, Jr., worked in a carpet mill for a year until he was promoted to sales work.

What could be more natural for the sons of "Rough Rider" Teddy Roosevelt, hero of the Spanish-American War, than that they should be leaders of America's forces in World War I ? Thus, Teddy, Sr., who saw that America must be drawn into the European conflict, inspired all of his sons to enroll in military training for officers. The father's plans for his sons were realized when, following the predicted entry of America into the European conflict, Teddy, Jr., was promoted to lieutenant colonel and served in France at the battle of the Argonne Forest. Gassed in 1918, Ted was awarded the Distinguished Service Medal and the Distinguished Service Cross and was decorated by several allied nations for gallantry.

Returning to the United States after the war, Ted ran for the New York Assembly in 1919. In response to the contention that he was running on his father's name, Ted replied, "My hat's in the ring too . . . and it isn't my father's."[124] From this beginning in politics, Ted's next step was an appointment by President Harding as assistant secretary of the navy, a position that was to involve young Ted in scandalous politics. The Teapot Dome scandal of the Harding administration concerned bribery and illegal payoffs. Oil lands, set apart as the navy's strategic reserve in case of war, were leased to high-level government officials and particularly to a petroleum magnate. Ted, himself, was never accused of any direct wrongdoing. But the question arose as to how the assistant secretary of the navy did not detect the oil lease conspiracy in his department. Undaunted by his proximity to the scandal, Ted decided to run for the position of Governor of New York against Democrat Al Smith. Naturally, Smith did not hesitate to recall to his audiences Ted's association with the Teapot Dome scandals, and Ted was soundly defeated in the election.

His father's son, the defeated Ted took his wife and went off to India and the Far East, later recounting his adventures in a book. There was a new president, Calvin Coolidge, when Ted returned to the United States. What could be more logical than Ted's being appointed governor of Puerto Rico by Coolidge? Senate confirmation was rapid. From Puerto Rico, Ted's next appointment, by yet another Republican president, Herbert Hoover, was as governor general of the Philippine Islands. Upon the election of his Democratic cousin, Franklin Roosevelt, presidential appointments ceased, forcing Ted back into the comparative calm of the business world. Teddy heartily disliked his cousin, Franklin, and swore to keep the Republican Roosevelts separate from the liberal Roosevelts.

It was World War II that again drew Ted from obscurity into the vortex of military action. With the rank of brigadier general, Teddy was placed in command of the Twenty-Sixth Infantry—his old unit from World War I. He served first in Africa and then in Italy, but it was in the landing at Normandy, while the world waited, that Teddy entered the spotlight as commander of a division landing on the French coast.

Teddy, Jr., died during World War II. The public assumption, in line with the Roosevelt aura of "dying with their boots on," was that he died in combat. In reality, Teddy, exhausted from the rigors of the Normandy battle, turned to London for well-earned rest. In July 1944, he died in his sleep. Posthumously, Teddy was awarded the Congressional Medal of Honor.

## KERMIT ROOSEVELT

Third child of Theodore Roosevelt; second child, second son of
Theodore Roosevelt and Edith Carow
*Born:* October 10, 1889      *Birthplace:* Oyster Bay, New York
*Died:* June 4, 1943      *Age at Death:* 53 years, 8 months
*Cause of Death:* Amoebic dysentery
*Education:* Groton Preparatory School, Harvard University
*Profession:* Businessman, executive, soldier
*Spouse:* Belle Wyatt Willand      *Number of Children:* 4

---

Beginning his life at Oyster Bay on New York's Long Island, Kermit attended Groton Preparatory School and earned his bachelor's degree while his father was running for the presidency under the 1912 Bull Moose party banner.

Shortly after Kermit's father left his almost two terms in office, Kermit traveled with his father on big-game hunts in Africa for almost a year. On later trips, Teddy introduced Kermit to South America, and the two explored the area extensively, including forages into uncharted river country. Like his father, Kermit enjoyed the strenuous life, but very much unlike his father and his brothers, Kermit had little interest in politics. It was due to these travels that upon Kermit's completion of his schooling, he chose to go to South America to work in both engineering and banking.

Well before the United States became involved in World War I, Kermit advocated America's involvement. But Kermit could not wait for the United States to enter the war, and when the British forces in Mesopotamia and Palestine offered Kermit a captain's rank, he jumped at the opportunity. For his service he was awarded the British Military Cross. When the United States entered the war, Kermit transferred to the U.S. field artillery, beginning a long experience with machine guns. Of all of the Roosevelt sons, Kermit was the only one to escape injury in World War I.

After the war, Kermit became an executive for a steamship line, and, in time, he formed his own Roosevelt Steamship Line, which eventually merged with the International Mercantile Marine Company. He became the firm's vice president and served as such until his 1938 resignation.

Aware that war was imminent on the Continent between Great Britain and Germany, Kermit went to Great Britain in September 1939 and joined the British army as a major, specializing in machine gun operations. Kermit was involved in the Norwegian campaign in 1940. He was then assigned to Egypt. Not bullets, but disease felled this old soldier and ended his service with the British army. In Egypt, he contracted amoebic dysentery and was sent back to England. Forced to resign from the British army, he returned to the United States to recover from his illness. After undergoing treatment for almost two years, Kermit was pronounced cured, and he immediately joined the American army, receiving the rank of major. Assigned to intelligence, he was transferred to Alaska where he died from what the Army described as "natural causes."

Of the five Republican Roosevelt children, Kermit was the only one to establish cordial relations with his cousin, Democratic President Franklin Roosevelt, even spending time on fishing expeditions with the president. Kermit, like his father, was not a man of mean and narrow temperament.

## ETHEL CAROW ROOSEVELT DERBY

Fourth child of Theodore Roosevelt; third child, only daughter of Theodore Roosevelt and Edith Carow
*Born:* August 13, 1891     *Birthplace:* Oyster Bay, New York
*Died:* December 10, 1977     *Age at Death:* 86 years, 4 months
*Cause of Death:* Unknown     *Education:* Private tutors
*Profession:* Housewife, mother     *Spouse:* Richard Derby
*Number of Children:* 4

Ethel Carow, the only daughter born to Teddy and his second wife, grew up in the Roosevelt compound at Oyster Bay, New York. When Ethel was ten years old, her father became president upon the assassination of President McKinley. Described as a character, though tame in comparison to her half-sister, Alice, Ethel was constantly in competition with her two older and two younger brothers. The liveliness of these children appealed to the American public and they took the Roosevelt children to heart with enthusiasm.

By the time she had become a teenager, Ethel was described as a perfect little lady, even a Sunday school teacher. In 1913 Ethel married a physician, ten years her senior. While her father's repeated offers to lead combat troops against the Germans in World War I were refused, Ethel and her husband took part in the war as working members of the Ambulance Hospital in Paris. Ethel and her husband had four children, several of whom became involved in politics in later years. Ethel, ever the party stalwart, reappeared on the national political stage when, in 1960, she made the Republican party's seconding speech for Richard Milhous Nixon's nomination as that year's Republican presidential candidate.

## ARCHIBALD (ARCHIE) BULLOCH ROOSEVELT

Fifth child of Theodore Roosevelt; fourth child, third son of Theodore Roosevelt and Edith Carow

*Born:* April 9, 1894      *Birthplace:* Washington, D.C.
*Died:* July 29, 1981      *Age at Death:* 87 years, 3 months
*Cause of Death:* Stroke
*Education:* Groton Preparatory School, Harvard University
*Profession:* Banker, soldier
*Spouse:* Grace Stackpole Lockwood
*Number of Children:* 4

Archie, the fourth of Teddy Roosevelt's children with Edith Carow, fought in both world wars, and was an avid American as well as a Republican party supporter throughout his long life.

Graduating from Harvard in 1914, he attended an officer training school with his brothers just prior to America's entry into World War I. Rising to the rank of captain in the army, Archie was awarded the Croix de Guerre by the French and was severely wounded when saving the lives of three of his men under enemy fire. His father, Teddy, was not immediately told of the full extent of Archie's wounds, which were a knee and arm shattered by bullets. His father, with an enthusiasm not dampened by comprehension of the extent of his son's wounds, expressed undiminished enthusiasm for Archie's valor and for the righteousness of the war.

Undaunted by wounds that plagued him long after the war's end, and well into his forties, Archie convinced the army to take him on active service during World War II. Serving as a lieutenant colonel and battalion commander in New Guinea, Archie was again wounded and again distinguished himself, earning the Silver Star with Oak Leaf Cluster.

Archie's business career began after World War I, when he established a bond company, and ended with his move to Florida where he was a bank chairman of the board. Following his father's example in peace as well as in war, Archie was an avid conservationist and became a member of the Boone and Crockett Club, which his father had founded.

Later years saw Archie extremely concerned with the Communist threat to America. In testimony before the House Un-American Activities Committee, he described the extensive infiltration (as he understood it) of the Communists into all levels of American life. At eighty-seven, the last surviving son of Teddy Roosevelt, Archie died in his Florida home from complications of a stroke.

## QUENTIN ROOSEVELT

Sixth child of Theodore Roosevelt; fifth child, fourth son of Theodore Roosevelt and Edith Carow
*Born:* November 19, 1897      *Birthplace:* Washington, D.C.
*Died:* July 14, 1918      *Age at Death:* 20 years, 5 months
*Cause of Death:* War casualty
*Education:* Groton Preparatory School      *Profession:* Pilot
*Spouse:* None      *Number of Children:* None

Quentin Roosevelt was four years old when his father succeeded President William McKinley into the presidency after McKinley's assassination. Quentin and his brother, Archie, earned a well-deserved reputation for their frequent White House pranks. On one occasion he and Archie managed to transport a massive snowball onto the White House balcony, whereupon they ceremoniously dumped it onto their father as he exited below with a guest. Typically, Teddy found the entire episode uproariously funny.

Quentin attended public schools in Washington, D.C., and in Alexandria, Virginia, while his father was president. In 1917, when the United States entered World War I, Quentin enlisted in the army. Fascinated by the new weapon, aeroplanes, Quentin managed to become a supervisor of a field used to train flyers for combat. Taking lessons while managing the field, Quentin qualified as an aviator and went to France to fight the Germans.

In July 1918, Quentin was shot down. General Pershing, commander of the American Expeditionary Force in France, informed the former president that his youngest son had been killed in action. Teddy's war, the Spanish-American War, described by an American secretary of state as "the splendid little war," had brought glory, renown, and even the presidency. His son's war was the greatest horror the human race had thus far inflicted on itself, and Quentin became one of the more than 8.5 million men to be sacrificed on its battlefields.

## FOR FURTHER READING

Blum, John Morton. *Progressive Presidents*. New York: W. W. Norton, 1980.

Burnham, Sophy. *The Landed Gentry: Passions and Personalities Inside America's Propertied Class*. New York: G. P. Putnam's Sons, 1978.

Churchill, Allen. *The Roosevelts: American Aristocrats*. New York: Harper & Row, 1965.

Conrad, P. Roosevelt. *Great American Families*. New York: W. W. Norton, 1977.

Egloff, Franklin R. *Theodore Roosevelt: An American Portrait*. New York: Vantage Press, 1980.

Hess, Stephen. *America's Political Dynasties*. New York: Doubleday, 1966.

Miller, Nathan. *Roosevelt Chronicles*. New York: Doubleday, 1966.

Morris, Edmund. *Rise of Theodore Roosevelt*. New York: McCann, 1979.

*New York Times*, February 21, 1980, 1:4.

Wilson, Dorothy Clarke. *Alice and Edith: The Two Wives of Teddy Roosevelt: A Biographical Novel*. New York: Doubleday, 1989.

Helen Taft (circa 1908). Photo courtesy of the Library of Congress.

# 22  WILLIAM HOWARD TAFT'S CHILDREN

## ROBERT ALPHONSO TAFT

First child of William Howard Taft and Helen Herron
*Born:* September 8, 1889     *Birthplace:* Cincinnati, Ohio
*Died:* July 31, 1953     *Age at Death:* 63 years, 10 months
*Cause of Death:* Cancer
*Education:* Harvard University, Yale University
*Profession:* Lawyer, politician
*Spouse:* Martha Wheaton Bowers     *Number of Children:* 4

It was Robert's sister, Helen, who observed that Robert had wanted to be president of the United States beginning with his attendance at his father's inauguration in 1909. This son of William Howard Taft made three unsuccessful bids for the Republican presidential nomination.

Robert, the eldest of the Taft children, was educated at both Yale and Harvard, and he graduated with the class's highest honors in 1913. He became a lawyer, but the practice of law did not satisfy this Taft. He had his sights set on the presidency. Beginning his political career in 1920, Robert was elected to the Ohio House of Representatives, where he served three terms, the last term as speaker. From the Ohio House, Taft's political career advanced to the U.S. Senate. Robert Taft had foresight when he married Martha Bowers, a woman who possessed the social skills to complement Robert's political acumen. The political team of "Bob and Martha" was successful in electing Bob to the Senate first in 1938, and in each campaign thereafter until his death.

During his service in the Roosevelt Democratic Congress, Taft earned the identity of "Mr. Republican" because of his strong and vociferous opposition to the social programs of the New Deal. While the titular head of the Republican party, in 1947, he sponsored the Taft-Hartley bill placing restrictions on organized labor. Despite this probusiness approach, he was considered by some a middle-of-the-roader because he also supported education and low-cost housing. Mr. Republican is also credited as one of the formative forces in the political education of the future Democratic president, Lyndon Baines Johnson.

Only two years after his election to the Senate, Bob Taft competed for the Republican nomination for the presidency. Out of that 1940 convention came not the name of Robert Taft, but that of Wendell Wilkie, a man who seemed even less likely than Taft to secure the bid. Taft's second bid for the presidential nomination came in 1948. Again, despite Taft's Senate experience and the name he had made for himself, he failed to capture the enthusiasm of the convention. The nomination went instead to New York's governor, Thomas E. Dewey. Taft's third and final attempt to fulfill his youthful dream of becoming president came in 1952. Unfortunately for Taft, his competition was the war hero, Dwight Eisenhower. In contrast to Eisenhower's warmth and fatherly bearing, Taft appeared cold and more of a political machine than did the flesh-and-blood leader of men, who went on to win the nomination and the presidency.

Taft died of cancer in 1953, only months after he had been elected as Senate majority leader and shortly after his wife, Martha, suffered a stroke. He died at the very time when a Republican Congress was elected along with a Republican president, and when he was the leader of the Republican Congress. Taft's untimely death was mourned by millions of Americans, both Republican and Democrat. Many believe that his loss to the Republican party was a severe setback to cooperation between Congress and the president.

## HELEN HERRON TAFT MANNING

Second child, only daughter of William Howard Taft and Helen Herron
*Born:* August 1, 1891    *Birthplace:* Cincinnati, Ohio
*Died:* February 1987    *Age at Death:* 95 years
*Cause of Death:* Pneumonia
*Education:* Bryn Mawr College, Yale University
*Profession:* Professor, dean, college president
*Spouse:* Frederick Johnson Manning    *Number of Children:* 2

Regarded as frank and highly intelligent by all who knew her, and considered more liberal than her parents, Helen Herron Taft pursued a career uncommon to women of her day. Beginning her education in the Philippines, where her father was governor general, she continued her education at the exclusive girl's school, Bryn Mawr, when the family returned from the Philippines. As an outspoken leader of the junior class, Helen set a pattern she would follow throughout her life, that of strongly but quietly speaking her mind to anyone who would listen.

In 1917, at the age of twenty-five, Helen was made acting dean of Bryn Mawr. In 1928 she was made acting president, and shortly thereafter she became that school's president. Considered a strong administrator as well as an excellent history professor, Helen had earned a Ph.D. for her study, "British Colonial Government after the American Revolution:1782–1820."

Helen married Frederick J. Manning, a Yale professor of history. Two daughters were born to the Mannings, both of whom also married professors.

During her father's term as president (1909–1913), Helen left Bryn Mawr to act as her father's White House hostess when her mother was temporarily ill. As the daughter of a president, Helen stands in marked contrast to her contemporary, Alice Lee Roosevelt, the daughter of Teddy. While Alice was flamboyant and conservative, Helen was quietly liberal. The press tried to play upon her popularity and, perhaps, even establish a rivalry with her contemporary, Alice Lee Roosevelt, often known as "Alice Blue" because she wore a blue wedding dress when she married Nicholas Longworth. The press endowed Helen with the title "Helen Pink." Not surprisingly, the nation preferred "Alice Blue" Roosevelt to the academic "Helen Pink."

At the age of ninety-five, this president's daughter died in a Philadelphia nursing home. She left behind a legacy of contributions to feminists of the twentieth century, to many of whom she had taught history and influenced while serving as president of the prestigious Bryn Mawr College. Her two daughters continued their mother's, and father's, contributions as teachers in institutions of higher learning.

Of the two presidents' daughters, both born in the last of the Victorian age, it was, in fact, Helen Taft Manning who attained a position of responsibility and personal excellence uncommon to her generation's women. She was part of the transition generation of women who were born into an exclusive, male-dominated world. But, Helen lived to earn prominence— and perhaps contributed to the development of a United States that during her adulthood made "full citizens" of its women.

## CHARLES PHELPS TAFT

Third child, second son of William Howard Taft and Helen Herron
*Born:* September 20, 1897    *Birthplace:* Cincinnati, Ohio
*Died:* June 24, 1983    *Age at Death:* 85 years, 9 months
*Cause of Death:* Long-term illness
*Education:* Yale University, University of Toledo
*Profession:* Lawyer, politician, author    *Spouse:* Eleanor Chase
*Number of Children:* 7

Charles Phelps Taft, the baby of the Taft family and eight years younger than his brother Robert, was a rambunctious, bright, mischievous child. The family favorite, Charlie, named after a wealthy uncle, was totally unlike his older brother as a child and as an adult, although comparisons were often made.

When Charlie was only two years old, his father became the governor of the Philippine Islands. The family moved to Manila, where the children received their early education. Charlie, as a youngster, was more interested in play than study. He was forever "cursed" with enthusiasm for his wide variety of interests, and his detractors would say that excessive enthusiasm was his major flaw.

Charlie, like his brother Robert, was educated at Yale and in the law. His education, unlike his brother's, was, however, interrupted when he decided to leave Yale and join the army as a private in the field artillery. While men of his social and economic standings obtained commissions, this son of a former president, characteristically, sought only to serve his country. Serving on active duty in France during World War I, Charlie was promoted from private to sergeant major.

After the war, Charlie completed his education and entered partnership with his brother. It did not work out. Indeed, a rift between the brothers was so deep that in 1927 Charlie refused to support Bob on the Ohio Republican slate. Bob Taft, never a man to forget injury or insult, returned the deed in kind when Charlie ran for governor of Ohio in 1952 by refusing to support Charlie in his bid for the governorship. In 1955 Charlie was elected mayor of Cincinnati, Ohio. During his lifetime, Charlie authored three books presenting his views of Cincinnati and government.

Throughout his life, Charles Phelps Taft involved himself in the public life of Cincinnati and the nation because of his passion for people. He earned for himself the reputation of a charming human being fully devoted to public service.

## FOR FURTHER READING

Anderson, Judith Icke. *William Howard Taft: An Intimate History*. New York: W. W. Norton, 1981.

Patterson, James T. *Mr. Republican: A Biography of Robert A. Taft*. Boston, Mass.: Houghton Mifflin, 1972.

Pringle, Henry F. *The Life and Times of William Howard Taft*. Vol. 2. Hamden, Conn.: Archon Books, 1939.

*New York Times*, February 23, 1987, I, 17:1.

# 23 WOODROW WILSON'S CHILDREN

## MARGARET WOODROW WILSON

First of three daughters of Woodrow Wilson and Ellen Louise Axson
*Born:* April 30, 1886     *Birthplace:* Gainesville, Georgia
*Died:* February 12, 1944     *Age at Death:* 57 years, 10 months
*Cause of Death:* Uremic poisoning
*Education:* Goucher College, Peabody Conservatory of Music, private music tutors
*Profession:* Pianist, singer, saleswoman, advertising writer
*Spouse:* None     *Number of Children:* None

Margaret Woodrow Wilson, the first of three daughters of Woodrow Wilson's first wife, wandered through life, dreaming of a success that appeared constantly just out of reach.

When her father entered the White House and became president in 1913, Margaret was twenty-six and had completed her formal education. Though her two younger sisters married during Wilson's first term, Margaret's interests did not lean toward marriage. Margaret wanted a career in music.

Though Margaret took lessons for piano and voice for many years, the results of her study were not all that she wished. Although she sang once with the Chicago Symphony Orchestra during her father's term as president, the critics were not impressed. Her performances were damned with faint praise. Said one critic, "[H]er voice had a sympathetic quality, which is its most commendable attribute."[125] Another critic observed that Margaret sang with "intelligence and feeling and without affectation."[126] Undaunted, she traveled to France to entertain World War I Allied soldiers through song.

After the White House, Margaret worked as an advertising writer for two years. Her father died in 1924, leaving his considerable estate to his wife, Edith. Margaret was to receive $2,500 per year, providing "she did not marry."[127] Trained as a musician, with only $2,500 a year for financial security if she remained unmarried, Margaret had to make her own way in the world. From advertising she next became involved in oil stock speculation. Unfortunately, her oil stocks were found to be fraudulent. In the resulting lawsuit, Margaret was ordered to pay in excess of $10,000. In late 1927, Margaret moved from personal oil stocks to general sales of stocks and bonds to pay off her debts. It was not long before the 1929 stock market crash occurred.

For the next decade, Margaret's press coverage is lost to the Great Depression. We may speculate that she earned a living through music or, more likely, she took whatever jobs were available. What is known is that sometime during the 1930s she began to study Indian cultures and religions during frequent visits to public libraries, as she later related.

In the early 1940s, Margaret surfaced again. She was living in seclusion with Guru Siri Abobindo, in Pondicherry, India. She had taken the name "Dishta" meaning "leading to the discovery of the divine self in every human being."[128] In an interview with a newspaper, Dishta stated, "I am not homesick, in fact I never felt more at home anywhere, anytime in my life."[129]

Daughter of a two-term president, once at the center of public affairs in the world's most powerful nation, Margaret Woodrow Wilson died of uremic poisoning while living in India under the tutelage and guidance of a guru.

## JESSIE WOODROW WILSON SAYRE

Second of three daughters of Woodrow Wilson and Ellen Louise Axson
*Born:* August 28, 1887      *Birthplace:* Gainesville, Georgia
*Died:* January 15, 1933      *Age at Death:* 45 years, 4 months
*Cause of Death:* Surgical complications
*Education:* Goucher College, Princeton University
*Profession:* Housewife, mother, politician
*Spouse:* Francis Bowes Sayre      *Number of Children:* 3

As a child growing up in the college atmosphere of Princeton University, the daughter of Professor Woodrow Wilson would acquire a higher level of formal education than most other women of her period. Jessie Woodrow Wilson attended Goucher College in Baltimore and Princeton University before beginning a three-year stint in social service work at a Philadelphia settlement house.

Jessie Wilson became Jessie Sayre in a White House wedding, the fifth daughter of a president to be married in the White House. Her husband, Francis Sayre, a professor of law at Harvard Law School, later served as both the Massachusetts state commissioner of corrections and assistant secretary of state.

In support of her father's peace program following World War I, Jessie became heavily involved in Democratic party politics and in working for the ratification of the Versailles Treaty and U.S. participation in the League of Nations. By 1928 she had achieved sufficient status within the party to be called upon to make the introductory speech for Alfred E. Smith's presidential nomination by the Democratic convention. She worked vigorously to elect the nation's first Catholic president. Smith lost, but Jessie had so impressed party leaders that she was asked to be a candidate for the Democratic nomination for the U.S. Senate from Massachusetts. She declined but continued to work for the party and a number of charitable causes.

Jessie died in January 1933. Just before her death, Franklin Delano Roosevelt began his many terms as president of the United States. As Jessie was, at the time of her death, secretary of the Massachusetts Democratic state committee, her death cut short a political career that would certainly have blossomed during the decades of the Democratic party's ascendancy.

## ELEANOR RANDOLPH WILSON MCADOO

Third daughter of Woodrow Wilson and Ellen Louise Axson
*Born:* October 16, 1889    *Birthplace:* Middletown, Connecticut
*Died:* April 5, 1967    *Age at Death:* 77 years, 5 months
*Cause of Death:* Long-term illness
*Education:* Princeton University
*Profession:* Housewife, mother, writer
*Spouse:* William Gibbs McAdoo    *Number of Children:* 2

She was considered the Wilson child who most resembled her father, both temperamentally and ideologically. Eleanor Randolph Wilson worked during her life as a writer, espousing her father's international viewpoints.

Her early years were spent on the Princeton University campus where her father was first a professor and then president of the university. In 1913, when Wilson entered the White House with his wife and three daughters, the Wilson girls were thrust into the center of national attention. Eleanor later wrote,

[W]hen father first went to the White House, I thought I would die. . . . Suddenly we became goldfish in a bowl. . . . Utter strangers passed judgment on us, and we were plunged into a sea of etiquette and customs that we didn't understand a thing about. There were times when [I] wanted to dig a hole into the floor and disappear down it.[130]

She, like her older sister Jessie, was married in a White House ceremony. At twenty-four years of age she married her father's secretary of the treasury, widowed fifty-two-year-old William Gibbs McAdoo. Two children were born to the McAdoos, but the marriage failed. In 1934 Eleanor divorced McAdoo, pleading mental cruelty, and received custody of the two girls. Following the divorce, Eleanor moved to California for the climate, which was more suited to her precarious health.

In California her life was active. She continued to write and participated in numerous charitable organizations, including an organization dedicated to preserving her father's memory—the Woodrow Wilson Foundation— still active in the 1990s. In 1959 Eleanor Wilson McAdoo made her last public appearance, attending a "Life with Father" luncheon held at the White House to honor sons and daughters of former presidents. The last few years were lived under the constant care of a nurse until she died at the age of seventy-seven.

## FOR FURTHER READING

Garraty, John Arthur. *Woodrow Wilson: A Great Life in Brief.* Westport, Conn.: Greenwood Press, 1977.

Mulder, John M. *Woodrow Wilson: The Years of Preparation.* Princeton, N.J.: Princeton University Press, 1978.

*New York Times*, April 7, 1967, 37:4.

Wilson, Woodrow. *President in Love: The Courtship Letters of Woodrow Wilson and Edith Bolling Galt.* Edited by Edwin Tribble. Boston: Houghton Mifflin, 1981.

# 24 CALVIN COOLIDGE'S CHILDREN

## JOHN COOLIDGE

First child of Calvin Coolidge and Grace Anna Goodhue
*Born:* September 7, 1906     *Birthplace:* Northampton, Massachusetts
*Education:* Mercersberg Academy, Amherst College
*Profession:* Businessman     *Spouse:* Florence Trumbull
*Number of Children:* 1

When President Warren G. Harding died in office, vice president Calvin Coolidge became president. The news reached John Coolidge, oldest of the Coolidge boys, while the seventeen-year-old was on military training exercises at Fort Devens, Massachusetts. When asked what it felt like to be the son of the president, John, in few words, observed, "It doesn't feel any different than when I was the son of the Massachusetts' governor."[131]

John, described as a "regular fellow" although his father was in the White House, graduated from Mercersberg Academy in June 1924 and entered Amherst College. Earning the nickname "Butch," which stayed with him throughout his college days, John was active in the sport of boxing, as well as acting in college plays and singing in Amherst's chorus. What Calvin Coolidge demanded, however, was excellence in scholastics. Even during the period of inauguration, John was not permitted to miss class for more than a single day. Coolidge's strict discipline and expectations for his sons' deportment were high. Thus, while John was allowed to visit in the White House, Coolidge reminded John, "You are dining at the table of the President of the United States, and you will present yourself promptly and in proper attire."[132]

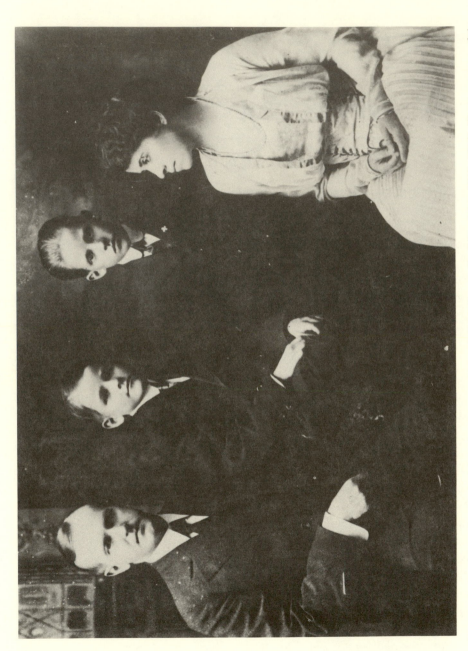

(Left to right) Calvin Coolidge, Calvin, Jr., John, and Mrs. Calvin (Grace) Coolidge (circa 1918–1920). Photo courtesy of the Library of Congress.

Despite John's rather ordinary college activities, his life on campus was not ordinary. The Secret Service was in constant attendance upon him. Nevertheless, the young man achieved some popularity with his fellow students. In 1928 John graduated from Amherst, not the recipient of the highest academic honors, but with an excellent record for achievement. At that point in his life John did not really know what he wanted for his future. He was caught between the attractions of studying law at Harvard and entering a business career, which he ultimately selected.

Despite the ever-present Secret Service during his days at Amherst, John managed to socialize and acquire a steady girlfriend. Indeed, the press speculated that John would elope with Florence Trumbull, the popular daughter of Connecticut's governor. The couple eventually married, though not until 1929.

Making his home in Connecticut, John embarked on a business career by becoming a traveling passenger agent for the New York, New Haven, and Hartford Railroad. He remained in that job for ten years. Seldom was his name mentioned in print, but in 1938 John did take a small role in politics, serving as a delegate to the Republican political convention and stressing his interest in helping the Republican party saying, "I'll be glad to do whatever I can locally to keep the Republican party alive."[133]

In 1940 John became ill and took a six-month leave of absence from his job. The illness persisted, and within a year, John resigned his position with the railroad. Recovering from his unnamed illness, John's next business venture was not as an employee, but as an entrepreneur. Impressed with the need for increased accuracy for new business systems, John invested in a concern manufacturing printed business forms which would facilitate accurate record keeping and reporting. His father's precision in all things thus characterized John's life, as it had his father's.

In 1985, having retired from the business world and returned to his family's Vermont beginnings, John astonished historians with the information that he had a dozen cartons of boxes of his father's papers kept in his attic in Plymouth, Vermont. Having found the papers, John turned them over for use in the public library, despite the fact that the papers, long abandoned, had served as appetizers for mice.

## CALVIN COOLIDGE, JR.

Second child, second son of Calvin Coolidge and Grace Anna Goodhue
*Born:* April 13, 1908     *Birthplace:* Northampton, Massachusetts

*Died:* April 7, 1924     *Age of Death:* 16 years
*Cause of Death:* Blood poisoning     *Education:* Mercersberg Academy

---

The short lifetime of Calvin Coolidge, Jr., ended when the young man stubbed his toe while playing tennis on the White House tennis court. The small injury caused blood poisoning, which ended his life.

Described as a rollicking boy, sixteen-year-old Cal was much like his mother, with a character full of fun and vigor and a ready ability to get along with his school classmates, very much unlike his father, who was called "Silent Cal."

Within a short time of Coolidge's elevation to the office of the presidency, Cal, Jr., was gravely ill. As Calvin Coolidge sat by his son's bedside, doctors tried to stop the spread of the infection that would cause the death of this much-loved son. Despite attempts at blood transfusions, by the time the seriousness of the illness was realized it was already too late. President Coolidge bemoaned the fact that, had he not been elected president, perhaps his son would not have died. The young man's death hit the family hard, and "silent Cal" was overcome by grief. Weeping unashamedly, he told a close reporter friend, "I just can't believe it happened."[134]

Cal and Grace Coolidge had arrived in the White House with two fine sons to whom they had emphasized the values of honesty, thrift, truthfulness, and valor. The death of the younger boy aroused the sympathy of the nation and very nearly crushed the parents. Grace Coolidge never got over the death of her younger son. She wrote a poem, later published, in which she described her intense emotions and feelings for her son.[135] She never overcame her feelings of despair over the tragic death of this special son.

## FOR FURTHER READING

Kane, Joseph Nathan. *Facts about the Presidents.* 4th ed. New York: H. W. Wilson, 1981.

Lathem, Edward C., ed. *Meet Calvin Coolidge: The Man behind the Myth.* Brattleboro, Vt.: Stephen Greene Press, 1960.

Lippman, Walter. *Public Person.* New York: Liveright Publishing, 1976.

Ross, Ishbel. *Grace Coolidge and Her Era: The Story of a President's Wife.* New York: Dodd, Mead, 1962.

# 25 HERBERT CLARK HOOVER'S CHILDREN

## HERBERT CLARK HOOVER, JR.

First child of Herbert Clark Hoover and Lou Henry
*Born:* August 8, 1903     *Birthplace:* London, England
*Died:* April 9, 1969     *Age at Death:* 65 years, 8 months
*Cause of Death:* Cancer
*Education:* Stanford University, Harvard University
*Profession:* Engineer, geologist, inventor, politician
*Spouse:* Margaret E. Watson     *Number of Children:* 3

The son of the "great engineer" also became a prominent engineer and geologist, highly respected for his contributions to geological exploration.

Born in London, England, where his father was working as an engineer, most of his childhood was spent accompanying his parents to far-flung points on the globe while his father practiced his profession. It was during his early childhood that Herbert Clark Hoover, Jr., began wearing a hearing aid because of partial deafness. But this handicap did not hinder his academic development. By 1925 he had earned his bachelor's degree from Stanford and shortly thereafter received his master's degree from Harvard, specializing in petroleum geology.

Among Herbert, Jr.'s, contributions to geology was the invention of a device to measure gasses that seeped to the surface from the earth, identifying probable oil deposits. In later years Herbert, Jr., developed and assisted in the invention of mechanisms that would be used on American planes in World War II, receiving many patents for his work.

(Left to right) Allan Henry Hoover and Herbert Clark Hoover, Jr. (circa 1912–1917). Photo courtesy of the Library of Congress.

But it was not only in engineering that Herbert, Jr., made his reputation. President Eisenhower appointed Herbert as under secretary of state, working with John Foster Dulles. Ike chose Herbert in recognition of his mediation of a dispute between Great Britain and Iran over the massive Iranian Abadan oil field. Herbert managed to satisfy all parties in the negotiations, a feat which earned Eisenhower's admiration and respect. Herbert, Sr., the former president, was still alive to see his son as the link between the "Grand Old Republican" party and Ike's modern Republicanism.

As secretary of state, Dulles was frequently ill, and Herbert, Jr., often acted in his stead. Despite Eisenhower's opinion, it was apparent that Herbert was not a born diplomat, though he did display excellent administrative ability in carrying out the policies established by others.

Herbert Clark Hoover, Jr., who earned recognition for his own contributions, never relied on his name for unearned advantage. Characteristically, with a modesty that endeared him to friends, when he spoke about his father he never mentioned the fact that his father had been president of the United States. Once, while reflecting on his past, Herbert observed, "[Y]ou know, my father was a mining engineer and we traveled a good deal."[136]

In 1969 Herbert died of cancer, leaving his widow and three children in California as the recipients of a large estate, earned by this president's son's own brilliance and ability. He was a self-made man, almost despite his father's position.

## ALLAN HENRY HOOVER

Second child, second son of Herbert Clark Hoover and Lou Henry
*Born:* July 17, 1907      *Birthplace:* London, England
*Died:* November 8, 1993      *Age at Death:* 86 years, 4 months
*Cause of Death:* Brief illness
*Education:* Stanford University, Harvard Business School
*Profession:* Rancher, miner, banker, businessman
*Spouse:* Margaret Coberly      *Number of Children:* 3

---

Born in 1907, Allan, the second of the two Hoover children, was a student at Stanford University when his father became president. Journeying to the capital for his father's inauguration, he found neither the city nor his father's new home at the White House to his taste. Allan went back to California, the family home, and completed his Stanford studies, earning a degree in economics.

Allan later returned to Washington, D.C., and the press found him an attractive subject both in personality and appearance. Father and son took some trips together, but they were marred by Allan's illness, which the press sensationalized as serious. The press even tried to drum up a romance between the handsome, socially active young man and the Philippines' American governor general's daughter. The press proclaimed the two would marry momentarily, but such was not to happen.

Instead of marrying, Allan went to Harvard Business School in fall, 1929, earning his master's degree in business administration.

Returning to California, Allan took over management of his father's northern California ranch, describing himself as a farmer, rancher, and even orchardist. Allan became wealthy. His father's successor to the presidency, Franklin Roosevelt, instituted, with congressional approval, farm-price support programs as one of the New Deal measures to combat the Depression, which contributed to Allan's wealth. One of the provisions of the law was payment to farmers for not growing crops. The program sought to end overproduction and keep prices high. Allan's management of the ranch profited from this program when he did not produce cotton on the ranch, and he received payment for nonproduction. (Whether the ranch was producing cotton prior to the program is not revealed in discussions on young Hoover's tactic, or even if the ranch could produce cotton.)

By 1937 Allan's investments were secure, and he expanded into banking and mining. When he married Margaret Coberly, his father, the only living former president of the United States at that time, attended his California wedding, in which Allan's older brother, Herbert, Jr., served as best man.

For a period of time, Allan lived in Greenwich, Connecticut, where he was active in association with charitable academic and study organizations established in his father's name. The organizations include the Hoover Institution of War, Revolution and Peace; the Hoover War Library, established in 1919 by the senior Herbert Hoover; and the Herbert Hoover Foundation, which continues active in the 1990s associated with expanding the scientific and public welfare principles associated with the former president, known during his era as "rugged individualism." Allan also played a major role in the restoration of Hoover's birthplace in West Branch, Iowa, which today is the site of this president's library and museum.

Though Allan lived to an old age, his long-time wife, Margaret, and two of his three children, Allan Jr., and Andrew, as well as six grandchildren survived him.

## FOR FURTHER READING

Best, Gary Dean. *Politics of American Individualism: Herbert Hoover in Transition: 1918–1921*. Westport, Conn.: Greenwood Press, 1975.

Burner, David. *Herbert Hoover: A Public Life*. New York: Alfred A. Knopf, 1979.

Lippmann, Walter. *Public Persons*. New York: Liveright Publishing, 1976.

Rice, Arnold S., ed. *Herbert Hoover: 1874–1964*. Dobbs Ferry, N.Y.: Oceana Publications, 1971.

Navy Lieutenant Franklin Delano Roosevelt, Jr. (circa 1940–1944). Photo courtesy of the Franklin Delano Roosevelt Library, Hyde Park, N.Y.

# 26 FRANKLIN DELANO ROOSEVELT'S CHILDREN

## ANNA ELEANOR ROOSEVELT DALL BOETTIGER HALSTED

First child, only daughter of Franklin Delano Roosevelt and Anna Eleanor Roosevelt
*Born:* May 3, 1906     *Birthplace:* Hyde Park, New York
*Died:* December 1, 1975     *Age at Death:* 69 years, 7 months
*Cause of Death:* Cancer
*Education:* Private schools, Cornell University
*Profession:* Housewife, mother, newspaperwoman
*Spouses:* Curtis Bean Dall, John Boettiger, James Addison Halsted
*Number of Children:* Roosevelt/Dall: 2; Roosevelt/Boettiger: None; Roosevelt/Halsted: None

Anna Eleanor, the only daughter of Franklin and Eleanor Roosevelt, moved to Washington, D.C., when she was only seven years old. She had already begun her education at an exclusive girl's school and she continued in that same style in Washington. It has been suggested, by Eleanor, that Anna was the recipient of too severe discipline. Her mother also observed that the excessive discipline was given in complete innocence and ignorance of child training. Sometimes her mother's innocence of child-rearing led to ludicrous situations, such as when Eleanor put Anna into a wire contraption and hung the baby outside of the home so that she might have fresh air, which Eleanor believed was crucial to the good health and robust development of her baby. Neighbors, however, were outraged and threatened to call the Society for the Prevention of Cruelty to Children.

Completing school in 1925, the tall, blonde Anna Roosevelt was taken abroad by the family's domineering grandmother, Sara Roosevelt. Anna was not, at that time, interested in going to college, and this suited her grandmother who cautioned her granddaughter to avoid becoming a "grind" because men would be intimidated by her and she would end up an old maid. Anna need not have worried for her ability to attract men, as she was to marry three times.

In spite of her grandmother's advice, Anna did decide to go to college, and attended Cornell where she studied agriculture because she loved the outdoors and animals. Her college days ended when she married Curtis Dall, a stockbroker about ten years her senior, when she was only twenty years old. Explaining her marriage to Dall, Anna pulled no punches: "I got married when I did because I wanted to get out."[137] What Anna referred to was the perpetual struggle between two strong-willed women, her mother and her father's mother, grandmother Sara. Anna's marriage did not last. Following the birth of two children in six years, the couple divorced. Thereafter, Anna's father became president of the United States, and the family moved into the White House.

During Roosevelt's first campaign for the presidency in 1931, Anna met and fell in love with John Boettiger, a reporter for the *Chicago Tribune*. Though the paper was staunchly Republican, and vehemently attacked Roosevelt and his policies during the presidency, the newspaper's political attitude did not prevent Anna and Boettiger from marrying in 1935. Boettiger left the *Tribune* for public relations work, and then, courtesy of another Roosevelt enemy, William Randolph Hearst, was made editor of the *Seattle Post Intelligencer*.

Leaving Seattle following public criticism of the Hearst and Roosevelt association, the couple purchased a shopping newspaper in Phoenix, Arizona, with the idea of turning it into a substantial daily newspaper. They poured every cent into the newspaper and borrowed from Anna's mother Eleanor and brother Jimmy. The paper failed, and so did the marriage. Boettiger left Phoenix while Anna continued the struggle until the summer of 1948. Justifying her persistence in the face of overwhelming opposition, she announced, "I love a fight against a reactionary monopoly, and I hate to see the latter winning out in so many fields of endeavor in this country today."[138] In 1949 she and John divorced. Boettiger remarried, but on October 29, 1950, he committed suicide by jumping from the seventh floor of a New York hotel.

Anna, never defeated by life, began again. In 1952 she married Dr. James A. Halsted, a physician with a deep interest in psychosomatic medicine. She and her husband lived a quiet life in California, though periodically she and her Fulbright professor husband traveled to Iran and later to Washington, D.C., where he was with the Veterans' Administration. By 1960 the couple were responsible for establishing a medical school in Iran.

In time, the couple retired to upstate New York. Anna died in 1975 of throat cancer and is buried in her birthplace at Hyde Park. Anna's son by her first marriage changed his name from Dall to Roosevelt.

## JAMES ROOSEVELT

Second child, first son of Franklin Delano Roosevelt and Anna Eleanor Roosevelt
*Born:* December 23, 1907     *Birthplace:* Hyde Park, New York
*Died:* August 13, 1991     *Age at Death:* 85 years, 9 months
*Cause of Death:* Stroke, long-term Parkinson's disease
*Education:* Groton Preparatory School, Harvard University, Boston University Law School
*Profession:* Businessman, politician, teacher
*Spouses:* Betsy Cushing, Romelle Theresa Sneider, Gladys Irene Owens
*Number of Children:* Roosevelt/Cushing: 3; Roosevelt/Sneider: None; Roosevelt/Owens: None

Described as having inherited "his father's charm, his father's boundless energy, and his father's speech and oratorial style," James, the eldest of Franklin and Eleanor Roosevelt's sons, was twenty-six years old when his father became president.[139] James was educated at the exclusive boy's preparatory school, Groton, and continued at Harvard, finally completing his education at Boston University Law School. James then entered the insurance business.

Upon his father's election to the presidency, Jimmy, as he was called, believed it his right and duty to make suggestions for appointments in the new administration, as he had been his father's campaign manager for the important state of Massachusetts. Public reaction to the son's advising the father was loud and negative. Jimmy escaped to Europe. Upon his return to the United States, there was talk that he was being considered for an appointment as the president's secretary; however, public reaction to the projected appointment was so unfavorable that Franklin dropped the idea. Anyway, Jimmy had another career in mind.

In 1935, before he was thirty years of age, Jimmy became president of the National Grain Yeast Corporation, which was involved in making industrial alcohol. Once more the public found fault with the president's son for it was rumored that backers of the company had underworld connections—that Jimmy's only credential for the presidency of the company was his connection to the chief executive of the United States. Under fire again, Jimmy resigned, giving as his reasons the conflict of time and the pursuit of other, more important, interests.

Next, Jimmy joined his father when he traveled to the inter-American conference in South America, and he served as his father's aide, with the rank of lieutenant colonel in the Marine Corps. Again there was public criticism, and Jimmy resigned from the Marine Corps, though he remained in his father's service.

In 1938 Jimmy was back at the insurance business, as a "super salesman" earning between $250,000 and $1 million per year in commissions. Yet again, the public was enraged. Jimmy defended both his integrity and his profits in a radio broadcast. From insurance, the young man went into the movie-production business and immediately became president of Goldwyn Studio Corporation, eventually establishing his own company and actually producing two movies.

During World War II, Jimmy went into the marines as a captain and was sent as an observer to the Middle and Far East. In order to see frontline duty, Jimmy had to use the authority of his father's name to convince his military superiors that his ulcers were not sufficient disability to hold him from such duty. He was right. Jimmy not only participated in combat, he won the Silver Star for gallantry and served at Guadalcanal, Tarawa, and Midway in the Pacific.

President Roosevelt died in 1945, the war ended, and Jimmy left active service and settled in California, where he became a spokesman for the state's Democrats.

In time, Jimmy ran for the position of California governor against Earl Warren. He was defeated. But Jimmy's political career was not ended. He served as a member of the House of Representatives for the Los Angeles congressional district, winning election to six terms, with a minimum of effort. Other political involvement of this president's son included his serving as a delegate to the United Nations in 1965 and 1966, though he resigned to return to business interests. Ever controversial, Jimmy Roosevelt participated in Democrats for Nixon in 1972, and even the 1980s found him involved with yet further concerns, particularly his founding of the National Committee to Preserve Social Security and Medicare.

Returning to live in California in his later years, he continued to lecture in colleges throughout the nation. He died in Newport Beach, California.

## FRANKLIN ROOSEVELT

Third child, second son of Franklin Delano Roosevelt and Anna Eleanor Roosevelt
*Born:* March 18, 1909     *Birthplace:* Hyde Park, New York
*Died:* November 8, 1909     *Age at Death:* 8 months
*Cause of Death:* Flu epidemic?

---

The third child of Franklin and Eleanor, the first namesake of his father, died before he was nine months old. We can only speculate as to the emotional impact on the Roosevelt family caused by this loss. Not unnaturally, the death of a child at such an early age, within such a vibrant family, must have caused great pain. The man who would be the presidential giant of the twentieth century had not achieved fame in 1909, and chroniclers of the day paid no attention to merely another death, even though in a well-to-do presidentially related family—as distant cousins of Theodore Roosevelt.

## ELLIOTT ROOSEVELT

Fourth child, third son of Franklin Delano Roosevelt and Anna Eleanor Roosevelt
*Born:* September 23, 1910     *Birthplace:* Hyde Park, New York
*Died:* October 27, 1990     *Age at Death:* 80 years, 1 month
*Cause of Death:* Congestive heart failure
*Education:* Groton Preparatory School
*Profession:* Businessman, soldier, writer
*Spouses:* Elizabeth Browning Donner, Ruth Josephine Googins, Faye Emerson, Minerva Bell Ross, Peabody
*Number of Children:* Roosevelt/Donner: 1; Roosevelt/Googins: 3; Roosevelt/Emerson: None; Roosevelt/Ross: None; Roosevelt/Peabody: None

---

Born only shortly before his father was elected to New York's state senate, Elliott was the third of five children to survive. He grew up in the family home at New York's Hyde Park. Elliott, like his other brothers, attended Groton. Elliott broke with family tradition when he went to work rather than continuing school. He entered the advertising business and was relatively successful before his father became president.

Elliott developed a long and profitable interest in aviation and eventually became well known as an expert on the fledgling aviation industry. It was this interest that brought to Elliott a brief association with Anthony Fokker and which caused international headlines and cries of favoritism by Roosevelt's enemies over Elliott's efforts on behalf of the German manufacturer of the Fokker airplane. Because of the notoriety, Elliott returned to the radio broadcast industry and settled at a ranch near Fort Worth, Texas, initially the home of his second wife, heiress Ruth Josephine Googins.

Just prior to the U.S. entry into World War II, Elliott received a commission as a captain in the U.S. Army Air Corps. His choice of military service again broke with the Roosevelt family tradition of the navy, with which his brothers, and even his uncle Theodore, had all been closely associated. During his wartime service, Elliott was awarded the U.S. Air Medal, the Legion of Merit, and the Distinguished Flying Cross with Oak Leaf Cluster; was made Commander of the Order of the British Empire; and received the French Legion of Honor and the Croix de Guerre with Palm. Nevertheless, Elliott's promotion to the rank of brigadier general, which had to be made with congressional approval, caused South Dakota's Senator Bushfield to argue that "General Robert E. Lee had thirty-six years of service in the Army before he became a Brigadier General, Eisenhower thirty years, General Pershing twenty-four years, and General MacArthur twenty-one years before reaching the rank of Brigadier General."[140] Despite Bushfield's objections, Elliott's four years of service were sufficient to earn him the promotion.

Bushfield's arguments had been exacerbated by news headlines that reported that Elliott's dog had received more favorable treatment than the lowly soldier returning from the Continent, who did not have a presidential father. It was claimed that Elliott had "bumped" a soldier returning from European duty so that his dog could journey home. The press had a field day with the dog incident.

Elliot's life was regularly associated with controversy. Another revelation brought the news that Elliott had borrowed some $200,000 in 1939, shortly before the war, and he had repaid only $4,000 of the debt. It was further claimed that the rest of the debt was written off—because he was the president's son. Defending himself, Elliott claimed the $200,000 had come from his wife. Following congressional inquiries nothing was proven or, for that matter, disproven.

After the war, Elliot traveled to Portugal, where he raised Arabian horses for a time. But, by the 1960s, he had returned to the United States and was elected mayor of Miami Beach, Florida.

In yet another period of his life, Elliot was an aviation editor for the Hearst newspapers. It was this avocation that became the focus of the balance of his life. His first book, about his father, *As He Saw It*, was published in 1946. The book was reviewed and, for the most part, it was agreed that the book was not a major contribution to FDR literature. One London critic even went so far as to observe that the book was so bad that it "proves nothing except that great men often have silly sons."[141] However, the critic was proved wrong, whether from failure at being a critic, or failure to account for Elliot's doggedness in pursuit of an interest. Elliot wrote thirteen more books, although he also pursued a variety of other interests while he wrote his books. The books often drew criticism for both their stylistics and their subject matters. Sometimes his stories included intimate, even shocking details of family members' lives and caused his sister and three brothers to disavow his claims publicly. In another series, Elliot fictionalized his mother, Eleanor, as an almost Angela Lansbury–like sleuth, solving mysteries in the White House.

After traveling the world, settling down for short times in other nations and in this country, Elliot died in Scottsdale, Arizona. Though the son of a president, it is difficult to imagine any other man of his generation being so successful at maneuvering the arrows hurled at him just because he was the son of a president. Elliot died having drunk deeply of the wine of life.

## FRANKLIN DELANO ROOSEVELT, JR.

Fifth child, fourth son of Franklin Delano Roosevelt and Anna Eleanor Roosevelt
*Born:* August 17, 1914
*Birthplace:* Campobello, New Brunswick, Georgia
*Died:* August 17, 1988     *Age at Death:* 74 years
*Cause of Death:* Unknown
*Education:* Groton Preparatory School, Harvard University, University of Virginia Law School
*Profession:* Lawyer, politician

*Spouses:* Ethel Du Pont, Suzanne Perrin, Felicia Schiff Warburg Sarnoff, Patricia Oakes
*Number of Children:* Roosevelt/Du Pont: 2; Roosevelt/Perrin: 2; Roosevelt/Sarnoff: None; Roosevelt/Oakes: None

---

Franklin was almost nineteen years old in 1933 when his father became president. That same year he graduated from Groton Preparatory School, where he had shown an aptitude for both scholarship and athletics. To continue his education, Franklin entered Harvard, but went traveling in France, England, and Spain before turning again to college studies.

As the press constantly demanded news of the Roosevelt family, Franklin's college days were dogged by reporters in their desire to find interesting, amusing, and, perhaps, even scandalous stories for the public's consumption of Roosevelt news. Franklin resented this intrusion into his private life. Not, by nature, the quiet type, he, in one instance, seized a reporter's camera and smashed it to pieces, thereby making a newspaper story out of the lack of a story prompting Franklin's action.

In 1937, following a long courtship, Franklin married Ethel Du Pont, a member of a family that despised Franklin's father. Because of the "Romeo and Juliet" aspect of the marriage, the public's demand for intimate details of the relationship was insatiable. Nevertheless, newlywed Franklin completed his Harvard education and earned, as well, a law degree from Virginia Law School. He began work as a clerk in a Wall Street law office for the munificent pay of $2,000 a year, a niggardly sum even in those days, but still a job in the midst of the Depression.

Unlike some of his generation, who became committed to social causes in the 1930s but dropped the causes with the coming of personal prosperity, Franklin remained committed to his causes throughout his life. In 1965 he was appointed as chairman of the Equal Opportunity Commission by President Johnson. Franklin's social consciousness compelled him to enter public service and work against racial discrimination and for expanded war veterans' benefits. President Truman appointed Franklin to the U.S. Civil Rights Commission. But young Franklin could win elected office as well. He was elected as a liberal Democratic party congressman from New York's twentieth district, and he served from 1949 to 1954, although he failed to be elected New York's governor when he sought the office in 1966.

Franklin, Jr., also distinguished himself in World War II as a naval officer, earning the command of a destroyer escort and serving in both Atlantic and

Pacific theaters of the war. He was awarded both the Silver Star and the Purple Heart, as well as other recognition for his military service.

Not only was this namesake of one of the nation's most renowned presidents successful in the political arena, he also made his mark in the business world. At one point in time, he owned the national distributorship for the Fiat automobile car company. However, married four times, and despite his patrimony, Franklin was dropped from New York's *Social Register*, the "blue book" of social acceptability. Even with such prestigious family credentials, social "bluebloods" found his behavior unacceptable for a time.

Franklin, Jr., observed of his life that being a president's son did not influence his life, as "We don't have royal families in America, only prominent families." He believed that each generation "must have the guts and talent to succeed on its own."[142]

## JOHN ASPINWALL ROOSEVELT

Sixth child, fifth son of Franklin Delano Roosevelt and Anna Eleanor Roosevelt
*Born:* March 13, 1916      *Birthplace:* Hyde Park, New York
*Died:* April 27, 1981      *Age at Death:* 68 years, 1 month
*Cause of Death:* Heart attack
*Education:* Groton Preparatory School, Harvard University
*Profession:* Businessman
*Spouses:* Anne Lindsay Clark, Irene Boyd McAlpin
*Number of Children:* Roosevelt/Clark: 3; Roosevelt/McAlpin: None

---

Seventeen years old when his father became president in 1933, John Roosevelt, along with the rest of the Roosevelt children, quickly gained reputations for their playful and boisterous behavior. His mother, however, referred to this youngest child as "the most dignified of all my children,"[143] in defending her son against charges that during a 1937 European tour, John "squirted champagne in the face of the Mayor of Cannes, and roughed him with a bouquet of flowers."[144]

Shortly after John's return to the United States he married a Boston debutante, Anne Lindsay Clark, in a "small" Massachusett's wedding that included 30,000 onlookers along the wedding party's route. Following the wedding, John joined a Boston department store as a store clerk, earning weekly $18.50. The press heartily approved of the young man and contrasted him with the sons of other wealthy men. Said one newspaper,

John Roosevelt, youngest son of the famous family, now happily married, is on his own, got himself a job, and is going to learn the art of merchandising. That's better than joining the colony of rich men's sons, idling away his times in a cocktail lounge and sponging on his parents as so many of them do.[143]

When the United States entered World War II, John joined the navy and served throughout the war. He was not in the United States at the time of his father's death near the conclusion of the war. When the war ended, John settled in California and resumed his business career, becoming an executive in a clothing store chain, Filene's Sons, Inc. Living a private life uncharacteristic of the Roosevelts, his name suddenly appeared in print when a large photo of John crossing picket lines at his company was published in 1947 by *Life* magazine.

With the exception of the 1957 attempt to win the mayor's race, following his return to New York City, John, unlike his political brothers, avoided political office, although he did act behind the scenes in supporting the candidacy of others. In New York, John became senior vice president of Bache, Halsey, Stuart, Shields & Company and devoted his spare time to charitable fund-raising activities, including the polio foundation, which was so dear to his polio-crippled father.

Surprisingly, this son of FDR in his later years took a more active interest in politics and gave his support to the Republican party. He firmly supported Presidents Eisenhower, Nixon, and Reagan, as well as New York's Rockefeller and Javits, and Chase of neighboring New Jersey. Only shortly after Ronald Reagan's term as president began, John died of a heart attack in New York City.

## FOR FURTHER READING

Boettiger, John R. *Love in Shadow*. New York: W. W. Norton, 1978.

Burnham, Sophy. *The Landed Gentry: Passions and Personalities Inside America's Propertied Class*. New York: G. P. Putnam's Sons, 1978.

Churchill, Allen. *The Roosevelts: American Aristocrats*. New York: Harper & Row, 1965.

Cook, Blanche Wiesen. *Eleanor Roosevelt*. New York: Viking, 1992.

*New York Times,* August 18, 1988; October 28, 1990, 38:5; August 14, 1991, D 19:1; August 14, 1991, A 3:1.

Perling, Joseph J. *Presidents' Sons: The Prestige of Name in a Democracy*. New York: Odyssey Press, 1947; Freeport, N.Y.: Books for Libraries Press, 1971.

Roosevelt, Elliott, and James Brough. *Mother: Eleanor Roosevelt's Untold Story*. N.Y.: G. P. Putnam's Sons, 1977.

Sadler, Christine. *Children in the White House*. NewYork: G. P. Putnam's Sons, 1967.

Zilg, Gerald Colby. *Du Pont: Behind the Nylon Curtain*. New York: Prentice-Hall, 1974.

Margaret Truman (1926). Photo courtesy of the Harry S Truman Library.

# 27 HARRY S TRUMAN'S CHILD

## MARGARET TRUMAN DANIEL

Only child of Harry S Truman and Elizabeth Virginia Wallace
*Born:* February 17, 1924     *Birthplace:* Independence, Missouri
*Education:* Gunston Hall, George Washington University
*Profession:* Housewife, mother, singer, author
*Spouse:* Clifton Daniel     *Number of Children:* 4

Margaret, born during the years when her father was a hard-working haberdasher in Missouri, grew up as the center of her parents' attention. Called "my baby," or "Margie," or even "skinny," because of her perpetual dieting, Margaret was the only child the couple had. Although she received the attention ofttimes reserved for only children, she never became the spoiled brat often associated with being an only child. Truman righteously observed of his daughter, "She's one nice girl and I'm so glad she hasn't turned out like Alice Roosevelt and a couple of the Wilson daughters."[145] It was Harry's highest accolade. She was, and remains, a down-to-earth person, so much so that Harry later credited both Margaret, and her mother, Bess, with keeping their feet firmly on the ground during the presidency as well as occasionally reminding Harry, when the power and prestige of the presidency elevated his own feelings of importance, that he, too, put on his pants one leg at a time.

Upon Truman's election to the Senate representing Missouri, in no small part resulting from his heroic opposition to a corrupt political machine in Missouri, the family moved to Washington, D.C. Margaret and her mother not unnaturally felt some dread of the Washington social world. The Washington establishment was unimpressed at the arrival of the new Missouri senator, and the family's penurious circumstances did nothing to change their impression until Truman became president of the United States. Money remained a perpetual family problem, even when Truman was the Democratic party's vice presidential candidate.

Franklin Delano Roosevelt died shortly after his fourth election. Truman became president in a manner not unlike that of his distant relative, John Tyler, who had become the first vice president to succeed to the office upon the death of the president. Margaret now had the opportunity to launch what she hoped would be a successful musical career, not unlike Margaret Wilson's—the former president's daughter referred to by her father. In spite of Margaret's arduous devotion to her craft (often practicing voice to the accompaniment of her piano-playing father) her efforts were less than well received. In fact, it was a music critic's scornful analysis of her singing and her father's vitriolic response to that critic for which Margaret is well remembered. On that occasion, a *Washington Post* critic, Paul Hume, described Margaret's performance, her voice quality, and her presentation in very unflattering terms. Harry, the presidential father, was enraged, and he publicly informed the nation of his opinion of the critic. Years later, in reminiscing about the incident, Harry, whose feelings had not mellowed, related the incident. "The next morning this Hume . . . wrote the dirtiest, meanest critique you ever saw. I wrote him a letter, saying that if I could get my hands on him I'd bust him in the jaw and kick his nuts out [chuckle]."[146]

Harry's protectiveness of his daughter is understandable, given an assassination attempt on his life by Puerto Rican nationalists. Security precautions strictly limited Margaret's romantic opportunities. Margaret would periodically be humiliated when her father would send Secret Service men to find her when she was late in returning home. In this respect, the role of president's daughter had its negative impact. Margaret referred to this aspect of living in the White House when she wrote a "Letter to the Editor" (castigating Chelsea Clinton's critics), observing "and [I] was incarcerated in the White House when [Harry S Truman] became president."[147] Nevertheless, there were also positive aspects for Margaret as child resident of the White House. Her father frequently sent her traveling in Europe as his personal representative. She made an excellent American ambassador, so much so that Harry laughingly remarked that the nation should fire its ambassadors and allow Margaret to fill their shoes.[148]

Shortly after her father left the White House, Margaret married. In 1956, having returned to the family home in Missouri, she married newspaperman

Clifton Daniel and entered a quiet time of raising their four boys. In 1974 Margaret wrote a book explaining her relationship with her father, and chronicling the Truman years in the White House.

An author of numerous books, primarily mysteries taking place in the Washington, D.C., she knows, Margaret has been seen periodically on television speaking about her newest book and addressing questions about her life as the daughter of one of the nation's most loved presidents. Other than during such appearances, Margaret has maintained a quiet, unobtrusive presence much as did her parents, Harry and Bess.

## FOR FURTHER READING

Hedley, John Hollister. *Harry S Truman: The Little Man from Missouri*. Woodburn, N.Y.: Barron's Educational Series, 1979.

Ferrell, Robert H., ed. *Off the Record: The Private Papers of Harry S Truman*. N.Y.: Harper & Row, 1980.

McCullough, David. *Truman*. New York: Touchstone, Simon and Schuster, 1992.

Miller, Merle. *Plain Speaking: An Oral Biography of Harry S Truman*. New York: Berkley, 1974.

Robbing, John. *Bess and Harry: An American Love Story*. New York: G. P. Putnam's Sons, 1980.

Robbins, Charles. *Last of His Kind: An Informal Portrait of Harry S Truman*. New York: Morrow, 1979.

Truman, Harry S. *An Autobiography of Harry S Truman*. Edited by Robert H. Ferrell. Boulder, Colo.: Associated University Press, 1980.

_____. *Memoirs: Years of Trial and Hope*. New York: Doubleday, 1956.

Truman, Margaret. *Harry S Truman*. New York: Pocket Books, 1974.

_____. *Bess W. Truman/Margaret Truman*. New York: Macmillan, 1986.

John Sheldon Doud Eisenhower in Paris (1928). Photo courtesy of the Dwight D. Eisenhower Library.

# 28 DWIGHT DAVID EISENHOWER'S CHILDREN

## DWIGHT DOUD EISENHOWER

First child of Dwight David Eisenhower and Mary Geneva Doud
*Born:* September 24, 1917    *Birthplace:* Denver, Colorado
*Died:* January 2, 1921    *Age at Death:* 3 years, 4 months
*Cause of Death:* Scarlet fever

Few Americans are aware that Dwight David Eisenhower and his wife, Mamie, had two sons. This first child, Dwight Doud Eisenhower, survived only a few years. After the little boy's death, the family rarely spoke publicly of their firstborn, whose life ended from the effects of scarlet fever.

However Ike, in his memoirs, later wrote that "this was the greatest disappointment and disaster in my life, the one I have never been able to forget completely."[149] After construction of the Eisenhower Library, the remains of this firstborn Eisenhower child, Dwight Doud, were transferred to the building where a plaque now marks his final resting place. At the dedication of the library, Eisenhower was seen to stare at the plaque with tears in his eyes.

## JOHN SHELDON DOUD EISENHOWER

Second child, second son of Dwight David Eisenhower and Mary Geneva Doud
*Born:* August 3, 1923    *Birthplace:* Denver, Colorado
*Education:* West Point, Columbia University

*Profession:* Soldier, White House aide, teacher, ambassador, writer
*Spouse:* Barbara Jean Thompson      *Number of Children:* 4

---

Born in Denver, Colorado, at the home of his maternal grandparents, John Sheldon Doud Eisenhower was named after his mother's father. By the age of two months, his mother, Mamie, overcame her dislike of the tropics and moved with her small son to join her military husband, Ike, in Panama. Reading accounts of the Eisenhower's family movements during John's young years is rather like reading a recitation of most of the nation's army military bases. Though he completed his schooling he attended many military-based schools.

John's memories of his father are based on a close feeling between father and son. They shared experiences such as hiking, flying lessons, and even cooking—comrades rather than superior versus inferior relationships which might characterize a career officer's association with his son.

General Eisenhower never attempted directly to influence his son's choice of a career, but the years spent on military camps made its mark. John chose a career like his father's, though he was also tempted by careers in journalism and law. Competing furiously with thirty-five other candidates from Kansas, Eisenhower's state of official residence, John earned a much-desired West Point appointment.

With a natural aptitude for academics, John, often called "young Ike," spent much of his time at West Point playing tennis, working on the yearbook, singing in the choir, and even acting as a tutor to lower classmen. He graduated from an accelerated three-year course in the 138th position in a class of 474. John's father was unable to attend his graduation, because he was directing his massive military operation on June 6, 1944—the Allied invasion of Europe.

John spent his graduation furlough with his father at the Normandy command post, and after further infantry training in the United States, he was assigned staff duty in Europe, specifically working under General Omar Bradley. At war's end, John returned to West Point, teaching, while he continued graduate studies in English and comparative literature, earning his graduate degree from Columbia University in 1950.

While serving as a frontline major in Korea, John was informed of his father's election to the presidency. When Ike visited Korea, in partial fulfillment of campaign promises to end the war, his son accompanied his president-father on a tour of the battlefront. In 1953 John returned to the

States, where he spent the next five years stationed at various posts, even doing a brief stint as a White House aide to his father until John Kennedy was elected to succeed his father into the presidency.

Resigning his army commission in 1963, John determined to pursue a literary career, first taking a position with Doubleday Publishing, and then moving on to association with the Freedom Foundation. In time, although he continued to serve on a variety of charitable interests, John Sheldon Doud Eisenhower turned his full attention to writing, initially focusing on the story of his father's life. Today John is a recognized scholar of history and an acclaimed and well-read author.

Married, the father of four children, including a son who is the husband of former President Nixon's daughter, Julie, John has moved far beyond his birthright as "the general's son" or as "little Ike." He has come full-circle in life, having had the opportunity to prove himself in his father's professional field, and also to make his own mark on history as a chronicler of history.

## FOR FURTHER READING

Cannon, Marian G. *Dwight David Eisenhower: War Hero and President.* New York: Watts, 1990.

Cook, Blanche Wiesen. *Declassified Eisenhower: A Divided Legacy.* New York: Doubleday, 1981.

Dulles, Eleanor Lansing. *Chances of a Lifetime: A Memoir.* New York: Prentice-Hall, 1980.

Eisenhower, John S. D. *Strictly Personal: A Memoir.* New York: Doubleday, Inc., 1974.

Eisenhower, Milton S. *The President Calling.* New York: Doubleday, 1974.

Ferrell, Robert H., ed. *Eisenhower Diaries.* New York: W. W. Norton, 1981.

Lee, R. Alton. *Dwight D. Eisenhower: Soldier and Statesman.* New York: Nelson-Hall, 1981.

Neal, Steve. *Eisenhower's Reluctant Dynasty.* New York: Doubleday, 1978.

Richardson, Elmo. *Presidency of Dwight D. Eisenhower.* Lawrence: Regents Press of Kansas, 1979.

# 29 JOHN FITZGERALD KENNEDY'S CHILDREN

## CAROLINE BOUVIER KENNEDY SCHLOSSBERG

First child of John Fitzgerald Kennedy and Jacqueline Lee Bouvier
*Born:* November 27, 1957     *Birthplace:* New York City, New York
*Education:* Radcliffe College, Harvard University
*Profession:* Copy girl, museum curator, wife, mother
*Spouse:* Edwin Schlossberg     *Number of Children:* 3

The phrase that is most descriptive of the young Caroline, the little blonde-haired, blue-eyed, dimpled daughter of the president was, to say the least, the "darling of the nation." Her handsome parents, Jack and Jackie, with their equally photogenic children, presented to the public the image of the ideal family. The name Caroline took a rapid jump in popularity; many parents named their daughters after the Kennedy firstborn. She was part of the Kennedy style, and the nation came to anticipate Caroline's appearance in her father's oval office—during times of her choosing, not his. The antics of the child and the obvious loving warmth between father and daughter further endeared both to the nation.

In the very public days following the president's assassination, the public faced new images of the Kennedy children. Caroline is well remembered as a silent, quiet, and very mature little girl as she stood with her mother and small brother, John, during the public's demonstrations of its sorrow over the loss of her much loved father.

Caroline's mother, Jacqueline Bouvier Kennedy, was not long a widow. The nation was shocked when she remarried, providing her two young children with a stepfather, Greek wheeler-dealer, billionaire Aristotle Onassis, a man much Jacqueline's senior. Caroline, naturally, could not escape public animosity to Jackie's new life. Both mother and daughter were chased throughout the world by photographers. Mother became a jet-setter, and her children often moved with her. The Kennedy image was tarnished though the glamour remained. Neither the death of Onassis, nor Jackie's permanent return to the United States (and even conscious removal from the public eye) immediately reinstated mother and daughter to the "Camelot" of former days. In time, Jackie and her children became again pleasantly welcomed images of the American scene—though through conscious efforts by Jackie their presence was often understated and very private.

Caroline moved through her teen years and graduated from Radcliffe, the exclusive women's college. She worked for a while as a copy girl and in a museum. She completed her education at Harvard University in 1980.

Married, the mother of three children—Rose, Tatiana, and John—Caroline has followed a path very like that of her mother who, until her death from cancer in 1994, successfully avoided regular contact with the press. However, though the images of Caroline during her childhood days in the White House remain, they have gradually come to be supplanted by images of an elegant young woman, regularly pictured in company with her mother—who doted on the Schlossberg children—until her death, and with her children and husband.

Today, though very involved in personally raising her children, she is also quietly associated with a variety of charitable causes, including serving, with her brother John, as an administrator of the estimated $250 million trust left by Jacqueline Kennedy Onassis upon her death. Though seeking privacy for herself and her family, it is likely that this daughter of one of America's most colorful presidents will continue to intrigue the public, both in memory of her parents and with interest in her own future contributions to the nation.

## JOHN FITZGERALD KENNEDY, JR.

Second child, first son of John Fitzgerald Kennedy and Jacqueline Lee Bouvier
*Born:* November 25, 1960      *Birthplace:* Washington, D.C.
*Education:* Brown University, New York University Law School
*Profession:* Public service, attorney
*Spouse:* None      *Children:* None

One of the enduring images of the Kennedy assassination is that of young John Kennedy, Jr., standing to attention before his father's grave and saluting the departed chief executive—his daddy. The agony of the nation was epitomized in the little boy's lost and bewildered appearance. The nation had lost its president and the boy had lost his father, and the double loss could be seen in the child standing by the grave.

Only weeks earlier, the nation had been charmed and delighted by the image of love between Jack Kennedy and his son "John-John" when the press photographed the young president tossing the little boy into the air; the obvious glee of the child captured the nation, as did the relationship of his sister Caroline to her father.

In years that followed the assassination, John, like his sister, traveled throughout the world with their mother, who had married the Greek shipping magnate, Aristotle Onassis. Onassis, having children of his own, made no pretense of anything more than acceptance of his new wife's children. The male role model in the boy's life was not his stepfather, but instead were his uncles Robert (assassinated in 1968) and Ted Kennedy, although Mother Jackie periodically advocated her son's distancing himself from the periodically eratic antics of his Uncle Ted. This admonishment came from her desire to see her son enter the public service arena in some, distant future.

John's world travels ended when his mother was again widowed, and the family returned to settle again in the United States. Upon returning to the United States, Jackie successfully sought privacy in her life, although she regularly worked as an editor for Doubleday Publishing in New York City. Jackie and her children moved between their city and vacation compounds with little public and press intervention into their lives.

John attended Brown University, where he expressed an interest in pursuing a career in acting. However, following the Kennedy family tradition of entering public service, John attended and graduated from law school at New York University, though his repeated attempts to pass the New York State bar exam did not go unnoticed by the press. After passing the bar, John became a New York City assistant district attorney, where he currently still works. Additionally, John is expected to publish a political magazine, and he serves with his sister, among others, as administrator of his mother's extensive estate.

The young John Kennedy has benefited from his heritage in terms of public image, responsibility, wealth, and his personal appearance. Considered extraordinarily handsome—identified in a poll as "the sexiest man in America"—his dating escapades regularly make the news. It is probable that his future too will be dominated by the public's memory of his father, as the young John's life is shown before the nation's cameras for decades to come.

## PATRICK BOUVIER KENNEDY

Third child, second son of John Fitzgerald Kennedy and Jacqueline Lee Bouvier
*Born:* August 7, 1963
*Birthplace:* Otis Air Force Base, Massachusetts
*Died:* August 9, 1963    *Age at Death:* 2 days
*Cause of Death:* Premature birth, respiratory distress syndrome (RDS)

Patrick Bouvier Kennedy, the second son of President Kennedy, was born five-and-one-half weeks prematurely, weighing only four pounds, ten and one-half ounces, and suffering from the same respiratory distress syndrome that had afflicted his brother John at birth. (RDS, common to premature or small birthweight children, is defined as an inability of the lungs to hold air, though they do inflate. Effectively, the lungs are underdeveloped.) A more effective treatment for RDS was found only a year after this Kennedy child died from its effects.

Named for his grandfather and great-grandfather, Patrick Joseph, and with his mother's maiden name, Patrick was beset with difficulties at birth. Delivered by caesarean section, he had difficulty breathing immediately. A day later, following attempts to stimulate his breathing, he was transferred to the Children's Hospital Medical Center in Boston and placed into a high-pressure oxygen chamber. His mother remained in Falmouth, Massachusetts, at Otis Air Force Base hospital, where the child had been delivered. Patrick's father, President Kennedy, spent the night in the Boston hospital as the baby's condition grew worse. Patrick died after living only thirty-nine hours. The nation joined in mourning for the Kennedy's loss of this, their third, child.

The first child born to a president in office at the White House in sixty-eight years, since the birth of Grover Cleveland's last daughter, Marion, in 1895, even his son's precarious condition did not allow the president of the United States to abandon his workload entirely. While on the way to the Boston hospital, during the limousine ride, the president signed four minor bills which had recently been passed by Congress into law. These bills became law with Kennedy's signature and permanently mark a moment's turmoil in this much-distressed family:

Public Law 88–90 Istle or Tampico Fiber—Duty-Free Importation
Public Law 88–91 Land Exchange—Wyoming
Public Law 88–92 Tanning Extracts—Duty-Free Import
Public Law 88–93 Heptanoic Acid—Duty-Free Import

All were signed on August 8, 1963, while a presidential father waited to hear whether his newborn son would live or die.

## FOR FURTHER READING

Heymann, C. David. *A Woman Named Jackie: An Intimate Biography of Jacqueline Bouvier Kennedy Onassis*. Secaucus, N.J.: L. Stuart, 1989.
Kennedy, Rose Fitzgerald. *Times to Remember*. New York: Doubleday, 1974.
Parmet, Herbert S. *Jack: The Struggles of John F. Kennedy*. New York: Dial Press, 1980.
Taylor, Richard. *Jackie: A Lasting Impression*. New York: St. Martin's Press, 1990.

# 30 LYNDON BAINES JOHNSON'S CHILDREN

## LYNDA BIRD JOHNSON ROBB

First child of Lyndon Baines Johnson and Claudia Alta Taylor
*Born:* March 19, 1944     *Birthplace:* Washington, D.C.
*Education:* University of Texas, at Austin
*Profession:* Housewife, mother, politician
*Spouse:* Charles S. Robb     *Number of Children:* 3

"She's the smartest one and the one I worry about the most" was her father's blunt appraisal about his elder daughter, Lynda.[150] Lyndon Baines Johnson, as a presidential father, approved of his daughter for displaying the qualities that he admired, intellect and strength of character, even going so far as to say that she was a woman who did not need to be taken care of by a man—as she was "so smart she'll be able to make a life for herself."[151] No idle flatterer, Johnson was so convinced of her abilities that he often consulted Lynda about his drafts of speeches. Lynda would reply by awarding the president's work an "A," "B," or "C" (there is no record of "D" or "F" papers).

Lynda, however, was not always comfortable with her father's political life. When Lyndon was still the House majority leader and Lynda was yet a small girl, she was negatively affected by her parent's ambition and success. Whereas her younger sister Luci's response to the situation was to resort to pranks, Lynda expressed her insecurity and resentment through compulsive eating, which had the expected results when she was described as a "butterball," a cause for further insecurity.

When her father entered the White House, Lynda was at the dating age and could not tolerate her "ugly duckling" self-image. Coincidentally with becoming the president's daughter, she developed a relationship with Hollywood's then perpetual "beach-boy bachelor," George Hamilton. Though the relationship was relatively short and its seriousness was strongly questioned by her father and the press, it was not questioned by Lynda. Lynda sought to make herself over in the Hollywood image. To satisfy demands of the publicity of her newly found glamour, Lynda even went to a Hollywood makeup artist for a makeover. Embarrassingly for Lynda, the nation's press detailed her makeover, complete with diagrams of her facial structure. Her dreams did not materialize; Lynda was not to be a Hollywood Cinderella. During this period of Lynda's enchantment with her own image and Hollywood, Lyndon ribbed his daughter, gently and cautiously. He waited until she had graduated from the University of Texas to give her a two-month vacation to Europe. He explained his purpose, in the down-home style for which he was famous, as "Shucks, now she might even come back with that slick Hollywood boy out of her hair."[152] Lynda returned and Hamilton exited. He was replaced by White House social aide, Marine Captain Charles S. Robb.

Robb, from an Ohio farm background, a recipient of a four-year scholarship, who would later be described as a mature "Ken doll," captured Lynda's attention. In the years following Kennedy's assassination, presidential families have lived under the constant surveillance of the Secret Service. Despite the guardianship of the Secret Service, Lynda's relationship with Robb developed until the Marine Corps officer and Lynda were married in a traditional military ceremony. The archway of crossed swords held by Robb's fellow officers set off one of the most beautiful of White House wedding ceremonies.

From the Marine Corps, in which Robb served in Vietnam and was recognized for bravery, Lynda's husband completed his law studies at the distinguished University of Virginia Law School. He then entered politics. Elected as lieutenant governor of Virginia in his first public office, Robb furthered his political career when he was twice elected Virginia's governor. In 1988 Robb captured a Democratic Senate seat for Virginia, and he was reelected in 1994. During his years in public service, the public has watched as his wife, Lynda, has stood by his side and has continued her ardent support for her husband, even when he was publicly accused of infidelity and when reports of marital rifts between the couple made the news.

Active in a variety of charitable interests, and serving as the wife of a senator, Lynda Johnson Robb has rarely been out of the public's view since her teenage years. It is likely that this situation will continue in the years to

come. Indeed, Johnson's assessment of his daughter was very accurate—
she has proven well able to take care of herself.

## LUCY (LUCI) BAINES JOHNSON NUGENT TURPIN

Second child, second daughter of Lyndon Baines Johnson and Claudia
Alta Taylor
*Born:* July 2, 1947      *Birthplace:* Washington, D.C.
*Education:* National Cathedral School
*Profession:* Housewife, mother, businesswoman
*Spouse:* Patrick John Nugent, Ian Turpin
*Number of Children:* Johnson/Nugent: 4; Johnson/Turpin: None

Luci, who represented an image of femininity to the public, was described
by her father as so "appealing and feminine that there will always be some
man around waiting to make a living for her."[153] But the president's
attractive daughter, crowned by her father as queen of the Shenandoah
Apple Blossom Festival in nearby Winchester, Virginia, was also tough-
minded enough to carve a social life for herself, even during the White
House years. She asserted, "[Y]ou have to be pushy to have any friends at
the White House. No one will call you any more. You have to call them."[154]

Years later, Luci elaborated on being a young daughter living in the White
House. She recalled hiding in her White House bedroom closet after
overhearing her mother, and presidential aide Jack Valenti, decide that Luci
should go campaigning on a weekend when she had two dates. In 1984 Luci's
recall of the unwanted campaign swing to Spearfish, South Dakota, included
her memory that "in fact, I wanted to give the people the spear. But they
turned out to be the nicest people in the world."[155]

Expected to personify all that was most wholesome in teenagers, Luci's
independence caused her to rebel occasionally. To her parents' dismay, she
periodically tormented her mother by playing the piano too loudly while her
mother was entertaining, or, in an even more shocking display, barging into
a room full of her parents' invited guests in her bare feet. Such behavior in
a president's child provoked comment, for the nation's people have come
to apply a higher standard of behavior to children of the White House. Yet,
first and foremost, children of the presidents are still children, needing and
seeking support of their very public parents. During a 1984 meeting of

several presidents' daughters, each concurred with the others' feelings about periodic resentment toward their mothers because they felt they were not receiving enough attention. Luci recalled how she sometimes went to her mother's room only to find a pillow hanging on the door knob announcing, "I want to be alone."[156]

Because of Kennedy's assassination, which had elevated her father to president, the Secret Service intensified the protection of the new president's family. One result, as Luci entered the dating age, was to turn the dating game into an obstacle course. Heightened security, combined with the press's scramble for a story, led at least one boyfriend to sacrifice his romance with the president's daughter for the sake of his own health. This boyfriend escaped, claiming he was developing ulcers.

A convert to Catholicism during her father's term in office, Luci graduated from Washington's Episcopalian National Cathedral School. Periodically she and her father would attend the city's Little Monk's Church, and it was, perhaps, during one of these times that Luci asked the question in which her father took so much delight, whatever its authenticity: "Daddy, as an outsider, how do you feel about the human race?"[157]

Despite problems with maintaining friendships and dating, Luci eventually met and married Airman First Class Patrick Nugent, a Vietnam veteran. The couple was married in Washington's National Cathedral which, in itself, caused an uproar because the privilege of marrying in the shrine was denied to other couples. The date chosen for the wedding—August 6, 1966—created another uproar. The date was the twenty-first anniversary of the day the United States dropped the atom bomb on Hiroshima. Luci explained to the complaining organization, the Friends of Japan, that the date was a personal choice and had nothing to do with Hiroshima, that she had been born after the bombing, and that the date would not be changed. The wedding, the first of a serving presidential daughter since that of Alice Roosevelt Longworth, early in the century, was held on a grand scale. Luci, object of the wedding engineered by her parents, proclaimed, "This all happened because I wanted just my immediate family and friends. My parents invited only the immediate nation."[158]

The Nugent marriage lasted almost thirteen years, and four children were born to the couple before their 1979 divorce. The marriage was annulled by the Roman Catholic Church. In 1984 Luci married an investment banker, Ian Turpin. Luci's four children, and her new husband's five-year-old son, all served as attendants in the wedding ceremony held in Stonewall, Texas, on the Johnson family ranch.[159] Although Luci often visits Texas, her most recent residency has been in Toronto, Ontario, Canada.

## FOR FURTHER READING

Bryant, Traphes, and Frances Spatz. *Dog Days at the White House: The Outrageous Memoirs of the Presidential Kennel Keeper*. New York: Macmillan, 1975.

Cormier, Frank. *LBJ: The Way He Was*. Garden City, N.Y.: Doubleday, 1977.

Miller, Merle. *Lyndon: An Oral Biography*. New York: G.P. Putnam's Sons, 1980.

Mooney, Booth. *LBJ: An Irreverent Chronicle*. New York: Crowell, l976.

Rulon, Philip Real. *Compassionate Samaritan: The Life of Lyndon Baines Johnson*. New York: Nelson-Hall, 1981.

# 31 RICHARD MILHOUS NIXON'S CHILDREN

## PATRICIA (TRICIA) NIXON COX

First child of Richard Milhous Nixon and Thelma Catherine Ryan
*Born:* February 21, 1946    *Birthplace:* San Francisco, California
*Education:* Finch College    *Profession:* Housewife, mother
*Spouse:* Edward Finch Cox    *Number of Children:* 1

Born only days after her father entered the race for California's Twelfth District congressional seat in 1946, Tricia, as she came to be called, developed a personality quite different from that of her sister, younger Julie. Tricia is more introverted; although "she is extremely effective whenever she has to do anything publicly, she doesn't like to do anything publicly."[160]

Twenty-two years old when her father became president in 1968, Tricia, a petite blonde weighing less than 100 pounds, worked as a tutor for third grade school children in the Washington, D.C., ghetto while living in the White House. Tricia, unlike many White House residents, never felt constricted by her home. "I never feel alone in the White House," she said. "If I want privacy, I go to private parties and I don't tell people. I can't go out in crowds, people always recognize you, but I've found it possible to have a private life."[161] Displaying her ease in the role of president's child she periodically served as hostess for White House parties, and she charmed the nation when she conducted a televised tour of the White House as a one-hour CBS television presentation.

It was on Tricia that her parents pinned their hopes for a truly "royal" daughter, for she was romantically linked in the press not only with many of the nation's leading bachelors, but also with Britain's Crown Prince Charles. However, Prince Charles and Tricia had other ideas. The Nixons' first daughter held out for her own choice, "Fast Eddy" Cox, whom she met in college. Edward Cox, whose family counted itself blue-blooded, tracing its ancestors to Chancellor Robert Livingston who swore into office the first president of the United States, George Washington, became Tricia's fiancé in spring 1971. Neither family was excited about their children's choice of a mate. The Nixons had hoped for more than a "blue-blooded liberal"—Cox was a member of consumer advocate (Ralph) "Nader's Raiders." From the Cox point of view, however, there were murmurs that the Nixons were certainly far beneath the Coxes' lofty family heritage.

Despite rumored objections on both sides, the couple married on June 12, 1971, in the first outdoor wedding in the 171-year history of the White House. Both sets of parents looked happy, although the wedding was slightly delayed by rain. The day after the wedding, political stormclouds gathered. On June 13, 1971, the lead story in the *New York Times*, "Pentagon Papers," initiated what would become a series of stories and events that would culminate in Richard Nixon's resignation from the presidency.

Newly married Tricia stayed in the background but proclaimed that the stories were "just jealous politicians who want his job" and predicted "that he would survive the ordeal and would not resign."[162] She was wrong. Her father resigned the presidency on August 9, 1974.

In 1981 Tricia's thirty-four-year-old husband moved from his job with a prominent New York law firm to work with the Reagan administration in the newly created synthetic fuels energy program, at a salary in excess of $52,000 per year. They later returned to the New York area where rarely has Tricia sought the public attention so often given to children of presidents.

With Nixon's 1994 death, Tricia Nixon Cox was again seen by the public when the Nixon family members were much photographed among the admirers and statesmen who came to pay their respects to the long-since resigned president, who had gradually returned to respectability and had even acquired, in some quarters, acclaim as an elder statesman.

## JULIE NIXON EISENHOWER

Second child, second daughter of Richard Milhous Nixon and Thelma Catherine Ryan
*Born:* July 5, 1948     *Birthplace:* Washington, D.C.

*Education:* Smith College
*Profession:* Housewife, mother, author, editor
*Spouse:* David Dwight Eisenhower II     *Number of Children:* 3

---

Julie—extroverted, gregarious, and constantly active—contrasts with the personality characteristics most commonly associated with the presidential Nixons. Born shortly after her father had become a member of Congress from California, Julie Nixon matured while her father acquired successively higher offices leading to the presidency.

When her father became president in 1968, Julie had already married her college sweetheart, David Dwight Eisenhower, grandson of former President Dwight David Eisenhower. The couple completed college, Julie at Smith College and David at Amherst, though at one time they both left their respective campuses to avoid possible difficulties from fellow college students during the U.S. bombing of Cambodia. During the early days of their marriage the couple rented, at an undisclosed rent, the $125,000 Bethesda, Maryland, home of her father's wealthy friend, Bebe Rebozo, which caused some press notice. Shortly thereafter the couple moved to a more modest apartment.

When the Watergate affair developed, Julie vehemently defended her father. Throughout the affair Julie's faith in her father's innocence remained steadfast. Indeed, just before her father's resignation, the first in the history of the office, she insisted, "[F]ather will not resign" and "he is stronger now than he has ever been in his determination to see this through."[163]

The Eisenhowers lived in Southern California before they moved back to the East Coast. Julie has authored a cookbook for children and another book that profiles people she met while she was a young woman living in the White House.


## FOR FURTHER READING

Atkins, Ollie. *White House Years: Triumph and Tragedy.* New York: Playboy Press, 1977.

Brodie, Fawn. *Richard Nixon: The Shaping of His Character.* New York: W. W. Norton, 1981.

Ehrlichman, John. *Witness to Power: The Nixon Years.* New York: Simon and Schuster, 1982.

Eisenhower, Julie Nixon. *Pat Nixon: The Untold Story*. New York: Simon and Schuster, 1986.

Klein, Herbert G. *Making It Perfectly Clear*. New York: Doubleday, 1980.

Morris, Roger. *Richard Milhous Nixon: The Rise of an American Politician*. New York: Henry Holt, 1990.

Wills, Garry. *Nixon Agonistes: The Crisis of a Self-Made Man*. New York: New American Library, 1979.

# 32 GERALD RUDOLPH FORD'S CHILDREN

## MICHAEL (MIKE) GERALD FORD

First child of Gerald Rudolph Ford and Elizabeth Anne Bloomer
*Born:* March 14, 1950      *Birthplace:* Washington, D.C.
*Education:* T. S. Williams High School, Wake Forest
University, Gordon-Conwell Theological Seminary
*Profession:* Businessman, minister, academic administrator
*Spouse:* Gayle Brumbaugh      *Number of Children:* 2

The eldest of the Ford children, Mike, was born the year his father began his first congressional term. Educated in public schools near the family home in Alexandria, Virginia, during which time his father was regularly reelected to Congress from his home district in Grand Rapids, Michigan, Mike was, and is today, considered the most introspective of the Ford children. He did everything with intensity, a Ford characteristic, but most prominent in Mike— whether skiing, studying, or even participating in youthful games.

When Ford became president of the United States following events that made him the only person to attain the presidency without having been elected as president or vice president, Mike was a twenty-three-year-old divinity student at a theological seminary working on his master's degree. When his father was sworn into the presidency, it was Mike's Bible, especially purchased for the occasion, on which the president placed his hand to take the oath stated in the Constitution of the United States. Ford's hand rested on the Twentieth Psalm which, appropriate to the situation of the United States on that day, begins, "The Lord hear thee in the day of trouble."

Susan and Gerald R. Ford before a White House reception (October 10, 1974). Photo courtesy of the Gerald R. Ford Library.

Mike and his wife, Gayle, traveled from Boston to be with his father and mother, when, shortly after Ford became president, Betty Ford underwent a mastectomy. The Fords' eldest son and his wife who were a major source of strength to the almost inconsolable president, often came to sit with the older Fords to pray.

More liberal than his father, Mike entered the academic setting. He served at the University of Pittsburgh with the Christian Outreach Program. In 1981 he became student affairs director at Wake Forest University.

## JOHN (JACK) GARDNER FORD

Second child, second son of Gerald Rudolph Ford and Elizabeth Anne Bloomer
*Born:* March 16, 1952      *Birthplace:* Washington, D.C.
*Education:* T. C. Williams High School, Utah State University
*Profession:* Businessman, journalist, publisher
*Spouse:* Juliann Felando      *Number of Children:* None

The middle son of Gerald and Betty Ford, John, or Jack as he is called, is considered the brightest of the four children by those who know them, although his school grades never reflected his intelligence. In fact, as a child, Jack's grades were so low that his teacher arranged for him to take special tests. As with some other children of high intellectual ability, he did not achieve his potential early or in the schoolroom setting.

Growing up in Washington, D.C., where his father was a representative from the state of Michigan, Jack constantly encouraged his father to aspire to higher, more prestigious offices, telling him, when the speaker's position was open, to "Go for it, Dad." Naturally, his father's ascendancy to the vice presidency following the resignation of Spiro Agnew thrilled the young Jack. Upon the resignation of Richard Nixon, the first ever such resignation, Jack's father became president of the United States. For Jack it meant traveling with his parents to European capitals and even venturing into the Soviet Union, as well as periodically serving as his father's representative on speaking tours in the United States—heady stuff for a Utah State University graduate in forestry.

Perhaps something of the young man's character is reflected in his statement, following his father's 1976 loss of the presidential office to

Jimmy Carter: "You know, when you come so close, it's really hard to lose. But at the same time, if you can't lose as graciously as you had planned to win, then you shouldn't have been in the race in the first place."[164]

By the 1980s, Jack had become a magazine and newspaper publisher in California, although he then moved into work in the field of public relations. Many observers believe that this presidential son will, one day, himself become involved in the nation's politics.

## STEVEN MEIGS FORD

Third child, third son of Gerald Rudolph Ford and Elizabeth Anne Bloomer
*Born:* May 19, 1956     *Birthplace:* Washington, D.C.
*Education:* T. C. Williams High School, Utah State University, California Polytechnical Institute
*Profession:* Actor
*Spouse:* None     *Number of Children:* None

---

Only seventeen when his father became president, Steve was a Washington "political brat," raised by the family nanny during his mother's and father's constant travels to fulfill the political duties of office. After completing his high school education, Steve was attracted to ranching, and in pursuit of his interests he went west to work on a ranch. At one time he was interested in dentistry because "a dentist can be his own man, set his own hours. I could never shuffle papers eight hours a day," but he later changed his mind.[165]

In 1981 Steve Ford, who was living in scenic San Luis Obispo, California, became involved in political activities designed to prevent the opening of the Diablo Canyon nuclear power plant near a major earthquake fault ten miles from Steve's home.

The skills developed by this son, whom many consider the most attractive of the Ford sons, during the time he spent working as a ranchhand in the Far West provided an unexpected opportunity to shift into a new career. Offered a small part in a Western, which made use of his riding skills, Steve became an actor.

In the early 1980s, Steve moved onto daytime television and became a regular player in "The Young and the Restless." Having moved away from show business, this most eligible son of President Ford now raises horses in northern California. With the passage of time, he too may follow his father's footsteps by seeking political office.


## SUSAN ELIZABETH FORD VANCE BALES

Fourth child, only daughter of Gerald Rudolph Ford and Elizabeth Anne Bloomer
*Born:* July 6, 1957      *Birthplace:* Washington, D.C.
*Education:* Holton-Arms School, Mt. Vernon College, University of Kansas
*Profession:* Photo journalist, wife, mother
*Spouse:* Charles Vance, Vaden Bales
*Number of Children:* Ford/Vance: 2; Ford/Bales: None

---

The only daughter and the youngest of the four Ford children, Susan was born in the Washington, D.C., suburb of Alexandria, Virginia, when her father was a House of Representatives member from Michigan. As had her brothers, Susan studied at that city's public schools, until, when she was sixteen, her father became the nation's vice president. Though she worked in the White House during summer vacations selling books as souvenirs, as well as periodically working for her father in his capitol building office, when Gerald R. Ford became president, Susan was elevated to that rarified atmosphere of a president's daughter living in the White House. Her teenage life changed.

Expressing the fear she often felt after her father was the victim of two assassination attempts, she later observed, "I remember the miserable nights of nightmares." And (after the assassination attempts), "I was never comfortable when he went out in a crowd and I was always looking to see whether he was wearing a bulletproof vest."[166] As many presidents' children have experienced, Susan quickly learned that the loss of friends was a consequence of having a presidential father and that others sought her friendship "because you're the daughter of the President."[167] Susan was not immune to the hazards of being a child of a president living in the White House.

Susan's father did not hesitate to make use of the Secret Service as a method of keeping tabs on his only daughter during both his vice presidency and presidency. On occasion when Susan would arrive home later than scheduled her father would refer to the agent's log for her arrival time. The use of the Secret Service with presidential children is well known, and privacy is little known. Father Ford, however, thought the Secret Service logs kept by the agents and designed to protect presidential families' children were a blessing for his parental role.

Susan, like the other Ford children, encouraged her father to run for the presidential office in 1976. When he was defeated, it was Susan, along with her mother and father, who made the final trip out of the United States, before Carter's inauguration, when the family took a late November 1976 presidential trip to China.

In 1979 twenty-one-year-old Susan, a California resident, married Charles Vance, ironically a thirty-seven-year-old Secret Service agent assigned to protect the former president's family. Later divorced from Vance, Susan married again and today resides in Tulsa, Oklahoma, where her many volunteer interests include a particular emphasis on breast cancer research fund-raising, an interest perhaps due to memories of her mother's bout with the disease during White House years.

In 1984, with the Ford Museum well established in Ford's Grand Rapids, Michigan, hometown, three presidential daughters, a presidential granddaughter, and two former first ladies joined together to entertain and inform museum visitors about life as a family member of the nation's chief executive officer.

## FOR FURTHER READING

Ford, Gerald R. *A Time to Heal.* New York: Harper & Row, 1979.

Mollenhoff, Clark R. *The Man Who Pardoned Nixon.* New York: St. Martin's Press, 1976.

Vesta, Bud. *Jerry Ford: Up Close.* New York: Coward, McCann and Geoghegan, 1974.

# 33 JAMES EARL CARTER'S CHILDREN

## JOHN (JACK) WILLIAM CARTER

First child of James Earl Carter and Rosalynn Smith
*Born:* July 3, 1947     *Birthplace:* Portsmouth, Virginia
*Education:* Georgia Institute of Technology, University of Georgia Law School
*Profession:* Businessman, lawyer
*Spouse:* Juliette Langford     *Number of Children:* 2

The eldest of the three Carter sons, John William, called Jack by family and media, became a successful businessman in Georgia. Though active in his political father's activities, he was first a businessman and then his father's campaigner. He claims to have developed an early political sense with this story: "Back when I was 13 my mother made me take a bath. I never liked it. Once I got in the bathtub, though, I liked it. The campaign is like that."[168]

Perhaps because Jack is the eldest of Carter's children, he was able to speak with authority about his father's interests once his father's quest for a second term as president failed. Thirty-three-year-old Jack told reporters that, though the loss of the office of the presidency was somewhat embarrassing, particularly the sound defeat at the hands of the electorate, "[N]either of my parents is taking it hard in the sense of being emotionally strung out about it."[169]

A veteran of the Vietnam War, Jack later moved to Calhoun, Georgia, where he practiced law and operated a grain storage business. In time, however, he left Georgia and moved to Illinois to work with the Chicago Board of Trade. With his father's increased political presence as a foreign affairs negotiator, during the Clinton administration in the early 1990s, Carter watchers do not discount the entry of this son into politics.

## JAMES EARL (CHIP) CARTER III

Second child, second son of James Earl Carter and Rosalynn Smith
*Born:* April 12, 1950     *Birthplace:* Honolulu, Hawaii
*Education:* Public schools
*Profession:* Businessman, politician
*Spouses:* Carol Griffith, Ginger Hodges
*Number of Children:* Carter/Griffith: 1; Carter/Hodges: None

---

Of the three Carter sons—his father's namesake—James Earl, called Chip by his family and the press, this son is often viewed as the most similar to his political father, both in appearance and ambition. However, the strong character of his mother is also to be seen in Chip, particularly in her "even-tempered, soft-spoken disposition."[170]

This son also claims to have been an active political campaigner by the time he was ten years old, when he worked to gain support for John Kennedy's 1960 election to the presidency. Campaigning actively for his father, in his first election when Jimmy successfully moved to the Georgia Senate, and helping his father win the Georgia governorship, Chip and his mother proved to be the most politically active and effective members of the immmediate family. The pair often substituted for father and husband, particularly during the period of the 1980 election when Carter chose not to engage directly in domestic politics—claiming the higher priority was the Iranian hostage crisis. For the most part, Jimmy campaigned from the White House rose garden, which eventually led to a political term —a rose garden strategy—that described a candidate's staying at home, on the job. Carter felt secure knowing that Chip, and other family members, were making political appearances and delivering speeches during the early stages of the 1980 election.

Chip's contributions to his father's second race for the presidency were so professional and traditional that "Chip kissed a few babies, cut one ribbon," and massaged local pride by stating that "Virginia [or Michigan, Wisconsin . . .] was one of the president's 'top targeted states.'" 171

After his father lost his bid for reelection, this son, considered to be the most politically active of the Carter sons, reentered business in Georgia. Chip, the father of James Earl Carter IV, divorced his first wife, but remarried in 1982.


## DONNELL JEFFREY CARTER

Third child, third son of James Earl Carter and Rosalynn Smith
*Born:* August 18, 1952     *Birthplace:* New London, Connecticut
*Education:* George Washington University
*Profession:* Businessman
*Spouse:* Annette Davis     *Number of Children:* None

---

In the heyday of mass media coverage and with a family which by itself attracted the most detailed attention perhaps ever experienced by a first family, Jeff Carter managed to remain a mystery to most of the public.

After graduating from George Washington University in Washington, D.C., where he specialized in computer cartography (a scientific technique used by demographers, city planners, and even energy developers in planning space use) Jeff joined with his college professor to found a computer consulting firm. It was a risk for both. At the beginning, the venture did not seem likely to succeed when earnings fell below a living wage for the two.

But in 1980 the future of Jeff's company dramatically brightened when Imelda Marcos, wife of then Philippine President Marcos, asked Jeff for assistance in her planned slum clearance project in Manila. Jeff's presidential father, informed of the potential business deal by his son, gave his approval, although he insisted that the business be run as would any other business, without a presidential father. Perhaps Jimmy Carter had in mind press coverage of his brother Billy's business with the Libyan government. Nevertheless, Jeff and his company received the Philippine government's contract, which would pay them $200,000, ensuring that his out-of-work father would not have to support this Carter child.

Maintaining his low profile throughout the years since his father left the presidency, Jeff has continued in his chosen career as a computer consultant, and he continues his association with the firm founded during his father's presidency. Clearly, his firm, Computer Mapping Consultants, has proven successful over the long haul.

## AMY LYNN CARTER ANTONUCCI

Fourth child, first daughter of James Earl Carter and Rosalyn Smith
*Born:* October 19, 1967     *Birthplace:* Plains, Georgia
*Education:* Thaddeus Stevens School, Brown University
*Profession:* Salesperson, clerk, wife
*Spouse:* Michael Antonucci     *Children:* None

---

Both public and press expected to enjoy the antics of a young child entering the White House, given the nation's previous delight with John Fitzgerald Kennedy's two children. But Amy Carter did not prove to be charming press material although, in fact, she may have merely been the object of press barbs really directed at her father. This treatment directly contrasted to Kennedy's John and Caroline, who could do no wrong and who, in fact, enhanced Kennedy's image.

Trouble with the press began almost immediately. Amy enrolled in a public school near the White House. The intent of this public school enrollment was considered appropriate because her parents decided that Carter's position as a man of the people should continue. But Amy was forced to withdraw when any semblance of a normal life was prevented by daily press attention to Amy, her teachers, and her fellow students. The president's daughter could not be just one of the people, and sending her to a public school proved to be a mistake. It was a mistake as well when, in some apparent attempt at normalcy, Amy was in attendance at state dinners with visiting dignitaries. She read books during what were clearly boring times for her, but the alternative of a young child's attempting to make polite conversation was impossible. The press even reported the titles of the books she was reading at the dinner table, which turned the entire attempt at living a normal life into a painfully comedic farce.

The president's effort to reach the people through the earthy simplicity of a child went from the absurd to the politically disastrous. In the hotly contested race for the presidency during a crucial nationally televised debate with Carter's opponent Ronald Reagan, the president referred to Amy as an authority when he observed that his young daughter informed him that the most important issue of the nation was control of nuclear proliferation. While the issue was clearly on the minds of the nation's citizens, the well-meaning president's implication caused the nation, and its prominent comedians and cartoonists, to howl with laughter. The image of the most powerful nation's head of state seeking the advice of a thirteen-year-old girl on fundamental issues facing the globe was too much for even the most ardent Carter supporters. Only days before the election, one of the nation's sports heroes, Roger Staubach, himself the father of a girl named Amy, tweaked the president's nose on national television when he said, "In fact, I talked to my daughter, Amy, this morning about [the loss of a football game] and she said the number one problem was the bomb."[172]

In general, children have been political pluses to a politician, hence the constant "baby kissing" so typical of politicians. But in Carter's presidency, little Amy repudiated the time-honored maxim. From the contrived normalcy of the Carter White House, Amy was thrust back into the family home in Plains, Georgia, when the bid for reelection failed.

In 1982 Amy returned to Washington as a page in the Senate, when she began her college education. In college, Amy became a student activist and was twice arrested for involvement in protests—over apartheid in 1985 and over the recruitment activities of the Central Intelligence Agency in 1986. Over the years, Amy's presence in the public eye has been associated with watching her mature and enter and leave college. Periodically, Amy has held a variety of jobs, including a longer period in a bookstore. She married longtime companion Michael Antonucci, a fellow student from Brown University whom she had met in the mid-1980s, prior to her dismissal for "academic reasons" from the school. The May 1994 ceremony was held at the Memphis, Tennessee, National Ornamental Metal Museum.

*NOTE*

As of November 28, 1994, the author was informed by Paul Kaplan, information director for the Carter Center in Atlanta, Georgia, that "[we] do not allow information on the president's [Carter] children to be given out due to the privacy factor." (Telephone conversation, November 28, 1994) Therefore, statistical information requested from this office on numbers of children and wives' names may not be current. Kaplan approved this statement's inclusion into this section on Carter as "That's perfectly fine!"

## FOR FURTHER READING

Baker, James T. *Southern Baptist in the White House*. New York: Westminster Press, 1977.

Blount, Roy, Jr. *Crackers: This Whole Many-Angled Thing of Jimmy, More Carters, Ominous Little Animals, Sad-Singing Women, My Daddy and Me*. New York: Alfred Knopf, 1980.

Carter, Jimmy. *Everything to Gain: Making the Most of the Rest of your Life/Jimmy and Rosalynn Carter*. Thorndike, Maine: Thorndike Press, 1987.

Kucharsky, David. *Man from Plains: The Mind and Spirit of Jimmy Carter*. New York: Harper, 1976.

Mazlish, Bruce, and Edwin Diamond. *Jimmy Carter: A Character Portrait*. New York: Simon and Schuster, 1979.

Meyer, Peter. *James Earl Carter: The Man and the Myth*. Mission, Kans.: Andrews and McMeel, 1978.

Miller, William Lee. *Yankee from Georgia: The Emergence of Jimmy Carter*. Los Angeles: Time Books, 1978.

Mollenhoff, Clark R. *President Who Failed: Carter out of Control*. New York: Macmillan, 1980.

Richman, Daniel A. *James E. Carter: 39th President of the United States*. Ada, Okla.: Garrett Educational Corporation, 1989.

# 34 RONALD WILSON REAGAN'S CHILDREN

## MAUREEN ELIZABETH REAGAN FILIPPONE SILLS REVELL

First born child of Ronald Wilson Reagan and Jane Wyman
*Born:* January 4, 1941    *Birthplace:* Los Angeles, California
*Education:* Marymount College
*Profession:* Businesswoman, politician, television and radio personality, author
*Spouses:* John Filippone, David Sills, Dennis Revell
*Number of Children:* None

A vocal, vivacious, and avid campaigner for her father in his quest for the presidency, Maureen Reagan, the eldest of the Reagan children, joined the Republican party well before her father moved from the Democratic party into Republican ranks. With an enthusiasm not unlike an aging cheerleader, Maureen often captured the attention of the press because of her readiness to speak out when asked her opinion. She was an early advocate of the Equal Rights Amendment, while Reagan was more modest in his advocacy of women's roles in society.

As the daughter of an actor and part-time politician, Maureen was educated in boarding schools. Eventually she attended Marymount College, in Virginia, until she dropped out to become a struggling actress and singer, although she discovered that that form of show business was not to her liking. She did, however, become involved with show business on both radio and television, and she has frequently sought out media attention to spotlight her interests. Maureen's venture into the political arena on her own proved unsuccessful when, in 1982, she sought the Republican nomination for senator from California. Her father was not loudly supportive of her quest, and his brother, Neal, even helped to bring Pete Wilson into the race—the same Pete Wilson who later became the state's governor. Maureen, however, came to be known as a frequent spokesperson and advocate for her father and his causes. After sixteen years in the radio and television business, Maureen moved into the export business. She developed a magazine to promote American exports and later became the chief executive of a firm specializing in assisting businesses to circumvent or overcome the hazards and pitfalls so common to international business. In 1989 Maureen added author to her already extensive resume when she wrote *First Father, First Daughter*, which recounts her experiences with her presidential father.

Three times married, little public notice has been given to Maureen Reagan of late. As with most cheerleaders of old, however, the potential of a resurgence of energy and public activism from this Reagan daughter should not be discounted.

## MICHAEL EDWARD REAGAN

Adopted son of Ronald Wilson Reagan and Jane Wyman
*Born:* 1945    *Birthplace:* Unknown
*Education:* Arizona State University
*Profession:* Businessman, radio personality
*Spouses:* Pamela Putnam, Colleen Sterns
*Number of Children:* Reagan/Putnam: None; Reagan/Sterns: 2

During his first marriage to actress Jane Wyman, Ronald Reagan adopted Michael. He attended various schools as a young man and received a football scholarship, but he turned down the offer, married, and devoted his time to motorboat sales and speedboat racing. His interest in the sport continued, and he became quite successful as a powerboat speedster. The marriage, however, ended.

Michael worked in various businesses and eventually became an executive with a title company. But, it was in connection with another business that Michael achieved some notoriety. As a firm's vice president, Michael sought government business for the firm's aircraft machine parts business, using his father's name (and by inference his position) in letters sent to potential clients. He was severely criticized by the press in his attempt to use presidential influence. Consequently, his father restated an earlier admonishment to exercise care not to seem to be using his father's position for personal gain. After first announcing that he would resign from the company, Michael recanted his intent and merely stated that under no conditions would he again make use of his father's name for business gain. He later left the firm and ventured into other interests in business until he too added show business to his already diverse experiences.

As the years have passed, Michael's interests have become more closely associated with the interests of all of his siblings. He has become an author, and he regularly hosts a late night talk show—not so far removed from the style of the show that so successfully propelled his father into the national political spotlight after the mid-1970s.

Outside of his business misstep, Michael appears to have developed into the most conservative of Reagan's four children. Living quietly with his second wife and son and daughter, Michael has provided the now-ailing Reagan and his wife Nancy with their only grandchildren.

## PATRICIA (PATTI) ANN REAGAN (DAVIS) GRILLEY

Third child of Ronald Wilson Reagan; only daughter of Ronald Wilson Reagan and Nancy Davis
*Born:* October 21, 1952     *Birthplace:* Los Angeles, California
*Education:* Northwestern University
*Profession:* Actress, writer, model
*Spouse:* Paul Grilley     *Number of Children:* None

---

An entertainer like both her father and her mother, although Nancy aborted her acting career when she married Ronald, Patti took her stage name of Davis from her mother's maiden name. Technically, Patti does not share her family's political interests, although she has acquired a certain renown for her ability to gain political attention. Patti did, however, actively campaign in her father's 1980 presidential race, despite her description of herself as "anti-political."[173]

Often called the family rebel, Patti dropped out, escaping to the company of a rock musician, with whom she lived for some time. Patti expressed opposition to the Vietnam War and became part of the counterculture of the early 1970s, but she and her family were temporarily reunited when her father won election to the presidency, although the reunion was often heated and eventually dissolved, much to the glee of the press with the resultant headlines. During Reagan's two terms in the White House, Patti herself made headlines, periodically expressing her disdain for her parents and for the social standards normally expected from children of presidents, often expressed by presidents themselves in word and correspondence to the rebellious children of any age.

Since the Reagans left the White House and moved to their California home in 1989, Patti has continued to make her own headlines, as well as to travel the talk and news show circuits. Among the causes for her headlines have been the books she has authored in which she presents her own, singular among her siblings, view of her parents. In 1994 Patti became a presidential daughter who will, perhaps, never be equaled in public exposure. She posed nude, with only a male's hands covering her breasts, for *Playboy Magazine.*

Always candid about her beliefs and experiences, Patti did not hesitate to acknowledge that her father's election to the presidency "has done wonders for my career."[174] On the other hand, Patti rejected accusations that she used her father's name and position to further her career, observing "but it's not as if I slid into it. For years I've been going to audition, getting a few parts, being turned down for others. I've worked as a waitress to pay the rent; I feel as if I've paid my dues."[175]

With Reagan's presidency moving into history, with both Bush and Clinton already following his name on the books, will Patti's paid dues and talent be sufficient to provide for her successful transition into a matured Patti Davis as activist, author, actress, and model? It seems unlikely that her future will include politics.

## RONALD (SKIP) PRESCOTT REAGAN

Fourth child of Ronald Wilson Reagan; second child, only son of Ronald Wilson Reagan and Nancy Davis
*Born:* May 20, 1958     *Birthplace:* Los Angeles, California
*Education:* Yale University
*Profession:* Dancer, television personality, journalist
*Spouse:* Doria Palmieri     *Number of Children:* None

Ronald Reagan, son of his father's second marriage, was a fine student, but very early in life he became fascinated by the entertainment business to which he was constantly exposed in his California home. Of all the artistic forms of the theatre, dance was the artistic medium that initially most intrigued the young man.

In his late teens Ron, who began to study dance seriously, earned a scholarship to New York City's Joffrey School of Dance and became a regular member of the traveling dance troupe, earning $90 for rehearsal weeks and $270 for performance weeks. In 1983 he resigned from the company; he later acknowledged, "When I danced I never had any illusions that I was going to be another Nureyev or Nijinski."[176]

In the years since his leaving dance, Ron Reagan has grown into a highly credible journalist in print, radio, and televison. Periodically since the mid-1980s, Ron has also demonstrated a sense of humor about himself, appearing in commercial ventures in print, television, and film spoofing his family association as well as his own assessment of his role as the son of a president.

Not unlike his father at a similar age, Ron's political beliefs tend to be much more liberal than those of his father as he matured and shifted from being a Democrat to becoming a conservative Republican. Therefore, although not all of his adventures into the entertainment world have proven successful, it may be well to remember that much the same could have been said about his father before his political activism took him into the nation's highest office. Ronald Prescott Reagan has many years before his contributions as an entertainer or even as a political activist will be subject to evaluation.

## FOR FURTHER READING

DeGregorio, William A. *The Complete Book of U.S. Presidents*. 4th ed. New York: Barricade Books, 1993.

Edwards, Lee. *Ronald Reagan: A Political Biography*. Belmont, Mass.: Nordland Publishing, 1980.

Grimes, Ann. *Running Mates: The Making of a First Lady*. New York: W. Morrow, 1990.

Kelly, Kitty. *Nancy Reagan: The Unauthorized Biography*. New York: Simon and Schuster, 1991.

Reagan, Maureen. *First Father, First Daughter*. New York: Little, Brown, 1989.

Reagan, Michael. *On the Outside Looking In*. New York: Zebra Books, 1988.

Smith, Hedrick, et al. *Reagan: The Man, The President*. New York: Macmillan, 1980.

Trimble, Vance H. *Reagan: The Man from Mainstreet U.S.A.* Oakville, Ontario, Canada: Mosaic Press, 1980.

# 35 GEORGE HERBERT WALKER BUSH'S CHILDREN

## GEORGE WALKER BUSH

First child of George Herbert Walker Bush and Barbara Pierce
*Born:* July 6, 1946     *Birthplace:* New Haven, Connecticut
*Education:* Andover Academy, Yale University, Harvard Business School
*Profession:* Oilman, businessman, politician
*Spouse:* Laura Welch     *Number of Children:* 2

Selecting a path already well worn by both his father and grandfather, this firstborn child of a potential American political dynasty rose to the top of the political scene with his 1994 election as Republican governor of Texas. (His grandfather, Prescott, was twice elected as Republican senator from Connecticut, and his father, President George Bush, a longtime resident of Texas, returned to live in Houston after he lost the presidency to Bill Clinton in 1992.) In seeking the governor's office, George had to overcome the political opposition of a well-organized, long-term, dominant Texas Democratic party. In 1995 he became the state's second Republican governor since the mid-nineteenth century. In the course of a "down and dirty" campaign conducted by the campaign managers of the nationally popular incumbent governor Ann Richards, George faced charges that he was able to run only because of his name. He responded by observing, "I'm proud to be George Bush's son, and I'm certainly not going to hide from the fact."[177] His performance as governor is sure to be closely watched and evaluated. The potential of joining such politically elite families, as the Adams, Tafts, Roosevelts, and Kennedys, with generations moving into national political prominence, cannot be lost on the public.

Educated in the Bush tradition of Ivy League schools, George entered both the business and political worlds almost simultaneously. After completing his M.B.A. at Harvard, he returned to Texas, and, as he observed, almost spontaneously decided to enter a race for the U.S. House of Representatives from the west Texas area, where he had moved for business interests. Soundly defeated, he focused his attention on developing an oil and gas company in Midland, Texas. Entering other businesses, sometimes through consolidation, George's business acumen led him to become the recipient of both plaudits and charges of mismanagement, particularly during his campaign for governor. By the late 1980s, George had become a part owner of the state's national baseball franchise, the Texas Rangers, and was made the team's executive manager.

Stories of his use of his father's influence to avoid service in the military were generally rejected when he proved that he did serve in the Texas Air National Guard as a pilot. Although he saw no combat, the military organization is well recognized for its frequent participation in heroic combat activities when called into action.

Married, and the father of twin daughters, Barbara and Jenna, Bush faces the nation's most strenuous test: whether he can live up to the heritage of the family members he seeks to emulate. Actively supported by his mother, Barbara, in his governorship quest, and tacitly supported by his father, George perhaps demonstrated his quick-witted abilities when, during a political photo-op, used by both George and his Democratic party opponent, Ann Richards, George went hunting. As is true of many Texans, he is skilled with hunting weapons. Drawing a bead on his target, he pulled, and found he had shot down a much smaller target—a killdeer, a protected bird. Quick on the uptake, George observed, "I thought it was a dove!"[178] Whether or not this president's son will continue the political dynasty initiated by his grandfather remains to be seen. Elected Republican Governor of Texas in November, 1994, this Bush is also well on his way to political grandeur.

## PAULINE ROBINSON (ROBIN) BUSH

Second child, first daughter of George Herbert Walker Bush and Barbara Pierce
*Born:* December 20, 1949     *Birthplace:* Compton, California
*Died:* October 11, 1953     *Age at Death:* 3 years, 10 months
*Cause of Death:* Leukemia

Born only two months after Barbara's mother and father were killed in a car crash, her devastated parents named this second child, the first Bush daughter, in honor of her deceased grandmother, Pauline. The small child, however, was soon called "Robin."

Approximately a year before her death, Robin was diagnosed with acute leukemia—only rarely cured even in small children in the 1950s. Both parents were heartbroken and spent every available hour at her bedside. (Barbara Bush's hair is alleged to have turned white during this tragic deathwatch over her daughter.)

After Robin's death, Barbara exerted her efforts on behalf of a variety of charities. Although her emphasis has been on the Leukemia Society, her contributions have extended to others including the March of Dimes and the Sloan-Kettering Cancer Center. Each hour spent in such volunteer work honors her deceased daughter.

## JOHN ELLIS (JEB) BUSH

Third child, second son of George Herbert Walker Bush and Barbara Pierce
*Born:* February 2, 1953    *Birthplace:* Midland, Texas
*Education:* University of Texas, at Austin
*Profession:* Banker, real estate developer, politician
*Spouse:* Columba Garnica    *Number of Children:* 3

Born and raised in Texas, unlike his sibling predecessors, Jeb Bush—his nickname derived from the initials of his first, middle, and last name—has made major marks in both the business and political worlds of Florida.

Jeb entered the banking business after completing his college education at the University of Texas, where he graduated Phi Beta Kappa in Latin American studies. Fluent in Spanish, he soon went to work in Caracas, Venezuela, in the same business until he returned to the United States and the Florida business world.

Successfully involved in real estate development in the Miami area, this Bush son soon became associated with the Dade County Republican party, and he assumed its chair position before he became Florida's secretary of commerce, just as his father's presidency drew to an end.

Converted to Catholicism upon his marriage to his Mexican-born wife, Columba, Jeb's experiences and lifestyle proved so successful in Florida that he ran for governorship of the state against a powerful Democratic incumbant, Lawton Chiles, in 1994—the same year his brother George sought the governorship of Texas. George won his race; Jeb did not, although his fine showing may bode well for future entries into the political arena.

## NEIL MALLON BUSH

Fourth child, third son of George Herbert Walker Bush and Barbara Pierce
*Born:* January 22, 1955     *Birthplace:* Midland, Texas
*Education:* Tulane University
*Profession:* Banker, oilman
*Spouse:* Sharon Smith     *Number of Children:* 2

---

Settling in Denver, Colorado, shortly after graduating from Tulane University, Neil Bush garnered the kind of publicity not sought by any member of a politically active family.

With Neil serving as an outside director of a Denver savings and loan association, the firm failed during the major S&L failures of the 1980s. Losses from this particular failure are measured in the hundreds of millions of dollars to taxpayers. In investigations later conducted concerning this particular S&L failure, Neil was castigated for his failure to identify his business relationships with some of the institution's defaulters. As a sanction, Neil was admonished to follow a pattern of strict behavior should he ever again become involved with any savings institution.

Though Neil had left Texas after completing his college studies, his heritage of a family involved in the oil and gas business prompted him to enter the business in Colorado soon after he arrived in the state. However, his successes in business ventures have been minimal if, indeed, they can be counted as successful.

Neil met his wife, Sharon, during some of his periodic political activities. He was campaigning in New Hampshire for his father in the 1980 presidential primary. Since that early political activism, Neil has stayed on the fringes of the Republican party. Perhaps it is just as well since it may take some time before the taint of the S&L scandal does not follow him or his family members into the voting booths.

## MARVIN PIERCE BUSH

Fifth child, fourth son of George Herbert Walker Bush and Barbara Pierce
*Born:* October 22, 1956     *Birthplace:* Midland, Texas
*Education:* University of Virginia
*Profession:* Businessman, investment consultant
*Spouse:* Margaret Molster     *Number of Children:* 2

---

When he was only thirty years old, Marvin Bush developed a serious health problem when intestinal ulcers necessitated the removal of his colon. Recognizing the importance of helping others understand the problem and the resultant problems of living with an ostomy, he has been a major contributor to the cause of the United Ostomy Association.

Carrying the name of his mother Barbara Bush's father, Marvin Pierce, who died in the 1949 car crash that also killed Barbara's mother, this Bush son has been associated with the business world since shortly after his 1981 graduation from the prestigious University of Virginia. In the years that have followed, he has maintained his business associations closely affiliated with investments.

It is interesting to note that the namesake of this young man presents a double affiliation with a former president of the United States. Franklin Pierce was a great, great, great uncle of Barbara's father, and the same president is also a distant cousin of his father, George Bush. Yet, of all of the Bush sons, this son seems to be the least likely to follow the political fortunes of his distantly related uncle and cousin or in the footsteps of his father or three older brothers. He has not publically demonstrated any keen sense of political activism.

## DOROTHY WALKER (DORO) BUSH LEBLOND KOCH

Sixth child, second daughter of George Herbert Walker Bush and Barbara Pierce
*Born:* August 18, 1959     *Birthplace:* Midland, Texas

*Education:* Boston College    *Profession:* Businesswoman
*Spouse:* William LeBlond, Robert Koch    *Children:* Bush/LeBlond: 2;
Bush/Koch: None

---

Perhaps the least known of the Bush children, Doro Bush has had a variety of experiences and opportunities associated with her father's public service since she was a young woman.

While her father was serving as a liaison officer in Communist China, she celebrated her sixteenth birthday as the first person to be publicly baptized in Communist China in modern times.[179] After graduating from Boston College, she remained on the East Coast and worked in a variety of business positions. Twice married, her 1992 wedding to Robert Koch took place at Camp David, shortly after he resigned his position as an aide to Richard Gephardt, the Democratic House leader.[180]

Rare are the photos and press releases of this very private young woman who has lived at the center of a most public family.

### FOR FURTHER READING

Bush, Barbara. *Barbara Bush: A Memoir*. New York: A Lisa Drew Book, Charles Scribner's Sons, 1994.

Kilian, Pamela. *Barbara Bush: A Biography*. New York: St. Martin's Press, 1992.

Radcliffe, Donnie. *Simply Barbara Bush: A Portrait of America's Candid First Lady*. New York: Warner Books, 1989.

Stefoff, Rebecca. *George H. W. Bush, 41st President of the United States*. Ada, Okla.: Garrett Educational Corporation, 1990.

# 36  WILLIAM JEFFERSON CLINTON'S CHILD

## CHELSEA VICTORIA CLINTON

Only child of William Jefferson Clinton and Hillary Diane Rodham
*Born:* February 27, 1980     *Birthplace:* Little Rock, Arkansas
*Education:* Sidwell Friends School

The potential for this first young girl in the White House since Amy Carter (1977–1981) to become constantly targeted by the press was short-circuited when her parents, as well as others, objected when some very unflattering images dominated the news. Margaret Truman wrote a letter to the editor of the *New York Times*, expressing her concerns for the damage that could be done to this president's daughter if the press was allowed to completely invade Chelsea's private life—as happened to Margaret.[181]  For the most part, after the first few days in the White House, Chelsea has been rarely photographed or interviewed.

Named after a song popular to the 1960s generation, "Chelsea Morning," Chelsea attended public school in Little Rock, Arkansas. Upon moving into the White House, however, she was not subjected to the problems associated with the Carters' attempting to educate their daughter, Amy, in public school. Instead Chelsea was enrolled in the very upscale, private, Quaker Sidwell Friends School in Washington, D.C.

Despite the successful quest to maintain Chelsea's privacy as she matures in her teen years, she has had the opportunity to travel with her parents and, in large measure, even to spend time visiting with youthful friends without the constant vigilance of the press. At age thirteen, Chelsea traveled to

Russia with her parents. Although she attended the Moscow Circus, she did not constantly take part in the political events associated with the trip.

Certainly as the latest daughter of a president to live in the White House, Chelsea Victoria Clinton will garner at least some attention by virture of her parents' activities.

# APPENDIX: SHARED CHARACTERISTICS OF PRESIDENTS' CHILDREN

As the years pass, further information, observations, and statistical data about many of these children will be collected. Although there are some shared experiences in the lives of presidents' children, it appears that these are not unique but are similar to those of children of other political, economic, and social leaders in America.

More male children of presidents, than might be expected of middle-income Americans, have achieved a professional status. Females, particularly those of the eighteenth and nineteenth centuries, generally married men of wealth and influence. Often in these earlier centuries, females had more opportunities for education than their counterparts from lower- or middle-income families. However, it is also apparent that there are exceptions to these very broad statements. There are clear indications of personal, economic, and social failures much as might be found in American society as a whole.

The stories told of the presidential children often reflect presidential fathers' willingness to assist their offspring in making their marks in the world, but, on the other hand, parents at all income levels regularly seek to assist their children, by easing transitions into academic or work settings. As the twentieth century has progressed, such assistance is no longer limited to males, but today includes females. (It may also be observed that some of the century's early presidential fathers sought to aid their daughters, and the daughters, in turn, were able to ease the path for successive generations of females.)

Other characteristics shared by children of presidents are included in the following pages for the various interests of readers. Regardless of reason, Americans love to read and know about experiences played out in the lives of their leaders.

## MONTHS OF BIRTHS OF PRESIDENTIAL CHILDREN (not including illegitimate children)

| *Months of Birth* | *Highest to lowest numbers of children born:* |
|---|---|
| January: 6 | August: 19 |
| February: 10 | July: 18 |
| March: 12 | April: 16 |
| April: 16 | September: 15 |
| May: 10 | October: 14 |
| June: 2 | March: 12 |
| July: 18 | December: 12 |
| August: 19 | February: 10 |
| September: 15 | May: 10 |
| October: 14 | November: 8 |
| November: 8 | January: 6 |
| December: 12 | June: 2 |
| Unknown: 5 | Unknown: 5 |

Total: 147

Adopted: 2 (Jackson and Reagan sons, exact birthdates unknown)

Supposed Illegitimate: 8 (Jefferson, 6; Cleveland, 1; Harding, 1)

## HOROSCOPE SIGNS OF PRESIDENTIAL CHILDREN

*Aries: March 21–April 19*     Males: 7     Females: 7

Jane Randolph Jefferson

George Washington Adams

Mary Tyler

Alice Tyler

John Alexander Tyler

Anne Margaret Mackall Taylor

Mary Abigail Fillmore

Benjamin Pierce

Thomas Lincoln

Mary Scott Harrison

Ida McKinley

Archibald Bulloch Roosevelt

Calvin Coolidge, Jr.

James Earl Carter III

*Taurus: April 20–May 20*     Males: 4   Females: 6
Lucy Elizabeth Jefferson II
John Tyler, Jr.
Letitia Tyler
Mary Elizabeth Taylor
Millard Powers Fillmore
Mary Johnson
Margaret Woodrow Wilson
Anna Eleanor Roosevelt
Steven Meigs Ford
Ronald Prescott Reagan

*Gemini: May 21–June 21*     Males: 3   Females: 1
Charles Adams
"Son" Jefferson
Pearl Tyler
Frederick Dent Grant

*Cancer: June 22–July 22*     Males: 9   Females: 1
Abigail Amelia Adams
John Quincy Adams
John Adams II
Elizabeth Tyler
David Gardiner Tyler
Ulysses Simpson Grant II
Ellen Wrenshall Grant
Rutherford Platt Hayes
Eliza Arabella Garfield
Marion Cleveland
Francis Grover Cleveland
Allan Henry Hoover
Lucy Baines Johnson
Julie Nixon
Susan Elizabeth Ford
John William Carter

George Walker Bush

*Leo: July 23–August 22*     Males: 12   Females: 6
Mary Jefferson
Charles Francis Adams
Octavia Pannel Taylor
Margaret Smith Taylor
Robert Todd Lincoln
Andrew Johnson, Jr.
Manning Force Hayes
Irvin McDowell Garfield
Chester Alan Arthur II
Russell Benjamin Harrison
Ethel Carow Roosevelt
Helen Herron Taft
Herbert Clark Hoover, Jr.
Franklin Delano Roosevelt, Jr.
John Sheldon Doud Eisenhower
Patrick Bouvier Kennedy
Donnell Jeffrey Carter
Dorothy Walker Bush

*Virgo: August 23–September 22*     Males: 8     Females: 3
Thomas Boylston Adams
William Henry Harrison, Jr.
Robert Tyler
Frank Robert Pierce
Fances Hayes
Esther Cleveland
Theodore Roosevelt, Jr.
Robert Alphonso Taft
Charles Phelps Taft
Jessie Woodrow Wilson
John Coolidge

*Libra: September 23–October 23*     Males: 8   Females: 6
Martha Washington Jefferson

Elizabeth Bassett Harrison
John Scott Harrison
George Crook Hayes
Harry Augustus Garfield
James Rudolph Garfield
Ruth Cleveland
Kermit Roosevelt
Eleanor Randolph Wilson
Elliott Roosevelt
Dwight Doud Eisenhower
Amy Lynn Carter
Patricia Ann Reagan
Marvin Pierce Bush

*Scorpio: October 24–November 21*     Males: 6   Females: 4

Lucy Elizabeth Jefferson I
John Cleves Symmes Harrison
Carter Bassett Harrison
Anna Tuthill Harrison
Martha Johnson
Sardis Austin Hayes
Abram Garfield
Ellen Herndon Arthur
Richard Folsom Cleveland
Quentin Roosevelt

*Sagittarius: November 22–December 21*     Males: 8   Females: 2

Abraham Van Buren
Martin Van Buren, Jr.
Tazewell Tyler
Lachlin Tyler
William Wallace Lincoln
Joseph Thompson Hayes
William Lewis Arthur
Caroline Bouvier Kennedy
John Fitzgerald Kennedy, Jr.
Pauline Robinson Bush

*Capricorn: December 22–January 19*     Males: 3   Females: 5
  Susanna Adams
  Smith Thompson Van Buren
  Julia Tyler
  Mary Garfield
  Edward Garfield
  Katherine McKinley
  James Roosevelt
  Maureen Elizabeth Reagan

*Aquarius: January 20–February 18*     Males: 7   Females: 3
  John Van Buren
  Mary Symmes Harrison
  Richard Taylor
  Franklin Pierce
  Jesse Root Grant
  Scott Russell Hayes
  Alice Lee Roosevelt
  Margaret Truman
  John Ellis Bush
  Neil Mallon Bush

*Pisces: February 19–March 20*     Males: 10   Females: 5
  Thomas Boylston Adams
  Robert Fitzwalter Tyler
  Sarah Knox Taylor
  Edward Baker Lincoln
  Charles Johnson
  Robert Johnson
  James Webb Hayes
  Elizabeth Harrison
  Franklin Roosevelt
  John Aspinwall Roosevelt
  Lynda Bird Johnson
  Patricia Nixon
  Michael Gerald Ford
  John Gardner Ford

Chelsea Victoria Clinton

*Unknown Months and/or Days of Birth*      Males: 6   Females: 5

Louisa Catherine Adams

Andrew Jackson, Jr. (adopted)

Lucy Singleton Harrison

Benjamin Harrison

James Findlay Harrison

Eliza Kortright Monroe

J. S. Monroe

Maria Hester Monrose

Anne Contesse Tyler

Lyon Gardiner Tyler

Michael Edward Reagan (adopted)

## STATES OF BIRTH OF PRESIDENTIAL CHILDREN

Ohio: 24

Virginia: 24

New York: 22

Massachusetts: 12

Washington, D.C.: 12

Indiana: 8

Kentucky: 5

Missouri: 5

Tennessee: 5

California: 4

Georgia: 4

Illinois: 4

Texas: 4

New Hampshire: 3

Colorado: 2

Connecticut: 1

Hawaii: 1

New Jersey: 1

Arkansas: 1

## FOREIGN NATIONS AS PLACES OF BIRTH OF PRESIDENTIAL CHILDREN

London, England: 2

Paris, France: 1

Berlin, Germany: 1

St. Petersburg, Russia: 1

## NUMBER OF CHILDREN PRODUCED BY PRESIDENTIAL CHILDREN, BY CENTURY

Eighteenth century: 23

Nineteenth century: 177

Twentieth century: 31

## COMMON SCHOOLS ATTENDED BY PRESIDENTIAL CHILDREN

Harvard University: 22

Columbia University: 6

Cornell University: 6

Groton Preparatory School: 6

Yale University: 6

Princeton University: 4

West Point: 3

University of Virginia: 3

## COMMON OCCUPATIONS OF PRESIDENTIAL CHILDREN

### Politicians: Elected, sought office, or appointed to office

John Quincy Adams

Thomas Boylston Adams

Charles Francis Adams

John Van Buren

William Henry Harrison, Jr.

John Scott Harrison

Robert Tyler

John Tyler, Jr.

David Gardiner Tyler

John Alexander Tyler

Lyon Gardiner Tyler

Richard Taylor

Robert Todd Lincoln

Frederick Dent Grant

Harry Augustus Garfield

James Rudolph Garfield

Russell Benjamin Harrison

Theodore Roosevelt, Jr.

Robert Alphonso Taft

Charles Phelps Taft

Jessie Woodrow Wilson Sayre

Herbert Clark Hoover, Jr.

James Roosevelt

Franklin Delano Roosevelt, Jr.

James Earl Carter III

Maureen Elizabeth Reagan

George Walker Bush

John Ellis Bush

## Lawyers

| | |
|---|---|
| Charles Adams | Robert Johnson |
| Thomas Boylston Adams | Ulysses Simpson Grant II |
| George Washington Adams | Sardis Austin Hayes |
| John Van Buren | Harry Augustus Garfield |
| William Henry Harrison, Jr. | James Rudolph Garfield |
| Carter Bassett Harrison | Irvin McDowell Garfield |
| Robert Tyler | Richard Folsom Cleveland |
| John Tyler, Jr. | Elizabeth Harrison |
| David Gardiner Tyler | Robert Alphonso Taft |
| Lyon Gardiner Tyler | Charles Phelps Taft |
| Millard Powers Fillmore | Franklin Delano Roosevelt, Jr. |
| Robert Todd Lincoln | John William Carter |
| John Fitzgerald Kennedy, Jr. | |

## Writers/Editors

| | |
|---|---|
| Thomas Boylston Adams | Elizabeth Harrison |
| Charles Francis Adams | Theodore Roosevelt, Jr. |
| Smith Thompson Van Buren | Eleanor Randolph Wilson |
| Robert Tyler | Anna Eleanor Roosevelt |
| Lyon Gardiner Tyler | Elliott Roosevelt |
| Richard Taylor | Margaret Truman |
| Andrew Johnson, Jr. | John Sheldon Doud Eisenhower |
| Jesse Root Grant | Julie Nixon |
| Russell Benjamin Harrison | John Gardner Ford |
| Charles Phelps Taft | Maureen Elizabeth Reagan |
| John Tyler, Jr. | Michael Edward Reagan |
| Patricia Ann Reagan | |

## Soldiers

| | |
|---|---|
| Abraham Van Buren | James Webb Hayes |
| Robert Tyler | Theodore Roosevelt, Jr. |
| Richard Taylor | Kermit Roosevelt |
| Robert Todd Lincoln | Archibald Bulloch Roosevelt |
| Charles Johnson | Quinton Roosevelt |

Robert Johnson                    Elliott Roosevelt
Frederick Dent Grant              John Sheldon Doud Eisenhower

## Presidential Aides/Secretaries

John Quincy Adams                 Robert Todd Lincoln
John Adams II                     Robert Johnson
Abraham Van Buren                 Ulysses Simpson Grant II
Martin Van Buren, Jr.             James Webb Hayes
Smith Thompson Van Buren          Russell Benjamin Harrison
Robert Tyler                      John Sheldon Doud Eisenhower
Millard Powers Fillmore

## Teachers

John Quincy Adams                 Francis Grover Cleveland
Letitia Tyler                     Helen Herron Taft
Lyon Gardiner Tyler               James Roosevelt
Mary Abigail Fillmore             John Sheldon Doud Eisenhower
Harry Augustus Garfield

## White House Hostesses

Martha Washington Jefferson
Eliza Kortright Monroe
Mary Elizabeth Taylor
Mary Abigail Fillmore
Martha Johnson

# COMMON NAMES OF PRESIDENTIAL CHILDREN

## John

Quincy Adams
Adams II
Van Buren
Cleves Symmes Harrison
Scott Harrison

Tyler, Jr.
Alexander Tyler
Coolidge
Aspinwall Roosevelt
Sheldon Doud Eisenhower
Fitzgerald Kennedy, Jr.
Gardner Ford
William Carter
Ellis Bush

## Mary/Maria

Jefferson
Hester Monroe
Symmes Harrison
Abigail Fillmore
Garfield
Scott Harrison

## James

Findlay Harrison
Webb Hayes
Rudolph Garfield
Roosevelt
Earl Carter III

## Charles

Adams
Francis Adams
Johnson
Phelps Taft

## Robert

Tyler
Fitzwalter Tyler
Todd Lincoln

Johnson

Alphonso Taft

## Anna/Anne

Tuthill Harrison Taylor

Contesse Tyler

Margaret Mackall Taylor

Eleanor Roosevelt

## Lucy

Elizabeth Jefferson I

Elizabeth Jefferson II

Singleton Harrison

Baines Johnson

## Margaret

Smith Taylor

Woodrow Wilson

Truman

## William

Henry Harrison, Jr.

Wallace Lincoln

Lewis Arthur

# LONGEVITY OF PRESIDENTIAL CHILDREN

## Survived Most Years

Alice Lee Roosevelt: 96 years

## Survived Shortest Period

Patrick Bouvier Kennedy: 2 days

## Died before Five Years Old

Susanna Adams: 1 year, 1 month
Jane Randolph Jefferson: 1 year, 6 months
"Son" Jefferson: 17 days
Lucy Elizabeth Jefferson I: 5 months
Lucy Elizabeth Jefferson II: 3 years, 6 months
J. S. Monroe: 2 years, 4 months
Louisa Catherine Adams: 1 year
James Finlay Harrison: 3 years
Anne Contesse Tyler: 3 months
Octavia Pannel Taylor: 3 years, 8 months
Margaret Smith Taylor: 1 year, 3 months
Franklin Pierce: 3 days
Frank Robert Pierce: 4 years, 3 months
Edward Baker Lincoln: 3 years, 11 months
Joseph Thompson Hayes: 1 year, 6 months
George Crook Hayes: 1 year, 8 months
Manning Force Hayes: 1 year
Eliza Arabella Garfield: 3 years, 5 months
Edward Garfield: 1 year, 10 months
William Lewis Arthur: 2 years, 7 months
Katherine McKinley: 3 years, 6 months
Ida McKinley: 5 months
Franklin Roosevelt: 8 months
Dwight Doud Eisenhower: 3 years, 4 months
Patrick Bouvier Kennedy: 2 days
Pauline Robinson Bush: 3 years, 10 months

## Died between Five Years and Twenty-One Years

Benjamin Pierce: 11 years, 8 months
William Wallace Lincoln: 11 years, 2 months
Thomas Lincoln: 18 years, 3 months
Ruth Cleveland: 12 years, 3 months
Quentin Roosevelt: 20 years, 5 months

Calvin Coolidge, Jr.: 16 years

## Survived beyond Seventy-Five Years

John Quincy Adams: 80 years, 7 months

Charles Francis Adams: 79 years, 3 months

John Tyler, Jr.: 76 years, 9 months

Letitia Tyler: 86 years, 7 months

David Gardiner Tyler: 81 years, 2 months

Lyon Gardiner Tyler: 81 years, 6 months

Pearl Tyler: 87 years

Mary Elizabeth Taylor: 85 years, 3 months

Robert Todd Lincoln: 82 years, 9 months

Ulysses Simpson Grant II: 77 years, 2 months

Jesse Root Grant: 76 years, 4 months

James Webb Hayes: 78 years, 4 months

Frances Hayes: 82 years, 6 months

Harry Augustus Garfield: 79 years, 2 months

James Rudolph Garfield: 84 years, 5 months

Mary Garfield: 80 years, 11 months

Irvin McDowell Garfield: 80 years, 11 months

Abram Garfield: 85 years, 11 months

Marion Cleveland: 81 years, 11 months

Richard Folsom Cleveland: 76 years, 3 months

Russell Benjamin Harrison: 82 years, 4 months

Alice Lee Roosevelt: 96 years

Ethel Carow Roosevelt: 86 years, 4 months

Archibald Bulloch Roosevelt: 87 years, 3 months

Helen Herron Taft: 95 years, 7 months

Charles Phelps Taft: 85 years, 9 months

Eleanor Randolph Wilson: 77 years, 5 months

Allan Henry Hoover: 85 years, 4 months

James Roosevelt: 85 years, 9 months

Elliott Roosevelt: 80 years, 1 month

## Living Presidential Children

John Coolidge
Margaret Truman
John Sheldon Doud Eisenhower
Caroline Bouvier Kennedy
John Fitzgerald Kennedy, Jr.
Lynda Bird Johnson
Lucy Baines Johnson
Patricia Nixon
Julie Nixon
Michael Gerald Ford
John Gardner Ford
Steven Meigs Ford
Susan Elizabeth Ford
John William Carter
James Earl Carter III
Donnell Jeffrey Carter
Amy Lynn Carter
Maureen Elizabeth Reagan
Michael Edward Reagan
Patricia Ann Reagan
Ronald Prescott Reagan
George Walker Bush
John Ellis Bush
Neil Mallon Bush
Marvin Pierce Bush
Dorothy Walker Bush
Chelsea Victoria Clinton

# CAUSES OF DEATH OF PRESIDENTIAL CHILDREN

## Illness/Disease

Alcohol or Alcohol-Related Illnesses:
   Charles Adams

John Adams II

William Henry Harrison, Jr.

Tazewell Tyler

Robert Johnson

Amoebic Dysentery:

Kermit Roosevelt

Bilious Colic:

Alice Tyler

Blood Poisoning:

Calvin Coolidge, Jr.

Cancer:

Abigail Amelia Adams

Frederick Dent Grant

Scott Russell Hayes

Mary Scott Harrison

Robert Alphonso Taft

Herbert Clark Hoover, Jr.

Anna Eleanor Roosevelt

Pauline Robinson Bush

Cholera:

Mary Abigail Fillmore

Convulsions:

William Lewis Arthur

Diphtheria:

Thomas Lincoln

Eliza Arabella Garfield

Ruth Cleveland

Dysentery:

John Alexander Tyler

Joseph Thompson Hayes

Heart Attack:

Ulysses Simpson Grant II

Chester Alan Arthur II

Theodore Roosevelt, Jr.

Elliot Roosevelt

Franklin Delano Roosevelt, Jr.

John Aspinwall Roosevelt

Influenza:

    Franklin Roosevelt

Kidney Failure:

    John Van Buren

Malaria:

    Sarah Knox Taylor

    Richard Taylor

Pneumonia:

    William Wallace Lincoln

    James Rudolph Garfield

    Alice Lee Roosevelt

    Helen Herron Taft

Scarlet Fever:

    George Crook Hayes

    Dwight Doud Eisenhower

Stroke/Cerebral Hemorrhage:

    John Quincy Adams (cerebral hemorrhage)

    Martha Washington Jefferson (apoplexy)

    Charles Francis Adams (stroke)

    Millard Powers Fillmore (apoplexy)

    James Webb Hayes (stroke)

    Archibald Bulloch Roosevelt (stroke)

    James Roosevelt (stroke)

Typhoid Fever:

    Katherine McKinley

    John Cleves Symmes Harrison

Uremic Poisoning:

    Margaret Woodrow Wilson

Whooping Cough:

    Lucy Elizabeth Jefferson II

    Edward Garfield

Yellow Fever:

    Octavia Pannel Taylor

    Margaret Smith Taylor

## Accidental Deaths

Benjanin Pierce (railroad accident)
Charles Johnson (riding accident)

## Complications of Childbirth

Mary Jefferson
Elizabeth Tyler
Julia Tyler

## Death from Surgical Complications

Ellen Herndon Arthur
Jessie Woodrow Wilson

## Suicide

George Washington Adams (drowning)

## War Death

Quentin Roosevelt

# NOTES

1. Joseph J. Perling, *Presidents' Sons: The Prestige of Name in a Democracy* (1947; reprint, New York: Arno Press, 1970), 358.

2. Ibid., 370.

3. William A. DeGregorio, *The Complete Book of U.S. Presidents,* 2d ed. (New York: Dembner Books, 1989). 435.

4. Lida Mayo, "Miss Adams in Love," *American Heritage* 16 (February 1965): 35–47. Cranch was Amelia's uncle on her mother's side. Letters to Royall were forwarded by Cranch.

5. Ibid., 87.

6. Ibid., 89.

7. Ibid.

8. Perling, *Presidents' Sons*, p. 9.

9. Ibid., 19.

10. Jack Shepherd, *The Adams' Chronicles* (Boston: Little, Brown, 1975), 210.

11. Ibid.

12. Perling, *Presidents' Sons*, 24.

13. Ibid., 28.

14. Fawn M. Brodie, *Thomas Jefferson: An Intimate History* (New York: W. W. Norton, 1974), 109.

15. Ibid.

16. Christine Sadler, *Children in the White House* (New York: G. P. Putnam's Sons, 1967), 55.

17. There is some disagreement as to whether the child was born in France or whether he was born in the United States shortly after Sally's return to Monticello.

18. Brodie, *Thomas Jefferson*, 23, 276–277, 392, 473.

19. Hope Ridings Miller, *Scandals in the Highest Office* (New York: Random House, 1973), 101.

20. Ibid.

21. Ibid.

22. William Penn Cresson, *James Monroe* (New York: Archon Books, 1971), 175.

23. Ibid.

24. Shepherd, *Adams' Chronicles*, 268.

25. Ibid., 310.

26. Ibid.

27. Ibid.

28. Ibid., 314.

29. Ibid., 271.

30. Ibid., 299.

31. Ibid., 322.

32. *New York Times*, November 22, 1886.

33. Shepherd, *Adams' Chronicles*, 41.

34. Ibid.

35. *New York Times*, November 22, 1886.

36. Shepherd, *Adams' Chronicles*, 244.

37. Sadler, *Children in the White House*, 103

38. Perling, *Presidents' Sons*, 58.

39. Ibid., 59.

40. Ibid.

41. Ibid., 64.

42. Ibid., 66.

43. Ibid., 71.

44. Ibid., 72.

45. A practice not uncommon in the day, as "bounties" were paid to those who supplied bodies for medical students' research and studies of anatomy.

46. Perling, *Presidents' Sons*, 77.

47. Robert Seager II. *And Tyler Too: A Biography of John and Julia Gardiner Tyler* (New York: McGraw-Hill, 1963), 107.

48. Ibid., 108.

49. Perling, *Presidents' Sons*, 90.

50. Ibid., 92.

51. Ibid., 98.

52. Ibid., 99.

53. Seager, *And Tyler Too*, 102.

54. Ibid., 256.

55. Ibid., 349.

56. Ibid., 105.

57. Ibid., 521.

58. *New York Times*, January 26, 1874, 2.

59. Seager, *And Tyler Too*, 100.

60. Ibid., 339.

61. Ibid.

62. Ibid., 356.

63. Ibid., 546.

64. Ibid.

65. *New York Times*, February 13, 1935, 19.

66. Ibid.

67. Sadler, *Children in the White House*, 128.

68. Irene Gerlinger, *Mistresses of the White House* (Freeport, N.Y.: Books for Libraries Press, 1950), 43.

69. Perling, *Presidents' Sons*, 118.

70. *New York Times*, January 19, 1889, 1.

71. Sadler, *Children in the White House*, 139.

72. Charles M. Snyder, *The Lady and the President: The Letters of Dorothea Dix and Millard Fillmore* (Lexington: University of Kentucky Press, 1975), 51.

73. Edward T. James, et al., eds. *Notable American Women*, vol. 3 (Cambridge, Mass.: Harvard University Press, 1980), 66.

74. Accidents of this type, which were common during the beginning of railroad expansion, were usually the result of faulty steel and poor construction.

75. James, *Notable American Women*, 67.

76. Perling, *Presidents' Sons*, 136.

77. Ibid., 137.

78. Ibid., 139.

79. Perling, *Presidents' Sons*, 140.

80. Ibid., 142.

81. Much information is available concerning Mary Todd Lincoln's illness, and particular attention has been given since the middle 1980s. Robert was later responsible for her commitment to a mental institution for a short period of time.

82. Perling, *Presidents' Sons*, 143.

83. The Pullman Palace Car Company earned a place in history books when its model town near Chicago was hit hard by the 1893 depression. The company cut wages by one-third but did not reduce the rent of company houses. Workers, inspired by Socialist leader Eugene V. Debs, organized a strike, which was crushed by intervention from Washington, D.C.'s bayonet-supported forces under President Cleveland. The legal ground for the government's intervention was that the strike interfered with mail delivery.

84. Garfield was assassinated in 1881.

85. Perling, *Presidents' Sons*, 142.

86. Ibid., 147.

87. Ibid., 148–49.

88. Carl Sandburg, *Abraham Lincoln: The War Years III* (New York: Harcourt Brace and World, 1939), 381.

89. Ibid., 283.

90. *New York Times*, February 21, 1862.

91. Perling, *Presidents' Sons*, 132.

92. Ibid., 134.

93. Ibid., 135.

94. Gerlinger, *Mistresses of the White House*, 56.

95. Ibid.

96. Robert W. Winston, *Andrew Johnson: Plebian and Patriot* (New York: Henry Holt, 1928), 494.

97. *New York Times*, April 5, 1863.

98. Perling, *Presidents' Sons*, 158.

99. *New York Times*, April 12, 1912.

100. Ibid.

101. *New York Times*, June 9, 1934, 15.

102. Perling, *Presidents' Sons*, 193.

103. Ibid., 151.

104. H. J. Eckenrode, *Rutherford B. Hayes* (New York: Kennikat Press, 1963), 47.

105. Perling, *Presidents' Sons*, 198.

106. Allan Peskin, *Garfield* (Kent, Ohio: Kent State University Press, 1978) 156.

107. Ibid., 545.

108. Margaret Leech and Harry Brown, *The Garfield Orbit* (New York: Harper & Row, 1978), 189.

109. Perling, *Presidents' Sons*, 218.

110. Peskin, *Garfield*, 390.

111. Thomas C. Reeves, *Gentleman Boss: The Life of Chester Alan Arthur* (New York: Alfred A. Knopf, 1975), 32.

112. Ibid., 35.

113. Ibid.

114. Ibid., 275.

115. *New York Times*, January 8, 1904.

116. Ibid.

117. Ibid.

118. Curtiss Candy Company, Chicago, Illinois, was established in 1916 and incorporated into Standard Brands, Inc., in 1965.

119. Perling, *Presidents' Sons*, 238.

120. *Washington Post*, February 21, 1980.

121. Ibid.

122. Ibid.

123. Ibid.

124. Perling, *Presidents' Sons*, 256.

125. *New York Times*, February 14, 1944, 1.

126. Ibid.

127. Ibid.

128. Ibid.

129. Ibid.

130. *New York Times*, April 7, 1967, 37.

131. Perling, *Presidents' Sons*, 296.

132. Ishbel Ross, *Grace Coolidge and Her Era: The Story of a President's Wife* (New York: Dodd, Mead, 1962), 216.

133. Perling, *Presidents' Sons*, 300.

134. John T. Lambert, "When the President Wept" in *Meet Calvin Coolidge: The Man Behind the Myth*, ed. Edward C. Lathem (Brattleboro, Vt.: Stephen Greene Press, 1960), 139.

135. Ross, *Grace Coolidge*, 128.

136. *New York Times*, July 10, 1969, 37.

137. Joseph P. Lash, *Eleanor and Franklin* (New York: W. W. Norton, 1971), 301.

138. Ibid., 347.

139. Anna Rothe, ed., *Current Biography: Who's News and Why, 1950* (New York: H. W. Wilson, 1950), 505.

140. Perling, *Presidents' Sons*, 330.

141. Ibid., 332.

142. Degregorio, *The Complete Book of U.S. Presidents*, 482.

143. Perling, *Presidents' Sons*, 332.

144. Ibid.

145. Robert H. Ferrell, ed., *Off the Record: The Private Papers of Harry S Truman* (New York: Harper & Row, 1980), 109.

146. Merle Miller, *Plain Speaking: An Oral Biography of Harry S Truman* (New York: Berkley, 1974), 87.

147. *New York Times*, March 21, 1993.

148. Miller, *Plain Speaking*, 33.

149. Dwight D. Eisenhower, *At Ease: Stories I Tell My Friends* (New York: Doubleday, 1967), 181.

150. Frank Cormier, *LBJ: The Way He Was* (Garden City, N.Y.: Doubleday, 1977), 112.

151. Ibid.

152. Ibid., 174.

153. Ibid., 85.

154. Ibid., 47.

155. *New York Times*, "First Daughters Tell of White House Years," by Judy Kelmesrud, April 21, 1984.

156. Ibid.

157. Cormier, *LBJ*, 151.

158. Ibid.

159. *New York Times*, March 4, 1984.

160. Helen Thomas, *Dateline: Whitehouse* (New York: Macmillan, 1975), 174.

161. Ibid., 176.

162. Ibid., 209.

163. Ibid., 207.

164. Gerald R. Ford, *A Time to Heal* (New York: Harper & Row, 1979), 436.

165. Bud Vesta, *Jerry Ford: Up Close* (New York: Coward, McCann and Geoghegan, 1974), 22.

166. *New York Times*, April 21, 1984, see note 155.

167. Ibid.

168. *Houston Post*, December 15, 1980, 10.

169. Ibid.

170. *Jacksonville Times-Union*, October 7, 1980.

171. *Grand Rapids Press*, September 25, 1980.

172. *New York Times*, November 4, 1980.

173. *Time*, "Four Reagans Used to Going Their Own Way," January 5, 1981, 24.

174. Ibid.

175. *People Magazine*, "A Reagan by Any Other Name, Star-Elect Patti Davis Hopes for Her Own Landslide," January 12, 1981, 37.

176. *Current Biography Yearbook* (New York: H. W. Wilson, 1992), 469.

177. *Texas Monthly Magazine*, "Son of a Bush," Skip Hollingsworth, May 1994.

178. *San Antonio Express News*, September 9, 1994, 1-A.

179. William A. DeGregorio, *The Complete Book of U.S. Presidents*, 4th ed. (New York: Barricade Books, 1993), 667.

180. Ibid.

181. *New York Times*, "Letters to the Editor," March 21, 1993.

# BIBLIOGRAPHY

## BOOKS

Anthony, Carl S. *First Ladies: The Saga of the Presidents' Wives and Their Power*. New York: W. Morrow, 1990.

Basler, Roy P., ed. *The Collected Works of Abraham Lincoln*, Vols. 1–3. New Brunswick, N.J.: Rutgers University Press, 1953.

Bonnell, John Sutherland. *Presidential Profiles: Religion in the Life of American Presidents*. Philadelphia, Pa: Westminster Press, 1971.

Bradlee, Benjamin. *Conversations with Kennedy*. New York: W. W. Norton, 1975.

Brodie, Fawn M. *Thomas Jefferson: An Intimate History*. New York: W. W. Norton, 1974.

Bruce, David K. *Sixteen American Presidents*. New York: Bobbs-Merrill, 1962.

Burnam, Tom. *The Dictionary of Misinformation*. New York: Thomas Y. Crowell, 1975.

Burner, David. *Herbert Hoover: A Public Life*. New York: Alfred A. Knopf, 1979.

Burnham, Sophy. *The Landed Gentry: Passions and Personalities Inside America's Propertied Class*. New York: G. P. Putnam's Sons, 1978.

Canfield, Cass. *The Iron Will of Jefferson Davis*. New York: Harcourt, Brace, Jovanovich, 1978.

Churchill, Allen. *The Roosevelts: American Aristocrats*. New York: Harper & Row, 1965.

Cormier, Frank. *LBJ: The Way He Was*. Garden City, N.Y.: Doubleday, 1977.

Cresson, William Penn. *James Monroe*. New York: Archon Books, 1971.

Davison, Kenneth E. *The Presidency of Rutherford B. Hayes*. Westport, Conn.: Greenwood Press, 1972.

DeGregorio, William A. *The Complete Book of U.S. Presidents*, 2d ed. New York: Dembner Books, 1989; 4th ed. Barricade Books, 1993.

Dulles, Eleanor Lansing. *Chances of a Lifetime: A Memoir*. New York: Prentice-Hall, 1980.

Eaton, Clement. *Jefferson Davis*. New York: Free Press, 1977.

Eckenrode, H. J. *Rutherford B. Hayes*. New York: Kennikat Press, 1963.

Eisenhower, Dwight D. *At Ease: Stories I Tell My Friends*. New York: Doubleday, 1967.

Eisenhower, John. S. D. *Strictly Personal: A Memoir*. New York: Doubleday, 1974.

Eisenhower, Milton S. *The President Calling*. New York: Doubleday, 1974.

Ferrell, Robert H., ed. *Off the Record: The Private Papers of Harry S Truman*. New York: Harper & Row, 1980.

Ford, Gerald R. *A Time To Heal*. New York: Harper & Row, 1979.

Gerlinger, Irene. *Mistresses of the White House*. Freeport, N.Y.: Books for Libraries Press, 1950.

Hardy, Stella Pickett, and Tobias A. Wright. *Colonial Families of the Southern States of America*. New York: Tobias A. Wright, 1911.

Hay, Peter. *All the Presidents' Ladies: Anecdotes of the Women Behind the Men in the White House*. New York: Viking, 1988.

Hess, Stephen. *America's Political Dynasties*. New York: Doubleday, 1966.

Jensen, Amy (LaFollette). *The White House and Its Thirty-five Families*. New York: McGraw-Hill, 1970.

Johannsen, Robert, ed. *The Letters of Stephan A. Douglas*. Urbana: University of Illinois Press, 1961.

Kane, Joseph Nathan. *Facts about the Presidents*, 4th and 6th eds. New York: H. W. Wilson, 1981, 1993.

Kennedy, Rose Fitzgerald. *Times to Remember*. New York: Doubleday, 1974.

Lambert, John T. "When the President Wept." In *Meet Calvin Coolidge: The Man Behind the Myth*, edited by Edward C. Lathem. Brattleboro, Vt.: Stephen Greene Press, 1960.

Lash, Joseph P. *Eleanor and Franklin*. New York: W. W. Norton, 1971.

Lathem, Edward C., ed. *Meet Calvin Coolidge: The Man behind the Myth*. Brattleboro, Vt.: Stephan Greene Press, 1960.

Leech, Margaret, and Harry Brown. *The Garfield Orbit*. New York: Harper & Row, 1978.

Lengyel, Cornel Adam. *Presidents of the United States*. New York: Golden Press, 1977.

Miller, Hope Ridings. *Scandals in the Highest Office*. New York: Random House, 1973.

Miller, Merle. *Plain Speaking: An Oral Biography of Harry S Truman*. New York: Berkley, 1974.

Monroe, Haskell M. *The Papers of Jefferson Davis*, Vol. 1 (1808–1840), edited by James T. McIntosh, et al. Baton Rouge: Louisiana State University Press, 1971.

Moore, Virginia. *The Madisons: A Biography*. New York: McGraw Hill, 1979.

Morgan, H. Wayne. *McKinley and His America*. Syracuse, N.Y.: Syracuse University Press, 1963.

Patterson, James T. *Mr. Republican: A Biography of Robert A. Taft.* Boston: Houghton Mifflin Company, 1972.

Perling, Joseph J. *Presidents' Sons: The Prestige of Name in a Democracy.* New York: Odyssey Press, 1947; Freeport, N.Y.: Books for Libraries Press, 1971.

Peskin, Allan. *Garfield.* Kent, Ohio: Kent State University Press, 1978.

Pringle, Henry F. *The Life and Times of William Howard Taft.* Vol. 2. Hamden, Conn.: Archon Books, 1939.

Reeves, Thomas C. *Gentleman Boss: The Life of Chester Alan Arthur.* New York: Alfred A. Knopf, 1975.

Rice, Arnold S., ed. *Herbert Hoover: 1874–1964.* Dobbs Ferry, N.Y.: Oceana Publications, 1971.

Richardson, James D. *A Compilation of the Messages and Papers of the Presidents: 1789–1897.* Vol. 4. Washington, D.C.: n.p., 1897.

Roosevelt, Mrs. Theodore, Jr. *Day before Yesterday.* New York: Doubleday, 1959.

Ross, Ishbel. *Grace Coolidge and Her Era: The Story of a President's Wife.* New York: Dodd, Mead, 1962.

Sadler, Christine. *Children in the White House.* New York: G. P. Putnam's Sons, 1967.

Sandburg, Carl. *Abraham Lincoln: The War Years III.* New York: Harcourt, Brace and World, 1939.

Seager, Robert II. *And Tyler Too: A Biography of John and Julia Gardiner Tyler.* New York: McGraw-Hill, 1963.

Shepherd, Jack. *The Adams' Chronicles.* Boston: Little, Brown, 1975.

Sievers, Harry J. *Hoosier Warrior: Through the Civil War Years 1833–1865.* New York: University Publishers, 1960.

Snyder, Charles M. *The Lady and the President: The Letters of Dorothea Dix and Millard Fillmore.* Lexington: The University of Kentucky Press, 1975.

Thomas, Helen. *Dateline: White House.* New York: Macmillan, 1975.

Thomas, Lately. *The First President Johnson.* New York: William Morrow, 1968.

Truman, Harry S. *Memoirs: Years of Trial and Hope.* New York: Doubleday, 1956.

Truman, Margaret. *Harry S Truman.* New York: Pocket Books, 1974.

Vesta, Bud. *Jerry Ford: Up Close.* New York: Coward, McCann and Geoghegan, 1974.

Whitney, David C. *The American Presidents.* 4th ed. Garden City, Doubleday, 1978; New York: Prentice Hall Press, 1990.

Williams, T. Harry. *Hayes of the Twenty-third: The Civil War Volunteer Officer.* New York: Alfred A. Knopf, 1965.

Winston, Robert W. *Andrew Johnson: Plebian and Patriot.* New York: Henry Holt, 1928.

Zilg, Gerald Colby. *Du Pont: Behind the Nylon Curtain*. New York: Prentice-Hall, 1974.


## REFERENCE BOOKS, NEWSPAPERS, AND OTHER SOURCES

*American Heritage*. Lida Mayo, "Miss Adams in Love." 16 (February 1965).
*Bibliographical Directory of the United States Executive Branch: 1974–1977*. Edited by Robert Sobel. Westport, Conn.: Greenwood Press, 1977.
*Colonial Families of the United States of America*. Vol. 7. Edited by Nelson Osgood Rhoades. Bratenahl, Ohio: Seaforth Press, 1960.
*Current Biography: Who's News and Why*. New York: H. W. Wilson, 1992.
Curtiss Candy Company. Telephone interview. Chicago, Illinois, April 1981.
*Cyclopedia of American Biography*. Vol. 3. 1891. Reprint. Ann Arbor, Mich.: University Microfilms, 1967.
*Grand Rapids Press*, September 25, 1980.
*Houston Post,* December 15, 1980.
*Jacksonville Union-Times*, October 7, 1980.
*New York Times*, February 21, 1862; April 5, 1863; January 26, 1874; May 31, 1878; November 22, 1886; January 19, 1889; January 27, 1896; January 8, 1904; April 12, 1912; August 31, 1922; August 1, 1927; September 27, 1929; October 23, 1930; October 28, 1930; June 9, 1934; July 27, 1934; August 1, 1934; February 13, 1935; December 14, 1936; July 19, 1937; September 29, 1937; December 13, 1942; February 14, 1944; December 31, 1947; March 25, 1950; July 20, 1951; December 26, 1955; October 17, 1958; April 7, 1967; July 10, 1969; January 11, 1974; June 6, 1975; June 18, 1977; February 21, 1980; November 4, 1980; June 25, 1983; March 4, 1984; April 21, 1984; August 26, 1984; November 22, 23, 28, 29, 1984; December 1, 4, 28, 29, 1984; February 27, 1987; August 18, 1988; December 31, 1989; October 28, 1990; February 24, 1991; July 28, 1991; August 14, 1991; August 29, 1991; August 30, 1991; August 28, 1992; January 6, 1993; January 7, 1993; January 26, 1993; February 28, 1993; March 21, 1993; March 26, 1993; March 21, 1993, September 16, 1993; November 9, 1993; November 9, 1994.
*Notable American Women: 1607–1950*. Edited by Edward T. James, et. al. Cambridge, Mass.: Belknap Press of Harvard University Press, 1971.
*Notable Men of Tennessee*. Edited by Oliver Perry Temple. New York: Cosmopolitan Press, 1912.
*People Magazine*. "A Reagan by Any Other Name, Star-Elect Patti Davis Hopes for Her Own Landslide," January 12, 1981.
*Playboy Magazine*. "The First Daughter: A Provacative Look at Ron and Nancy's Wildest Child," by Micheal Angeli, July 1994.
*San Antonio Express News*, September 9, 1994.

*Texas Monthly Magazine.* "Son of a Bush," by Skip Hollingsworth, May 1994.
*Time.* "Four Reagans Used to Going Their Own Way," January 5, 1981.
*Washington Post*, February 21, 1980.
*Who's Who in America 1978–1979.* Vol. 2. Chicago: Marquis Who's Who, 1978.
*Who's Who in the South and Southwest 1976–1977.* 15th ed. Chicago: Marquis Who's Who, 1976.

# INDEX

## About the Authors

SANDRA L. QUINN-MUSGROVE is Associate Professor of Political Science and Public Administration at Our Lady of the Lake University, San Antonio. She has authored academic and trade books, journal articles, and has written two weekly newspaper columns over the last eleven years.

SANFORD KANTER is an instructor in the Department of History at San Jacinto Community College in Houston. He has authored articles on military history for academic journals and is coauthor with Quinn-Musgrove of *How to Pass Essay Examinations.*